FATAL ALLIANCE

Other books by E. William Henry

Triumph and Tragedy: the Life of Edward Whymper

FATAL ALLIANCE

The Prosecution, Imprisonment and Gangland Murder of Jimmy Hoffa

E. William Henry

ANDOVER
PRESS

Jacket design by Liz Trovato

All photos printed
by permission of Corbis Images,
except those on p. 60, 153.

Published by Andover Press
271 Main St. Great Barrington, MA 01230

Manufactured in Canada
ISBN: 978-1938183010

Library of Congress Catalog Card No: 2012936177

0 9 8 7 6 5 4 3 2 1

Andover Press and the Andover Press colophon are registered trademarks of
Vantage Press, Inc.

To the memory of Tony Schulte
and
For Taylor, Nora, Madeleine,
Parker and Emil III, paragons all

Contents

Acknowledgments

As in the case of my earlier literary effort, the first person I turned to for advice while writing *Fatal Alliance* was my friend and college classmate Anthony M. Schulte, former Executive Vice-President of Alfred A. Knopf. Now sadly departed, Tony was a man for all seasons, always available and ready with helpful suggestions. Like the many who knew him well, I miss him greatly.

I am ever grateful to John L. Seigenthaler for his many hours spent with me during the research and writing of this book. His encyclopedic memory enlarged the scope of my inquiry and lent cohesion to my thoughts. Through him I gained access to the *Tennesseean* newspaper's library of clippings, a nourishing well-spring from which I drank freely. "Sig" remains, at his core, the courageous investigative reporter who climbed to the top of his profession and inspired so many to follow in his footsteps.

James F. Neal, the leading light of Vanderbilt Law School's class of 1957, gave me much of his time and memories of encounters with Jimmy Hoffa. From Neal I gained a front row seat at Hoffa's criminal trials, along with firsthand accounts of the contentious legal and political problems he dealt with in prosecuting the notorious Teamster boss. My sessions with Jim also gave me new insights into the talents that made him a leading trial lawyer on a national scale.

My introduction to Bob Kennedy came through John Jay Hooker Jr., my law school classmate, who suggested I join him in working as a volunteer in the presidential campaign of 1960. Lawyers would say John Jay's suggestion was not the proximate cause of my writing a book featuring the Kennedy-Hoffa face-off. Almost certainly, however, I would not otherwise have experienced the events that generated my interest in this subject. I recognize the role my old friend played in opening this wider road, and thank him for it.

My most unexpected assistant was James Rosen, Fox News's Chief Washington Correspondent and the author of *The Strong Man*, the definitive biography of former Attorney General John N. Mitchell. I met with James seeking clarification on allegations of Mitchell's involvement in illegal transfers of cash from suspect sources to President Nixon's re-election campaign of 1972. Rosen persuaded me these allegations were highly doubtful. He also pointed me to the source of Oval Office tapes disclosing Nixon's reasons for barring Hoffa from union office upon the latter's release from prison, a veritable time bomb of information in the Hoffa story. I heartily thank James for his interest in my work, and his help.

Gay Campbell, John Seigenthaler's efficient and devoted assistant was of great help to me in tying up loose ends and pinning down innumerable pieces of essential information. Throughout, she was an efficient and gracious intermediary in my dealings with her boss. Thanks also to Christine Irizarry, the *Tennessean's* former Librarian, who faithfully navigated me through the voluminous stacks of clippings at the newspaper's library. Without her assistance my time there would have doubled and my discoveries diminished.

Patrick J. Haverty, a member of the jury that convicted Hoffa, shared with me his impressions of Hoffa and other trial participants along with his remembrances of a sequestered juror's isolated life. Craig Pollack of the Ingram Book Company responded cordially and helpfully to my inquiries. In various ways my three children—Elizabeth, Sherrye Jr., and Emil Jr.—worked to stir interest in my book. Friends Nancy Schwartz and Jenny Peters were also helpful members of my bandwagon.

Finally, I wish to thank David Lamb, Fiona Hallowell, Brenna Filipello and Selina Peyser at Vantage Press for their dedicated help during the publication process.

Introduction

Delegates to the 1957 national convention of the International Brotherhood of Teamsters (IBT), soon to be the nation's largest and most politically powerful labor union, unanimously elected James R. Hoffa their new president. As the rank-and-file's overwhelming favorite, Hoffa held that office for fourteen years, serving the last four in a federal prison. Robert F. Kennedy—initially as chief counsel to the investigative McClellan Committee of the US Senate and then as the nation's attorney general—was the Teamster boss's main antagonist and the principal agent of his undoing. Out of prison in the final years of his life, Hoffa became his own worst enemy.

Differences in the family origins and youthful environments of Jimmy Hoffa and Bob Kennedy could hardly have been greater. Hoffa's family was dirt poor, his father a coal miner, his mother a farmer's daughter. The father's early death left his widow with four children under the age of twelve. For several years she supported the family with poorly paid jobs ranging from home laundress to assembly-line robot. From her, young Jimmy learned the value of frugality, fortitude and self-reliance. There was no male role model in his adolescent years until he joined the Teamsters union at age eighteen. Rising to power and wealth solely through his own efforts, he was the epitome of a self-made man.

Robert Kennedy was the seventh of nine children born to upper-middle class parents lately made wealthy by the father's exceptional business acumen. Kennedy's mother, an ardent Catholic and dedicated homemaker, oversaw her children's daily needs and set the course of their religious training. Her husband spent most of his time at the office or away on business, making cameo appearances at the dinner table and on intermittent weekends. Paying particular attention to his sons, he repeatedly stressed their duty to enter politics and public service. Through them he was determined to gain the family's acceptance into the powerful Protestant establishment that had long excluded the Kennedys for their lace curtain, Irish-Catholic roots. Young Robert, desperate for the parental care and attention given to his two older brothers, wholeheartedly embraced his mother's religion, his father's social ambitions and the latter's emphasis on personal achievement. In his determination to contribute to the family's goals in equal measure, Kennedy's energy and enthusiasm were exceeded only by his intensity of purpose. This sense of mission became the guiding force of his adult life.

Comparisons of Kennedy with Hoffa—one a US Senator and presidential candidate, the other a corrupt labor boss and convicted felon—surprisingly reveal striking similarities in their positive traits. Most noticeable is each man's will to succeed, driven by a need to demonstrate individual worth. As Kennedy strove to rise above Protestant prejudice and prove himself the equal of his older brothers, Hoffa fought aggressively to overcome poverty and powerlessness in a hostile world. Both were charismatic natural leaders who courageously pursued their goals in the face of intense criticism and threats of physical harm. Both had an enduring love of family but put hard work and job completion ahead of time with wife and children. Each had simple tastes, shunned large social gatherings and addictive substances, and stayed unshakeably loyal to close friends and associates.

As adversaries the two men seemed equally matched and neither was above reproach. They had no patience for slackers and little concern for the feelings of anyone perceived as wrongly or arbitrarily standing in their way. In their separate struggles to resist marital infidelity, rumors arose that both were unsuccessful. But these attributes did not represent their moral cores or their basic codes of conduct, and it was here they diverged. At the deepest levels of their psyches they were fundamentally different, distinguished primarily by their disparate views on the nature of good and evil. Kennedy was moralistic, driven by lessons learned at his mother's knees and in her Church. He adopted and sought to live by a strict set of ethical rules and, in the final analysis, judged others by the degree to which they followed suit. Hoffa was essentially amoral, choosing each course of action on the basis of its value to a planned objective. Accordingly, he never acknowledged to himself or others the true nature of his motivations.

In early 1961, despite his awareness that charges of nepotism would follow, the recently elected president appointed Robert as the nation's new attorney general. RFK immediately put the power of his brother's administration behind a campaign to bring criminal charges against the leader of the country's fastest growing union. To this end he personally assembled, within the Department of Justice (DOJ), a team of lawyers and investigators the media soon tagged as the "Get Hoffa Squad." The Teamster boss proved an elusive target. His defense lawyers, known as the "Teamsters Bar Association" for their large numbers, included the "magic mouthpiece" Edward Bennett Williams. They flooded the courts with motions, arguments and charges of illegal surveillance by wiretaps and other means, an issue as current today as it was then. The fierce rivalry between these two powerhouses became the reality TV of the 1960s, trumpeted by savvy media outlets of every kind and relished by a voracious public.

The Teamsters' public relations team also joined the fight. They brought former heavyweight champion Joe Louis into court to embrace Hoffa before a mostly black jury. They persuaded US Senators and Representatives, along with elements of the national media, to parrot their claim that Hoffa was the innocent victim of the attorney general's personal vendetta. During Hoffa's trials, Teamster loyalists threatened opposing witnesses with bodily harm. They attempted to bribe jurors in return for votes of acquittal. It took ten years of investigative and prosecutorial persistence to surmount these formidable barriers and accomplish Kennedy's goal.

At every stage of his career as a union official, Hoffa partnered with the bosses of organized crime. During his rise to power in Detroit's Local 299 he justified bringing known gangsters into his union because they owned or controlled businesses whose employees he wanted to organize. To solidify those relationships he allowed mobsters to hold union office and to use those offices to acquire exorbitant personal profits, often at the expense of their own employees. They also brought money and muscle. For good measure the Teamster boss found similar means to reward himself, characterizing his actions as the only way to survive and prosper in a corrupt world. This pragmatic but self-serving logic, coupled with Hoffa's consummate powers of persuasion, convinced a range of people from courtroom juries to members of the US Congress that he was the subject of an unlawful persecution. Robert Kennedy, he repeatedly told friendly audiences and eager reporters, was a spoiled rich kid, misusing the enormous power of the federal government and maliciously intent on putting a man of the people behind bars.

As Hoffa struggled to gain the presidency of the International Brotherhood of Teamsters, the IBT faced widespread charges of violence and corruption from within and the growing influence of organized crime from without. One account of the Teamsters' corrupt practices came from Nashville, the capital city of Tennessee. The unlikely source of such damning information was a young investigative reporter for the *Tennessean,* the town's leading newspaper. For four years John Seigenthaler wrote regularly of malfeasance within Teamster Local 327, and of Hoffa's role in facilitating its growth in Nashville and elsewhere in the state. Seigenthaler's compilation of names, dates and specific acts of violence, bribery and extortion gave rise to nine days of testimony before the McClellan Committee. These hearings led to Hoffa's indictment and trials in Tennessee that marked the beginning of the Teamster boss's downfall.

Bob Kennedy's choice as the chief prosecuting attorney in these trials was thirty-two-year-old James F. Neal, a rising star in the Department of Justice's Get Hoffa Squad. Though he possessed limited courtroom experience, the young lawyer's self-confidence, aggressive style and incisive legal mind made him a standout trial lawyer. When a hung jury in the first case led to Hoffa's second trial, the attorney general added John Hooker Sr., a colorful veteran of the Tennessee trial bar, as Neal's co-counsel. With the assistance of DOJ investigators,

FBI agents and the dramatic testimony of a surprise witness straight out of television's *Perry Mason,* these two lawyers accomplished what had eluded other government prosecutors for half a generation.

Behind prison bars Hoffa's first concern was survival. Prison officials showed their celebrated prisoner some slight favoritism, but his main allies were gang members also serving time. These included a powerful Mob underboss with close Teamster relationships, and a Mafia capo who had served earlier as a Hoffa-appointed IBT vice-president. Under their protection Hoffa attempted to retain control of his union through emissaries to Frank Fitzsimmons, the man he had installed as the IBT's caretaker president. He also sought help from the Nixon administration to gain early release from prison. As revealed in previously unpublished excerpts from the infamous Oval Office tapes, the president took a strikingly cynical approach to the prisoner's plea. Designed to cut short the incarcerated labor boss's time served while barring him from union office for a fixed period, Nixon's decision set the stage for disaster. Public disclosure of the president's motives at that time might well have saved Hoffa's life.

Once again on the outside, Hoffa pressed hard to regain his old office. Misled by his own hubris he refused to concede that the Mafiosi and their gangland cousins within the IBT no longer gave him their support. Finally realizing that these mobsters were no longer his friends, he threatened to expose their dealings with his successor and the ways they had benefited in recent years at the expense of the Teamsters' rank and file. Though clearly warned that he was treading a minefield, Hoffa would not be deterred. In the end, his grand illusion of immunity from Mob vengeance was the root cause of his death, an event that removed from the American labor scene its last mega-boss and folk hero.

After six months of investigation, FBI agents got the facts of Hoffa's last hours essentially correct. Ignoring the wild speculation that surfaced at the time, the Bureau astutely applied Occam's razor to minimize the assumptions used to create a picture of what probably happened that fateful day. Its summary of those events and their participants withstood serious challenge for thirty years. Its two missing pieces—the killer's identity and the disposition of Hoffa's body—have emerged only recently from the mists of time. These crucial elements of the story bring a credible solution to the mystery of Hoffa's disappearance.

****

The prosecution, imprisonment and gangland murder of James R. Hoffa is a cautionary tale, bathed in irony by heroes and villains alike. Featured players hold high office in the American labor movement, the national media and all three branches of the federal government. Business and labor interests willfully violate the law in pursuit of higher profits or greater influence. Advocates from both groups promote known falsehoods. Pandering politicians echo the claims of their major donors with no concern for the facts at issue. Political campaign managers willingly accept bags of cash from suspect sources. Zealous defense lawyers flout the rules of professional conduct; government investigators skirt the boundaries of accepted legal restraints. Adversaries spend equal time in open conflict and cloistered conspiracy. As circumstances change, fast friends become lethal enemies. Organized crime bosses skulk in the shadows before taking center stage in the final act. In short, the magnetic labor leader's fatal alliance with organized crime and his consequent fall from grace comprise a classic story of greed, corruption and lust for power, played out in a uniquely American context.

Prologue

Friday, the 12th of April, 1957, was the last day of a two-week seminar on investigative reporting being held at Columbia University in upper Manhattan. Attending this class were twenty-five newspaper reporters from as many cities, gathered in New York to hone their skills at the nation's preeminent School of Journalism. Each of the men had been selected by his local editor for initiative and trenchant writing. Among them was John Seigenthaler, a thirty-year-old prize-winning investigative reporter for the *Nashville Tennessean*, one of the southeastern United States' most highly regarded publications.

As his group took their seats in the lecture hall after the morning break, Seigenthaler found it difficult to focus on the subject at hand. Uppermost in his thoughts was a meeting he had been trying to arrange for more than three months and was now scheduled for 12:30 that very afternoon. It would be a face-to-face session with Robert F. Kennedy, chief counsel of the recently formed Senate Select Committee on Labor-Management Improprieties chaired by John McClellan, an Arkansas Democrat. Kennedy had agreed to see the persistent reporter only after Vic Johnson, a Nashville businessman familiar with Seigenthaler's reportorial record, called Sargent Shriver, RFK's brother-in-law and Johnson's Yale College classmate, to request Shriver's help in setting up the meeting.

The young reporter was bursting to discuss with Kennedy the articles he'd written in the *Tennessean* over the last eighteen months on Teamster violence. During this period—in Tennessee's major cities and some of the state's smaller communities—Teamster agents and hired thugs had beaten uncooperative drivers with tire irons and clubs, sending several to hospitals. They had blasted non-union trucks with shotguns, slashed their tires, and locked up their engines with sugared water forced into their gas tanks. They had dynamited, burned, and smashed windows at the offices of recalcitrant employers. They had paid city officials to look the other way, and bribed the corrupt judge of a state criminal court.

Seigenthaler had clipped and arranged his articles in a bound volume recounting this lawless behavior in gripping detail. His investigation showed a larger hub of Teamster malfeasance in his state than in any area the McClellan Committee had yet to survey. Surely this would light the eyes of the Committee's aggressive legal counselor who had finally agreed to spend a few moments of his busy schedule with the young Nashville reporter.

****

The day was overcast and unseasonably cold as Seigenthaler left the Columbia classroom shortly before noon, turning up the collar of his jacket against a brisk wind as he hailed a cab to take him downtown. In those days of less congested Manhattan streets he had plenty of time to make his meeting at Kennedy's temporary office space in the federal courthouse at 40 Centre Street on Foley Square near the foot of the Brooklyn Bridge.

The taxi moved at a steady pace and left its occupant at the courthouse entrance about 12:15, well before the time of his appointment. A uniformed guard gave Seigenthaler's briefcase a cursory look and waved him in, with no metal detectors or X-ray devices to slow him down. He took an elevator to one of the upper floors where Angie Novello, the secretary who would remain Bob Kennedy's loyal assistant for the rest of his career, made him welcome.

After sitting down he immediately stood up again. Through an inner office doorway strode Kennedy, already in his overcoat and scarf, outward bound. As recounted by Seigenthaler, Ms. Novello introduced them. "You're late," her boss said. "No," replied Seigenthaler, "I'm early.

Our meeting was set for 12:30." "Angie, what time was our meeting?" "12 noon, Bob." "No," the undaunted newsman repeated, "I have a note here from Sarge Shriver that plainly says 12:30. There's the clock and I'm ten minutes early." Kennedy stared silently at his visitor for a heartbeat. "Sarge Shriver is on Central Standard Time," he said, with the shadow of a grin. He then turned to his secretary. "Angie, I've got to move on. Please ask Jerry to see Mr. Seigenthaler." And that was that—a plainspoken exchange characteristic of each of these hard-driving, stubborn young men. They would later understand and appreciate each other but at that moment their relationship was off to a shaky start.

Indeed, Seigenthaler was furious. After almost four years of hard work and three frustrating months of trying to arrange this meeting, he had been curtly dismissed by a man who would not admit his own mistake or rearrange his schedule to accommodate an out-of-town visitor. Granted, the Senate Committee's chief counsel was incredibly busy but that was no excuse. Maybe he was in fact the man his critics claimed: a rich kid spoiled by a life of privilege, icily impersonal and ruthless in the pursuit of his goals. Well, to hell with him and his kind!

Unmoved by his guest's obvious frustration, Kennedy walked out the door as Jerome Adlerman, an assistant counsel to the Committee, entered the room and shook Seigenthaler's hand. For a couple of hours the two men reviewed the heavy scrapbook of clippings about Teamster violence and corrupt practices in Tennessee. As they finished, Adlerman said excitedly, "This is terrific stuff! I've *got* to get you with Kennedy. Can you stay over the weekend if I can arrange for you to meet with him in Washington early next week?" Mollified by Adlerman's attention and obvious interest, Seigenthaler agreed. He later received word that Kennedy would see him in the chief counsel's D.C. office at 1:00 p.m. the following Monday.

Punctual once again, Seigenthaler showed up at the Senate Office Building just north of the nation's Capitol on the appointed day. Already seated in the cramped reception area of the McClellan Committee's basement offices was Harold Brislin, a fellow investigative reporter from the Scranton, Pennsylvania *Scrantonian*. Brislin, who had recently supplied the investigative committee with useful information about Teamster violence in Pennsylvania, was a friend of Seigenthaler's. Theirs was a fraternal relationship, a bond of mutual respect and camaraderie shared by investigative reporters in different cities engaged in a common calling.

Kennedy walked in as the two reporters chatted warmly, gave Seigenthaler a weak handshake and said to Breslin, "Come on in, Harold, I'm glad to see you." The receptionist then told the *Tennesseean's* reporter that he was scheduled to meet again with Mr. Adlerman.

This brought Seigenthaler's simmering frustration again to the surface, compounding it with bewilderment. He had spent the weekend away from his wife and son on the promise that he would finally meet personally with this arrogant aristocrat, only to receive another Kennedy brush-off. Stifling his anger he closeted himself once more with Adlerman. The Committee aide apologized for his boss's actions, explaining that the chief counsel was simply overburdened with information and had not yet been able to review the *Tennessean* stories, important as they were. They discussed the clippings again; Seigenthaler answered the assistant's additional questions and flew back to Nashville early that evening. In his office the next day the disgusted reporter told his colleagues how badly he had been treated. And he made no effort to hide his conviction that Robert F. Kennedy was a snot-nosed little shit.

About a month later a telephone rang in the *Tennessean's* busy editorial headquarters. The nearest reporter, unhappy at being distracted from his typewriter, grabbed the jangling phone's receiver and spoke abruptly: "Newsroom…yeah…yeah…just a minute." Putting his hand over the mouthpiece he yelled at his colleague a couple of desks away: "Sig! Some joker's on the phone pretending to be Bobby Kennedy. Says he wants to talk to you." Knowing that the caller was the genuine article but too experienced to be shocked out of his professional demeanor, Seigenthaler said "hello" as if the two had seen each other the day before. "I'm sorry not to have gotten back to you before this," said Kennedy. "I read your stuff over the weekend, and it's dynamite. When can you be in my office to talk more about it?"

At the time Seigenthaler did not recognize this moment as the beginning of a beautiful friendship. Yet that was exactly what it would become, and his package of dynamite would, in time, blast a huge hole in Jimmy Hoffa's insistent claim of innocence.

CHAPTER 1

"The Sincerest Little Guy I've Ever Seen"

In a fiery exchange of words with his foreman, nineteen-year-old Jimmy Hoffa slammed down a carton of fresh produce at his boss's feet and stormed off the loading dock of the Kroger Grocery Company's warehouse in Detroit. The object of his defiance was Al Hastings, the dock workers' small but pugnacious supervisor, known behind his back as the "little bastard." A sadistic taskmaster, Hastings berated his charges at every opportunity. On bad days he fired any man bold enough to offer a mild complaint or muttered curse sent in his direction. On some days he let workers go to make room for his friends or relatives, and occasionally for no reason whatsoever. Jimmy had worked the Kroger warehouse's night shift for almost two years, enduring the little bastard's daily threats until his repressed misery finally exploded in anger.

The youngster's bold move was a rare event in those deep Depression days of 1932. Unskilled laborers could ill afford to vex their bosses even when provoked. Every day in most American cities and especially in hard-hit Detroit, unemployed workers hung around industrial plants and commercial facilities hoping for a call. Kroger's Motor City warehouse was no exception. Within minutes of Hoffa's exit another man was helping to offload the truck being worked on.

Hoffa shared his fellow employees' anger at low wages, oppressive working conditions and job insecurity. Several months earlier he had helped to manage a sit-down work stoppage that forced Kroger management to recognize the Detroit dock workers as a new labor union. Since then, as one of the rebellious group's more outspoken members, Hoffa had been a continuing irritant to Hastings, his workplace nemesis. The inevitable confrontation between them occurred during a transfer of crates of fresh celery from a large incoming load to small trucks bound for Kroger stores. According to Hoffa, the little bastard "had been on me all night, nagging me and whispering obscenities. Finally, I'd had all I could take. He was right on my heels and I whirled around and threw the crate on the floor at his feet. It split open and showered him with vegetables. 'All right Hoffa, ya did it, ya dumb bastard, you're fired!' 'Like hell I am,' I yelled back at him, 'I quit.'"[1]

The brash youngster was not unemployed for long. During the workers' successful effort to unionize Kroger's warehousemen, Hoffa's precocious talent for leadership of men of all ages had attracted the attention of Ray Bennett, a local Teamster official and administrator of the American Federation of Labor's Joint Council 43 in Detroit. On the day following young Hoffa's departure, Bennett offered him a job as the Council's general organizer. The position would pay no salary, only a small commission for each man he brought into the Teamster fold. This was likely to generate less than his weekly average of $15 at Kroger but he welcomed the chance to devote full time to union work and immediately accepted Bennett's invitation.

Hoffa had found his calling. More accurately the labor movement had recognized him as one of its own and brought him into its ranks. He would never again work for a commercial enterprise. From this date forward the International Brotherhood of Teamsters or one of its affiliated organizations would be his only employer.

****

Brazil, Indiana, lies in the heartland of the American Midwest. In the early 20th century, with a population of around ten thousand, it was known principally for the bricks and tiles made from clay deposits in the surrounding countryside. Its first son to achieve national recognition was Orville Redenbacher, the future popcorn king, born in

Brazil in 1907. Its second, James Riddle Hoffa, came into the world on Saint Valentine's Day, 1913. John Hoffa, Jimmy's coal-drilling father, died there of a stroke in 1922. He was survived by his wife, the former Viola Riddle, along with the four children of their eleven-year marriage: Jennetta, Billy, Jimmy and Nancy, born in that order.

At the time of the father's death there was no welfare system for the family to turn to. He had left them no savings account or employment pension. Viola was a homemaker with limited income-producing skills, and jobs in Brazil were scarce. Now alone as the family's sole provider she worked as a domestic maid, washerwoman and restaurant cook. Discouraged by paltry earnings and the lack of better opportunities in such a small town, she discussed her plight with Lizzie Guinn, a childhood companion who lived across the Indiana state line in Clinton, Illinois. Encouraged by Lizzie's description of this larger town and heartened at the thought of being near an old friend, Viola moved her family to what looked like a greener pasture.

In Clinton the Hoffas rented a two-room house for six dollars a month. Viola decided that her best opportunity in the more populous town was a home laundry, something she had tried in Brazil but abandoned for lack of customers. Taking in washing would keep her close to the children and maximize whatever contributions they could make. She did the ironing, and with Jennetta's help scrubbed and washed the clothes. The two boys picked up and delivered the neighbors' washables in their wagon and gathered and chopped the firewood needed to heat the water. All helped with the care of young Nancy.

The work was hard and the income meager but it kept them going. In her rare contemplative moments Viola pictured life as little brighter than when they left Brazil, but she knew her children would not stay homebound indefinitely. After four years in Clinton, with considerable courage for a family-burdened, unskilled widow in a still-struggling economy, Viola decided to move her family to Detroit in the hope of finding less backbreaking toil at a living wage.

In Motor City her determination paid off in steady employment if only slightly higher earnings. She worked first as a laundry presser but soon looked for better pay in the automobile industry. Nominally those jobs required some prior experience in a factory, so Viola falsely but brazenly claimed assembly-line work as one of her earlier jobs. Hired by an auto parts manufacturer, she was assigned the robotic task of screwing valve mechanisms onto the bolts of parts as hundreds of them went down the line each day. A few years later, following an appendectomy, she found better paying but no less boring employment at Fisher Body's Fleetwood plant. Her new job was polishing decorative radiator caps to the intense luster demanded by Cadillac owners of the day. On the sidewalks of Detroit, sighting a particularly shiny hood ornament on a passing or parked car, the Hoffa siblings would agree, "That must be one of Mom's!"[2]

These were stressful times for Viola and her brood. The children were a boisterous lot but also helped their mother in making ends meet. After school the boys worked at bagging groceries, dumping ashes and other odd jobs to supplement their mother's small salary. Jennetta helped with the cleaning, cooking and household chores; she also babysat young Nancy in the afternoons. Their small house was cluttered enough, but for extra money Viola opened her home's one available room to boarders. She thus managed to keep the children together and in good health but their combined earnings left nothing for savings. In time her child-raising responsibilities and long hours at tedious factory jobs took their toll on the family's breadwinner. Her face became haggard and her disposition increasingly bitter. In later years the children never forgot her concern for their welfare, and when she retired during her sixth decade they supported her for the rest of her life. Her example endowed all of them with a strong work ethic and a lasting commitment to family.

Viola had rented a house in a west Detroit neighborhood populated mainly by families of Slavic origin. The Hoffa children's heritage was Dutch through their father John and Irish on their mother's side. Despite the older ancestral roots of the new arrivals, their Motor City neighbors considered the Hoffas country folk. Viola often felt snubbed, particularly when passing strangers silently shot her inhospitable looks. The two boys and Jennetta attended the Neinas Intermediate School, a nearby unit of Detroit's public school system. The children of the Hoffa family's critics were more vocal than their parents, calling the newcomers "hillbillies" to their faces, which was a mistake. One look at either of the boys should have warned their tormentors to go easy.

Jimmy, though not yet at his adult height, had inherited the strength of his brawny six-foot father and the sturdiness of his compact mother. Billy was only slightly less imposing and equally bold. With their fists the Hoffa boys quickly taught their rash schoolmates to show them and their sisters greater respect.

In the spring of 1927, at age fourteen, Jimmy graduated from the ninth grade. He had been an indifferent student but took books home to read when he could find the time. Though Viola wanted him to go on to high school he was tired of the classroom and yearned to make enough money to stand on his own. The issue was resolved when they saw an ad in the local newspaper for a "stock boy" at Frank & Cedar's department store in downtown Detroit. Accompanied by his mother Hoffa applied for the job and was hired.

The position called for sixty hours per week and paid twenty cents an hour, about three dollars twenty cents today. Still living at home, the newly employed teenager proudly gave Viola his first week's earnings of $12. In what would become an established pattern, she put the money in the family coffers and doled out nickels and dimes to Jimmy for his minimal adolescent needs. He cared little for movies or other diversions and had a date only once in a blue moon. He liked to fish, to stretch his legs walking, and to read, not books any longer but magazines and newspapers about people and events happening in the world around him.

For two years Hoffa applied himself diligently to the work of the stockroom, earning the approval of his bosses and the goodwill of his fellow employees. He was a fast learner and showed himself able to take on jobs of increasing responsibility. He had visions of becoming a clerk and finding a career in the retail business. Then came Black Monday in late October 1929, followed by a sharp downturn in the economy. The convivial atmosphere at work became tense as business slackened, and what began as a trickle of employee layoffs soon swelled to a stream.

Like Viola, the young Hoffa regularly assessed the present and contemplated the future. Department store employment in the waning months of 1929 seemed unprofitable at best and untenable at worst. As his mother had done, he followed the advice of a friend: "Get into the food business. No matter what happens, people have to eat."[3]

The family's boarder at the time was James Langley, a man in his twenties who worked at the Kroger Company's distribution warehouse located within walking distance of the Hoffa household. Langley had his eye on Jennetta, the oldest of the Hoffa children, whom he subsequently married. Probably as a goodwill gesture flowing from dinner table conversation and perhaps also to ingratiate himself with his future mother-in-law, the boarder took Jimmy to Kroger for a job interview with the warehouse's night foreman. To increase the youthful applicant's employability they conspired to add two years to the sixteen Hoffa had actually accumulated.

Passing off the future labor leader as a young adult was as easy as falling off a Teamster's truck. Hoffa was close to his mature height of 5 feet, 5½ inches and weighed a solid 170 pounds. He had the build of a slightly overweight amateur wrestler with a bull neck, a barrel chest and un-sculpted muscular arms whose upper mass pushed his elbows slightly away from his body. He had big hands, a thick torso and tree-trunk legs. His defiant air and fiercely penetrating look had already begun to show. The Kroger foreman sensed at a glance this youngster was a hard worker who could hold his own among the rough crew of older warehousemen. He hired Hoffa on the spot as a member of the night shift, much to his later regret.

A Kroger warehouseman's salary was thirty-two cents an hour, paid only for the time actually worked. Hoffa checked in daily at 4:30 p.m. and typically spent twelve or more hours at the warehouse to receive nine hours of pay. In a good week he could make about fifteen dollars, an effective rate of twenty-five cents for each hour on the job. Nothing was withheld for benefits and nothing offered in the way of job security. Management had all the power, which included open shop hiring and "lockouts" of employees during labor disputes. Strikes were prohibited in Michigan at the time but when legalized a few years later, strike breakers were hired to replace workers who walked off the job.

Besides "Jay" Langley, his future brother-in-law, Hoffa had other acquaintances among these warehousemen before he joined them and in short order made friends with several more. Chief among the latter were Bobby Holmes, Frank Collins, and Sam Calhoun. Langley had belonged to a union in a prior job and was a strong proponent of organized labor. Holmes was an English immigrant; he, Collins, and Langley were only two or three years older than Hoffa. At thirty-four, Calhoun was the old man of the group, its unofficial leader and spokesman.

Though no one had selected these five employees to act for the Kroger warehousemen, they began to think of themselves as leaders. In slack periods—on the warehouse steps in the summer heat, and around a coal fire in the cold days of winter—they found plenty of time to talk. Along with fellow workers they feared the loss of their jobs and seethed under the Little Bastard's unremitting lash. Their conversations thus inevitably focused on ways they might band together to seek job security and improved working conditions. Gradually they developed a plan to form an independent union composed of Kroger's roughly one hundred seventy-five warehousemen. Their goal was a written contract with management, spelling out the benefits and protections they sought.

The efficient operation of the Kroger warehouse depended on coordinated teamwork among this large group of dockmen. The night shift's job was to unload railroad boxcars and over-the-road trucks upon their arrival at the receiving platform laden with canned goods, packaged foods, or fresh meat and produce cooled by melting ice. Items designated for later distribution were put into temporary storage; all were eventually sorted into groups destined for specific Kroger stores and loaded into waiting trucks. Smooth handling was particularly important when a large shipment of spoilable food had to be put quickly into the local distribution system. In that situation Hoffa and his colleagues had to move alertly and harmoniously through their paces to assure the perishables' arrival at retail outlets in marketable condition.

After much discussion the gang of five agreed on the concessions they would seek from management and the circumstances in which they would make their move. Holmes felt they should not reach for the stars on this first effort. Calhoun emphasized the need "to hit 'em in the pocketbook" by stopping work while offloading a particularly expensive cargo.[4] Over several months each of the five had buttonholed fellow workers to stress the benefits of forming a union and the need for everyone's support when the proper time came.

Midnight marked the approximate mid-point of a dockman's working day. One night in April of 1931 two workers went to a street cart just off the company's premises to buy sandwiches for their midnight "lunch." This was a customary practice, but when the duo returned to the warehouse foreman Hastings told them he had hired replacements and they were no longer Kroger employees. Perhaps the men had taken a few extra minutes, or maybe their overseer thought they had not been carrying their weight. But as usual the Little Bastard gave no reason for his action, confirming to the entire workforce that his decision was arbitrary and vindictive. This was the catalytic event the five leaders had been waiting for. As word of the abrupt discharges quickly spread, the warehousemen went about their jobs as usual but their unrest was palpable and rebellion was in the air.

A few nights later a large truckload of fresh strawberries, an especially delicate crop, pulled up at the Kroger distribution facility. About halfway through the unloading process the word was passed to all workers: "Lay down your crates and assemble on the dock," which they did promptly, to a man. Foreman Hastings immediately launched into demented overdrive. "This is private property," he screamed. "Get back to work, you bums, or get the hell out!"[5] Calhoun told him they wanted to talk to the foreman's boss. "Get Blough," the warehouse manager and Hastings's boss, Calhoun said sharply. "We'll deal only with him." This merely heightened the Little Bastard's apoplexy. Again he yelled "This is private property, get back to work," obviously believing that on Kroger's turf he could do as he pleased.[6]

But the crewmen were now fully energized. "The hell with you, Bandy Legs! We want Blough! We want Blough!" Hearing the commotion, the big boss himself came out to the loading platform, sized up the situation, and quickly understood he had to take action. His dock workers' anger had boiled over. A valuable truckload of strawberries would be lost if not soon transferred to cool storage. After giving the leaders a chance to express the men's grievances, Blough defused the crisis by promising that Kroger management would meet with them the next morning and negotiate their demand in good faith. With that, the strawberry rebellion ended. The men went back to work, their stoic skepticism now infused with a modicum of hope.

After several days of discussion the gang of five essentially got what they asked for. Led by the low-key but persistent Calhoun, and adhering to their earlier decision not to overreach, the leaders negotiated "a pay raise of thirteen cents an hour, the guarantee of at least half a day's pay, a modest insurance plan and the designation of an eating room for the men."[7] The company also agreed to put its commitment in the form of a union contract and to recognize the men's union once they sought and obtained a charter. Within a few weeks Kroger's warehousemen belonged to Federal Local 19431, an affiliate of the American Federation of Labor.

Recognizing Calhoun as the guiding force behind their movement, the leaders nominated him for the office of union president and elected him by acclamation. On the slate with him were Hoffa as vice-president and Holmes as secretary-treasurer ("without treasure," said the latter some years after the event).[8] Calhoun chose his vice-president not out of the blue but in recognition of the energy and empathy with which Hoffa had addressed and assuaged the fears of so many, priming them for a work stoppage whenever the order might come.

Jimmy displayed uncanny ability in enlisting the support of his fellow workers. He was a born organizer. William Crow, one of his earliest recruits, said: "He stood right up close to you and looked right at you.... He was the sincerest little guy I've ever seen. He gave me confidence. Up to then I'd been scared to join a union but Jimmy made me feel that it was just the right thing to do."[9]

The five stalwarts of the strawberry rebellion stayed on their jobs at Kroger, working openly to solidify the feeling of union brotherhood among their fellow workers. Hoffa took a leading role in recruiting new employees to the organization, and in dealing with the men's ongoing employment issues. A few months later, in response to the urging of a visiting Teamster organizer, the members decided to affiliate their Local with the International Brotherhood. In this new relationship, IBT officials began to take notice of Hoffa's organizing skills and the vigorous enthusiasm he brought to the job.

Although the atmosphere at Kroger's loading dock remained tense, relative calmness prevailed for some time. About a year after the showdown at the warehouse Hoffa and his irascible foreman Hastings had their inevitable confrontation. It happened during a transfer of crates of fresh celery from a large incoming load to small trucks bound for Kroger stores. Fed up with the Little Bastard's incessant badgering, Hoffa threw down a celery crate and stormed off of the loading dock.

The very next day Ray Bennett offered him an organizer's job at the AFL's Joint Council 43, which he took without a second thought. At the time, Hoffa could hardly imagine how far he would go or the obstacles and temptations he would meet along the way. Nor could he foresee the risks he would take or the consequences of embracing them. For now he was simply feeling the exhilaration of his new freedom from the Little Bastard and from the limited opportunities of his past employment. He also saw his new job as a chance to put his natural talents to their highest and best use.

****

Detroit in the mid-1930s was hostile terrain for the newest organizer hired by Joint Council 43. The city's automobile manufacturers were not merely anti-union; they were private property fundamentalists whose perceived rights were enshrined in the principle of laissez-faire, protected by the US Constitution. To them an open shop was an entitlement essential to their industry's profitability. Henry Ford, the town's earliest business icon, was the group's most spirited advocate. Denouncing the United Automobile Workers in 1937, he famously called labor unions "the worst thing that ever struck the earth, because they take away a man's independence." The Ford Motor Company and the half-dozen other auto makers of the day kept lists of thugs for hire, ready to be loosed on strikers at the first hint of trouble. These goons were also available to guard scabs who crossed picket lines to perform striking workers' jobs. Other local businesses, though less powerful than the auto makers, were equally adamant in their opposition to labor unions' growth.

Detroit's employers spent freely to put political power in friendly hands at City Hall and the state legislature. When labor turmoil led inevitably to violence, the police responded as agents of the business establishment. With billy clubs they lacerated scalps and broke bones, then loaded their paddy wagons to capacity with roughed-up strikers for repeated trips to the jailhouse. To sit at the table with this business-government alliance, union leaders felt they had to smash through a bolted dining room door. Angry workers wielded baseball bats or makeshift clubs in self-defense and in open assaults on hired muscle men. Even peaceful protests would occasionally get out of hand, as at Ford's plant in Dearborn, Michigan in March of 1932. "Nobody could look at the marchers themselves," said one historian, "and accuse them of any destructive purpose."[10] But the policemen and company security guards standing at the factory gates grew nervous. As the crowd of some three thousand workers approached, the armed defenders drew their guns and fired into the crowd. Five marchers were shot dead and nineteen others were injured.

This was the rough and tumble arena in which Hoffa began his union career. Ray Bennett had chosen his man wisely; the job of organizer at the IBT's Joint Council 43 fit the burly young man like a tailored suit. Honing the skills that had persuaded the Kroger dock workers to support the strawberry rebellion, he went after his former company's employees at other locations. Before the end of his first year he had led almost four hundred of them into the Teamster fold, along with an equal or greater number of warehousemen employed by other Detroit companies. In the process he had learned new techniques of persuasion, sometimes starting with the lowest paid workers and moving up, often approaching management in advance to soften their opposition. The fruits of his efforts were satisfyingly evident; conversion to union membership usually brought instant improvements in pay and working conditions. These successes sustained Hoffa's self-confidence and fueled his seemingly inexhaustible supply of vitality and stamina.

Pleased with the young organizer's success, his Joint Council superiors gave him an important new assignment: the recruitment of "haulaway" truck drivers employed by Detroit's auto makers to carry new models to local car dealers around the country. These "car haulers" were an independent breed, willing to accept the dangers of the highway and the long, dull hours on the road away from family and friends. Like most over-the-road truckers they had not served apprenticeships in other areas of their employers' businesses. They were simply "drive-away" truckers with no special knowledge or particular skill. Dan Tobin, the IBT's craft-oriented president at the time, considered them "riffraff" and "rubbish," but they were becoming an important segment of Detroit's truck driver pool. The Teamsters could no longer afford to ignore them.

Organizing the car haulers was a difficult, time-consuming job. They were usually out of town, and hardly approachable in their homes or at factory loading docks. The only way to pitch them for union membership was to go where they worked, on the open road. Truck stops were few and small-town hotels were miles apart and pricey. The drivers found it easier to pull off on the side of the road, eat a homemade sandwich washed down with a bottle of pop, have a cigarette and sleep in the driver's cab until the first pre-dawn light. Hoffa developed a technique for approaching them that became the organizers' standard. He would drive his car along the road until a parked truck came into view, pull up behind it, get out and bang on the driver's door to get his attention. The door would be opened by a suspicious operator, half-asleep, angry and often clutching a tire iron in his right hand to ward off a possible attack. As Hoffa described it he would then identify himself with a rapid-fire introduction: "'Hi-I'm-Jimmy-Hoffa-organizer-for-the-Teamsters-and-I-wonder-if-I-could-talk-to-you.' Then I'd duck back."[11]

One trucker recruited by Hoffa in those days remembered him well. "I was about half-way between Detroit and Cleveland. Guess I'd been sawing the wood for about twenty minutes when the door opening woke me up. I was still half asleep. This little guy looked up at me, grinning. I thought he was a bum looking for a ride. But he said, 'My name is Hoffa. Can I talk with you about the Teamsters?' I said, no, you can't. Now get out of here and let me sleep."[12]

But Hoffa would not be denied. "'Just five minutes,' he would say, 'that's all I ask.' Well I was awake anyhow so I told him to go ahead. He really bore in on me. I told him I was scared I'd get fired if I joined a union. He said that by the time I got back to Detroit everybody would have joined. I told him I couldn't afford the dues. He said that once we got organized I'd make it up in pay raises and more besides. I told him I didn't like unions anyhow. Them union guys was always causing trouble. He said that in the Teamster Union I would be invited to all the meetings and the members called the shots. He had an answer for everything and he never let up. If I hadn't signed that membership card we'd still be there."[13]

With other Council organizers following Hoffa's lead, the trucking companies retaliated be seating hired thugs alongside their drivers. Hoffa told of one encounter with these ruffians. "I spotted a rig parked off the highway in a lonely stretch … I pulled up behind it and when I couldn't open the door … I yelled 'Hey, you awake?' The door shot open and two goons piled right on top of me … [and] beat me right into the ground. Just before I passed out, one of them grabbed me by the throat and lifted my head off the ground. 'That's just a sample,' he growled. 'Stay away from our trucks. Next time you're dead.'"[14] To counter this practice the union organizers went out in pairs, able enough, thought Hoffa, to take care of any goons they might meet. Management responded by loading trucks with gangs of muscle men to scour the highways for marauding union organizers. They also prodded the police to find pretexts to search the Teamsters' cars, which the cops now knew by sight. Complained Hoffa, "We were stopped … for every imagined traffic violation, … and anything that might pass as a weapon—a tire iron or a jack handle—was confiscated."[15]

In 1935 the IBT's Tobin made Ray Bennett the trustee-manager of the Teamster's faltering Detroit Local 299. One of Bennett's early actions was to choose young Jimmy Hoffa, whom he had hired three years earlier, as the local union's Business Agent and chief administrator. With the appointment came a weekly salary of twenty-five dollars—higher pay and a more reliable source of income, at least in theory, than Hoffa's contingent pay as an organizer. In fact, however, the Local's finances were dismal and for several months its new day-to-day manager was lucky to take home a small portion of his weekly due. But Hoffa was a man of simple tastes and spartan habits and as yet unmarried. Personal ambition and a sense of mission, not a hunger for money, drove him to work harder than ever.

By the mid-1930s, having brought most of the "car haulers" into the Teamster ranks, Hoffa turned his attention to the wider Detroit scene. During his time at Joint Council 43 he had developed a close friendship with Owen "Bert" Brennan, a fellow organizer who had been a truck driver in Chicago before moving to Detroit. Growing up in a poor family in the Windy City's rougher neighborhoods, Brennan had learned to defend himself on its mean streets. Thin and wiry but with a steely glare and an oversized temper that easily boiled over, he could give as good as he got. Pound for pound he was as tough as his stockier friend and they hit it off from the beginning. The two of them now worked together, their goal to make Teamsters out of every local truck driver and warehouseman and, as well, the "inside" workers at retail outlets and other sites receiving goods by truck.

A case in point was the battle between the Teamsters and the United Brewery Workers whose Locals, like those of the Teamsters, were affiliated with the AFL. Begun in January 1938, Detroit's beer war raged on and off for more than two years. Members of Local 271, a Teamster union formed specifically to recruit UBW drivers, simultaneously picketed all seven of the city's breweries. When brewery trucks tried to cross the picket lines, swarming Teamsters pulled the drivers from their cabs and beat them, some severely enough to require hospitalization. They used their own cars and trucks to block roads leading to the breweries, stretching the ranks of policemen sent to keep order. When a beer truck escaped, a Teamster vehicle gave chase, trying to force it off the road. Teamsters not participating in the picket lines waylaid and beat UBW dolly-handlers with clubs and brass knuckles as they delivered cases of beer to taverns and hotels. Brewery workers fought back, once firing shots at Owen Brennan's car. He was not hit but later showed bullet holes and a shattered window as proof of the assault.

During an uneasy truce the combatants tried to settle their dispute with non-binding arbitration. When that failed both sides went to court but were turned away by judges unwilling to enter the fray. That brought appeals to the AFL Executive Council which overturned a local ruling favoring the UBW but essentially maintained the status quo. Unable to win a definitive recruiting victory through legitimate means the Detroit Teamsters sought help from tavern owners. Most of these owners were former bootleggers, many of them former members of the East Side Sicilian Mob or the Jewish Purple Gang, the city's most notorious criminal organizations.[16] Cash payments to bartenders and continuing threats of violence to recalcitrant UBW drivers brought many new members into the Teamsters' fold. These early connections between the Detroit Teamsters and organized crime took root and steadily grew stronger.

As Detroit's labor battles raged on, Hoffa and Brennan set about reorganizing the employees of the Kroger Company from which the Teamsters had been ousted a year or so earlier. One of Kroger's armed security guards shot and wounded Martin Haggerty, a Teamster organizer. Sam Calhoun, the strawberry rebels' elder statesman, was mauled by an ex-prizefighter hired by Kroger. In 1940, while on a picket line, Hoffa's brother Billy was shot, a non-fatal but serious wound to the stomach.

Hoffa spoke of these times self-servingly, but his words had the ring of truth from one who had been in the trenches. "In the early days you couldn't get recognition without a strike, ... and every strike was a fight ... [W]e kept the picket lines going day and night, sleeping in cars on the ground. The strikebreakers tried to run us away and the police helped them. ... Our cars were bombed out. Three different times someone broke into the office and destroyed our furniture. Cars would crowd us off the streets ... I got my head busted a few times. ... One of our business agents was killed. There was only one way to survive—fight back."[17]

Hoffa himself swung a baseball bat at a strikebreaker attempting to cross a picket line at Sears Roebuck. On another occasion he used an automobile tire chain to flog a CIO organizer during an inter-union face-off. Said an approving colleague who had stood at his boss's side during those early days, "Jimmy did whatever he had to do"[18] And the hot-tempered Hoffa readily conceded, "I'm no angel."

He scorned anyone afraid to mix it up physically when the need arose. On one occasion Hoffa and several union cronies sat in their headquarters when a larger group of disgruntled Teamsters burst into the room, "for one purpose only," said a union colleague later, "to whip our ass."[19] After a free-swinging melee the loyalists managed to push the intruders back out the door, chastised and no longer threatening. Hoffa turned immediately to one of his fellows, an ex-prizefighter named Brady, furious at the man's inadequate performance. In his book this failure meant only one thing: Brady was a coward, and cowards had no place in the Teamster organization. "You son of a bitch; you don't work here no more!" And with that cursory dismissal Brady was not seen again in the halls of Local 299.[20]

Hoffa had the instincts and bold determination of a natural leader. When his men went to jail he was right beside them. On one occasion, in an effort to demoralize Teamster picketers by removing their leader, the police arrested and carried him to jail eighteen times in a single day and night. Unable to be held for any specific offense, he returned each time to the picket line to the men's cheers for his willingness to defy authority. He accepted these arrests as a symbol of honor and effective leadership. "A union organizer who didn't get in trouble with the police was either buying them off or he wasn't doing his job."[21] Despite his involvement in so many incidents in the tumultuous labor disputes of the 1930s, only once in that decade was Hoffa convicted of a crime: assault and battery on a picket line at a local laundry, for which he was fined ten dollars. This record reflected Hoffa's street smarts as well as the Depression era's tolerance of non-lethal violence.

It was on another laundry picket line, coincidentally, that he met Josephine Poszywak, an active member of the American Laundry Workers Association and a spirited young granddaughter of Polish immigrants. She and her fellow washers, ironers, and mangle operators had gone on strike in May of 1936, seeking guaranteed hours of work and higher wages. The inequities of the laundry workers' pay structure were similar to those of the Kroger dockmen when Hoffa first joined the latter's ranks. Poszywak and her co-workers received payment only for the time the mangles were in operation, not while waiting for enough dirty clothes to pile up to make a tub-load. They then received a sweat-shop rate of seventeen cents per hour, sometimes for only two or three loads per day.

At that time Teamster Local 299 boasted only four laundry drivers. Anxious to bring more of them into his union Hoffa agreed to help the laundry workers' latest effort to improve their lot. After visiting the strike scene to see what was needed, he brought forty Teamsters to join the women's picket line. Local police called to the plant by management seized him as the new picketers' ringleader, shoved him in a paddy wagon and took him to jail on a charge of disturbing the peace. Quickly released because he had done nothing illegal, he returned the following day and joined the picket line himself.

His decision to march with the women strikers changed his life. The picketers had formed two concentric circles marching in opposite directions. Among them was an eighteen-year-old "looker" who immediately captured his attention. "I dropped into the outside line and as I passed … women [in the inner line] I tried to give each of them a smile to encourage them. Then it happened. I was looking into the brightest pair of blue eyes I'd ever seen. They crinkled in the corners when she smiled back at me. Her hair was shining blond and although she was small and looked frail, she walked erect and proud. I felt like I'd been hit on the chest with a blackjack."[22] The "looker" was Josephine. After they had passed each other a couple of times the twenty-three-year-old Jimmy saw his opportunity and seized it. He stepped over into her line and fell in behind her. "I'm going after coffee and donuts for the picketers," he said, "so how about coming with me?" She agreed and at the sweet shop accepted his invitation to go to the movies with him that night.

Arriving at Jo's house to pick her up Hoffa tapped the horn of his used Chevrolet instead of going into the house for her, a serious tactical mistake. When she failed to show he blew louder and longer, compounding his error. Finally he went up to the door and was greeted coldly, first by Mrs. Poszywak and then by the daughter, who said flatly she was not going out with him as planned. Flustered by this unexpected rejection he fled, but the next day, back on the picket line, he asked her what happened. "You blew your horn," she said, "and you don't do that in my neighborhood. The neighbors were looking out at you, and if I'd gone with you they would think I'd go out with any young man who drove up and tooted his horn." Pleading ignorance and begging her pardon, he convinced her to give him another try. That night at her door he was introduced to her mother as if they had never met. Jo left with him, unabashed by stares of curious neighbors. In the theater he reached for her hand. "Polish girls don't hold hands unless they mean it," she said. "Well, I sure hope you mean it," Jimmy whispered, "because I *really* mean it."[23]

Following that first evening the two dated steadily as Hoffa gradually gained the confidence of his girlfriend's mother. Four months later, on a Saturday in September, he and Jo were married by a Justice of the Peace in Bowling Green, Ohio. After spending only two nights in a Cleveland hotel they returned to Detroit, the new husband pressed for time to prepare for an upcoming special Teamster assignment in

Minneapolis. From then on the two were out of each other's sight only when Hoffa was on the road. Because that was often, he telephoned her daily from wherever he might be. With two children, first a daughter and then a son, they spent virtually all of the busy unionist's home time with the children at a lakeside cabin about forty miles north of the city. In later years when the media interviewed her as the wife of a noted labor leader, Jo said she was still hoping that one day they would find time to have a real honeymoon. In the early years of their marriage the cabin and its lake would provide their only mutual recreation.

In June of 1938 Hoffa gained greater awareness of labor's larger picture. Ray Bennett sent him westward to work with the Teamsters' resourceful organizer in Minneapolis, Farrell Dobbs. Dobbs and his colleagues were socialists in the Trotsky mold, advocating unionism—rather than Stalin's state socialism—as a method of gaining labor's control of the means of production. Dan Tobin, the IBT president and a staunch Roosevelt supporter, tolerated the Trotskyites for their extraordinary organizing skills. Hoffa considered all such far left-wingers "nuts" and "screwball" communists, but he quickly came to admire Dobbs's brilliance as an organizer and a theorist of union growth. It was Dobbs more than any other who conceptualized the strategic value of the over-the-road driver in the Teamster's planning, and the use of secondary boycotts he called "leapfrogging" as an effective way to organize truck terminals in consecutive cities along the drivers' routes. In his later years Hoffa would say that in Minneapolis he had studied "at the knees of a master."[24]

In July of that year the Teamsters began a serious effort to bring local unions together to bargain for the rights of their over-the-road drivers on a regional basis. Dobbs had begun to work with Teamster units in the Dakotas, Iowa, and Wisconsin. Detroit's three Locals were spreading their influence toward Indiana and Ohio. Teamster unions in Nebraska, Illinois and Missouri were thinking along similar lines. Now, with intercity drivers working for hundreds of trucking companies along this broad east-west swath, a mechanism was needed to force their employers to negotiate a single contract for the entire region. With this as their goal, Teamster officials from these states met in Chicago in March and formed the North Central Area Committee. The new Committee then wrote to the American

Trucking Association, a group of the nation's largest trucking companies, demanding that it bargain with them for an agreement covering over-the-road Teamsters in their region. The ATA turned them down cold.

Led by Dobbs, the NCAC developed an imaginative plan to use Chicago as the focal point of their campaign. To the commerce of the north-central United States, the Windy City of the late 1930s was like ancient Rome to its empire: all roads passed through it. Dobbs wisely reasoned that if pressure could be put on that critical hub, the numerous trucking companies daily entering and leaving Chicago would feel the pain. Reaching agreement with them would then encourage other Midwest companies to follow suit. Following their turndown by the ATA, the NCAC wrote a letter to all unionized truck operators in their eleven-state region carrying goods to or from the Windy City: send a negotiating team to meet with us, it said, or our drivers will go out on strike. This threat hit the trucking industry like an earthquake. A regional settlement in the heart of the country would seriously undermine the power of truck operators everywhere vis-à-vis the local truck driver unions.

Recipients of the NCAC letter agreed to its demand with unexpected speed. Within two weeks they had formed a committee and sent it to Chicago with no restrictions on what might be discussed. The results of that meeting were startling. In August of 1938, after fourteen days of "grueling negotiations, … the operators' committee and the NCAC agreed on a contract that established uniform minimum wages, maximum hours, seniority rights and safety guarantees for 125,000 workers at 1,700 companies in the eleven-state area."[25] The Teamster hordes had invaded Chicago, clashed with the country's largest trucking companies, and come away with unprecedented spoils of victory. Hoffa and his two Detroit bosses, Ray Bennett and Joseph O'Laughlin, returned to Detroit as conquering heroes.

The regional contract, despite its breadth, did not cover all trucking companies in the eleven-state area but proved the enormous power of collective bargaining. It became the foundation of Teamster efforts to bring recalcitrant employers within its scope. Once again it was the fertile mind of Farrell Dobbs that saw how to corral the holdouts. Large operators in Omaha and Sioux City had not only refused to sign the agreement; in its wake they had locked out their Teamster drivers and hired non-union members to replace them. Focusing on Omaha, Dobbs decided that the road to Teamster success in the heart of Nebraska began in Kansas City, Missouri. If the movement of trucked goods between those two cities could be interrupted, even for a relatively short time, employers in both places would suffer. The head of the Teamster Local in Kansas City respected Dobbs and saw the value of his plan. He advised all trucking companies in his Missouri territory that his Teamsters would be ordered to strike unless the Kansas City companies agreed to cease handling goods moving to and from Omaha. Surrender to this mandate came quickly. The Omaha companies, pressured by their KC colleagues and desperate to restore the huge flow of traffic between the two cities, soon capitulated by signing onto the master regional contract.

Hoffa observed the working of this innovative strategy and never forgot its lesson about the power of a secondary boycott: "When [we] push[ed] a button in Kansas City, Omaha jump[ed]."[26] In the years to come he would often order Teamsters to refuse to handle goods at one company or industry group as a highly effective means of organizing or increasing the working conditions at another commercially connected city. After negotiating his own regional agreements he raised his sights to a higher level: a nationwide agreement with trucking companies covering all of the IBT's over-the-road drivers. Indeed, a contract of this enormous scope became his holy grail, a goal that would eventually become a reality.

The biggest threat to the power of the Detroit Teamsters came in June of 1941, when the IBT's executive board announced its decision to expel from its ranks members of "subversive, revolutionary" organizations.[27] The clear targets of this edict were Dobbs and the Minneapolis Trotskyites whose socialist politics had long rankled Tobin, the IBT president. With the country facing the threat of war and Detroit's businesses brimming with Defense Department contracts, Tobin had finally reached the boiling point. John L. Lewis, the head of the CIO, had no such qualms. When Dobbs and his band applied for CIO affiliation Lewis promptly issued them a charter, welcoming the outcasts like wandering children coming home from the wilderness. Denny Lewis, John L.'s brother, went to Detroit and announced that

"We [see] this move on the part of the Minneapolis truck drivers into our organization as the first step towards the complete organization of truck drivers in the United States in the CIO."[28] For Hoffa and Brennan, who had been fighting the CIO in Detroit for the better part of three years, this was a trumpet call to battle.

The anticipated invasion of the Teamsters' Detroit stronghold by a reinforced CIO was made even more menacing by reports that Walter Reuther's United Automobile Workers would lend their potentially decisive support. Tobin and other IBT officers knew they were in trouble. Publicly Tobin warned the UAW hierarchy not to disturb the "harmonious relations" between their two organizations. Privately he sent his Detroit lieutenant Hoffa to the Twin Cities to persuade the members of Local 544 to rejoin the Teamsters and the AFL. The future Teamster boss later professed to having been reluctant to antagonize his Minnesota mentors, perhaps disingenuously, given the high stakes of the threat. At the time, however, he saluted smartly, filled a caravan of automobiles with strong-armed supporters, and headed west.

In Minneapolis Hoffa increased his army to an estimated 200 men with a mix of Teamster loyalists from surrounding areas, local thugs, and a few Chicago mercenaries enticed westward by Bert Brennan. The Trotskyite unionists swelled their ranks with professional ruffians, and the fight was on. In the streets of the Twin Cities, armed with bats, sticks and brass knuckles, Hoffa's motorcades searched out gatherings of their former union brothers and forced them to sign membership cards renewing their Teamster loyalty. Injuries were common, some serious. Local police, backed by the staunchly anti-socialist Minneapolis mayor and the state's similarly inclined governor, did little to maintain order. President Roosevelt's Department of Justice sent FBI agents to raid and make arrests at the Minneapolis headquarters of the Socialist Party Workers. In the end the battle was won and Local 544 was again a Teamster stronghold.

IBT officialdom knew, however, that a victory obtained by force alone was unstable. If Teamster affiliation brought no tangible benefits, member loyalty would soon turn to unrest. To solidify their recent success they ordered the new Local 544 leaders to use all their resources, including strike threats as necessary, in a full-court press on Minneapolis employers for higher wages and more favorable working conditions. In recognition of Hoffa's leadership, Tobin gave him Dobbs's old position of vice-president of the Central States Drivers Council and kept him also as the chairman of its negotiating team. With those titles, and as the de facto head of ten local unions in the lower Michigan area, the star of the twenty-eight-year-old Hoffa was rising steadily.

America's entry into World War II marked the end of an uncommon decade of growth for the Detroit Teamsters. When the Strawberry Rebels organized Kroger warehousemen into a fledgling local in 1931, about four hundred Motor City truck drivers called themselves Teamsters. Ten years later, Teamster affiliates in the greater Detroit area represented more than twenty thousand employees in a wide variety of jobs. Though he had not yet turned thirty, and was not yet a union president, Hoffa ran the show with Brennan as his second in command. Deferred from military service as an executive of an industry essential to the nation's wartime effort, he kept up his trademark intensity in the recruitment of drivers and inside employees, primarily those in the food distribution business. And by calling strikes he largely ignored Tobin's pledge to President Roosevelt that the Teamsters would not use this tactic in wartime. In short, Hoffa remained Hoffa as his countrymen took up arms, preeminently concerned with the expansion of his union and the amassing of personal power within it.

The decade of the 1930s had shown Hoffa's brilliance as a union organizer and his courage as a fighter for the Teamsters' rank and file. The drain on civilian personnel during five years of war and demobilization highlighted his leadership talents to other home front civilians, particularly among union officials anywhere near his age. His energetic opportunism was undiminished by any guilt for avoidance of military service. With the public's attention elsewhere he was freer than ever to continue his unusually aggressive tactics, and he did so. Teamster growth remained his highest priority, above the country's wartime imperatives and their emphasis on national unity and military success.

During the years of World War II Hoffa grew and consolidated his power within Teamster organizations in Michigan and other states located in a wide arc between Ohio and Minnesota. In 1940, IBT President Tobin appointed him the negotiating chairman of the Central States Drivers' Council, an organization representing

Teamster unions in twelve midwestern states, and a year later named him the CSDC's vice-president. A few months later Hoffa brashly created the Michigan Conference of Teamsters, appointing himself as the new organization's chairman. Tobin further polished Hoffa's reputation in 1943 by selecting him as one of three Trustees to make semi-annual reviews of the international union's financial records. Accompanying his ascendancy within IBT officialdom during these war years was his increasing popularity among rank and file Teamster members in his backyard and beyond.

In June of 1945, two months before the war's end, Hoffa sought the presidency of Detroit's Local 299 and was elected by voice vote without opposition.[31] Two years later the members of Joint Council 43, the burgeoning organization of Teamster unions within metropolitan Detroit, unanimously elected him as their president. Seattle's Dave Beck, the western states' most powerful Teamster boss and the IBT's executive vice-president, was then emerging as the man to succeed Dan Tobin as the international union's president at its next general convention in 1952. Delegates to that convention elected Hoffa to the IBT's executive board as one of its thirteen vice-presidents, at age 39 the youngest person yet to hold that office. With his growing power rapidly coalescing, Hoffa now controlled the votes of several hundred delegates from the Central States, Southern, and Eastern Teamster Conferences. When a "stop Beck" movement began to circulate among the convention delegates, Hoffa pledged his full support to the Seattle boss. This move put Beck over the top and the new IBT president heavily in debt to his powerful new supporter. From that point on, as a full-fledged member of the IBT hierarchy and with some six hundred thousand IBT members as his loyal supporters, the ambitious Teamster boss from Detroit was widely recognized as Beck's heir apparent.

Concurrently with his rise to national leadership, Hoffa sowed the seeds of the destructive forces that would ultimately bring him down. He hired recognized criminals as Joint Council organizers, including Tom Burke, a pistol-wielding thug known for obtaining Teamster contracts with employers held at gunpoint. Also on his payroll were James Cassily, a professional burglar; and Harry Ames, an ex-con who had served time for dynamiting a building for an owner seeking insurance proceeds.[32] His connections to Detroit mobsters grew stronger, and through them he met and empowered Mafia bosses and *caporegimes* to exert influence and often take control of Teamster operations. A sampling of these included Johnny Dio in New York City, Tony Provenzano in northern New Jersey, Paul ("Red") Dorfman in Chicago, Russell Bufalino in eastern Pennsylvania, Carlos Marcello in New Orleans, and Santos Trafficante in Miami.

Some Teamster unions, however, spawned anti-Hoffa cabals. Dissidents within these groups gradually became aware of Hoffa's relationships with organized crime members and filed complaints about them with local law enforcement agencies and state legislators throughout the country. Their grievances eventually reached the halls of the US Congress, resulting in the formation of committees in the Senate and House of Representatives to conduct hearings on the issues raised. Foremost among these, and the last to be created, was Senator McClellan's Select Committee to investigate the growing influence of organized crime within the nation's larger labor unions. Although the McClellan Committee cast its net widely over several major unions and their officials, David Beck and Jimmy Hoffa soon became the Committee's primary targets.

Leading the charge to incriminate the incumbent Teamster boss and his presumed successor was the Committee's Chief Counsel, Robert F. Kennedy. At Kennedy's side was a team of young, bright investigators and lawyers, equally dedicated to putting the two men and their ilk behind bars. Publicizing their efforts were a coterie of inquisitive and highly motivated journalists in cities all too familiar with the Teamsters' modus operandi. Though experiencing crushing setbacks, this crusade—for it was indeed that—would achieve ultimate victory. In a book summarizing the findings of the McClellan Committee, Kennedy would indelibly label big labor's affiliation with organized crime *The Enemy Within*. His best seller would recount a story unique in the annals of the American labor movement.

CHAPTER 2

"If Hoffa's Acquitted I'll Jump Off the Capitol Dome"

Bob Kennedy contributed more than anyone else to Jimmy Hoffa's downfall. As chief counsel to a US Senate investigative committee in the late 1950s, the young lawyer developed indisputable evidence of organized crime's growing influence within several of the nation's largest labor unions. Most shocking among the committee's findings were Hoffa's alliances with Mafia bosses whose representatives held positions of power throughout the Teamsters organization. In the eyes of the conscientious young investigator, Hoffa personified the Mob's corrupting influence on labor union management. In 1961, as the new attorney general in President John Kennedy's administration, the younger Kennedy formed a "Get Hoffa Squad" within the Department of Justice and grimly set out to put Hoffa behind bars. With a tenacity acquired in his youthful striving for acceptance amid a fiercely competitive family, he pursued Hoffa's prosecution through massive opposition from the Teamsters' army of lawyers, lobbyists and powerful political supporters. Buffeted by threats and vicious criticisms, Kennedy stayed resolutely on course throughout a long but ultimately successful battle.

****

Robert Francis Kennedy was born November 20th, 1925, the seventh of Joseph and Rose Kennedy's nine children. Known in his youth as "Bobby," he was the apple that fell closest to the family tree. Stories of his life and the lives of his well-known relatives are legion. Biographers describe his desperate struggle for acceptance by his elder brothers and their imperious father, a fight that began when he was only five years old. Impatient even at that age with the slow pace of his swimming lessons in the shallows off the family's Hyannis Port home, he longed to show his teenage brothers how far he had progressed. Out sailing with them one day, he threw himself into the deep waters of Nantucket Sound and likely would have drowned had not Joe Jr. jumped in and hauled the spluttering youngster back on board. And because father Joe demanded punctuality at family gatherings, Bobby became "spectacularly prompt," once bloodying himself by accidentally crashing into an unseen glass partition in a frantic rush to arrive on time at his designated dinner table seat.[1]

Young Bobby also showed a Zen-like attitude toward physical pain. As an eight-year-old, exploring the basement of the family's new house in Bronxville, New York, he tried to move an old radiator that stubbornly held its ground. Finally, with a last tug he pulled so hard it fell over, crushing one of his toes. Hearing the commotion Joe Jr. rushed to him and asked if he was hurt. "No," came the answer, and only when the toe ballooned and turned purple a few days later was it discovered to have been broken.

This habit of silently nursing his injuries, both physical and emotional, persisted as he grew older. At Harvard College he made the varsity football team through sheer guts and determination. In early practice scrimmages he recklessly slammed his five-foot ten-inch, 155-pound frame head-on into players like Vinnie Moravec, a 230-pound fullback. After several of these bone-rattling encounters, Moravec said to the team's coach, "For Christ's sake, stop him before he gets killed."[2] Later in the season Bob crashed into an equipment cart on the sidelines, then got up and played until he collapsed on the field and had to be carried off. Post-game Xrays revealed a fractured leg.[3] This compulsion to risk physical harm, and his reverence for the bravery of his older brothers and other heroes, were deeply ingrained and stayed with him to the end of his life.

As young Bobby sought to match his male role models through stoicism and risk-taking, he wholeheartedly embraced his mother's Catholicism and her religiosity. At age eight he became an acolyte at Saint Joseph's, the family's church in Bronxville, and at age ten prided himself on knowing more Latin than his older siblings. Receiving Holy Communion also gave him a satisfying sense of belonging, and of his worth as a beloved child of God. "Waiving the [censer's] perfumed smoke in the processional or ringing the bell as the priest consecrated the bread and wine, [Bobby] could forget, for a moment, his insignificance at the family dinner table."[4] In his mature years the Church's influence waned, its teachings moderated to fit his active role in law and politics. But his moral compass remained permanently aligned with the magnetic field of the Roman Catholic faith.

At its end, World War II had heightened the disparity between his accomplishments and those of his older brothers. On a classified and highly dangerous mission as a volunteer, Joe Kennedy Jr. died while piloting a bomb-laden experimental airplane that vaporized in mid-air. Brother Jack attained hero status as captain of a PT boat who saved the lives of his crew when Japanese guns destroyed their craft following its sinking of a large enemy ship. Only sixteen years old at the start of the conflict, Bob—as his friends and colleagues now called him—spent the war years finishing high school, studying as an officer candidate in the Navy's V-12 program, and finally, frustrated at the V-12's slow pace, volunteering for service as a seaman on the *USS Joseph P. Kennedy Jr.,* a destroyer named for his deceased brother. No wonder that when asked in a parlor game during a Georgetown dinner party in 1960 what he would choose to be in another life, he replied "a paratrooper."[5]

In the decade following the war Robert Kennedy grew to manhood, found his bearings and gained his balance. He bore the scars of emotional turmoil, physical pain and deep personal loss in the deaths of two siblings. Neglected to the point of humiliation by the family in his early years, he retained smoldering embers of anger and resentment. Inherited wealth had brought him little satisfaction. Driven to seek relevance and a deeper sense of worth he chose various areas of public service, eventually emerging as John Kennedy's chief political adviser and closest confidant. By that time he had outgrown his shyness and feelings of inferiority. He had wooed and won Ethel Skakel as an ebullient wife who fit him like an old sweater. She also brought him the affection, understanding and companionship he had long been without. In contrast to his lackadaisical approach to prep-school and college studies, he had graduated from Virginia Law School with a solid foundation in the law.

Withal, however, his life still lacked the sense of fulfillment and accomplishment which Kennedy males had been taught was their birthright. But in late 1956, a career opportunity Kennedy had perceived only dimly began to come into focus. Senator John McClellan, an Arkansas Democrat, had hired him as chief counsel to a select investigative committee of the US Senate. This job would focus Bob's energies and offer him a previously missing purpose. It would also show his loathing for sloth, pomposity and half-hearted commitment, along with a unique talent for attracting intensely loyal associates as dedicated as he to a common cause.

The McClellan Committee's accumulated evidence showed that unsavory criminals from the ranks of organized crime were infiltrating American labor unions, contaminating their leadership structure and distorting their basic mission. Politicians and the public began to see this as a cancerous growth threatening hard-working men and women with the loss of job security and stability for their dependent families. Dominating this picture in Kennedy's view was the pugnacious image of the corrupt boss of the International Brotherhood of Teamsters, Jimmy Hoffa. The resulting conflict would evolve into a battle of two unyielding wills—Hoffa representing big labor and Kennedy big government— who fought mano-a-mano in the harsh glare of Congressional hearings, media exploitation and courtroom trials of titanic proportion. In Hoffa's ten-year fight to stave off the government's effort to put him behind bars, he attempted to manipulate the power of the White House and the US Congress. In so doing, he threatened to undermine the foundations of the nation's federal court system and almost succeeded. Many would say that Kennedy's determination to prevent that from happening was his defining accomplishment in a lifetime of public service.

****

The Democrats regained control of both houses of Congress in the mid-term elections of 1954. In the game of musical chairs traditionally following such power swings, John McClellan of Arkansas succeeded Wisconsin's Joe McCarthy as the chairman of the Senate's Permanent Subcommittee on Investigations. Before his election to the Senate in 1948, McClellan had served two terms in the House. A thoughtful lawyer, he was a vocal opponent of McCarthy's cruel use of innuendo and unidentified witnesses to support charges of disloyalty within the State Department and other government agencies. He was also a scornful critic of Roy Cohn, McCarthy's shadowy aide, and when he got the opportunity lost no time in naming Bob Kennedy to replace Cohn as the Subcommittee's chief counsel. The Arkansas Senator became one of Kennedy's heroes. "McClellan," he said, was "a man of great patience and innate fair[ness]" who challenged "both labor and management wherever he found wrongdoing." These traits earned him the young lawyer's "highest affection and respect."[6]

In 1956 McClellan's Subcommittee, predecessor of the later-formed Select Committee, turned its attention to allegations of corruption within the national labor movement and to the rising influence of organized crime in union affairs. One such report came from Frank Hogan, district attorney for New York City's Manhattan borough. Hogan supplied evidence that gangsters Antonio ("Tony Ducks") Corallo and Giovanni John Ignazio Dioguardi, alias "Johnny Dio," had infiltrated the City's labor movement, imposing "protection" charges on non-unionized businesses and siphoning off a percentage of paid-in union dues to line their own pockets.

At about the same time, Clark Mollenhoff, Washington Bureau Chief for the *Des Moines Register*, began pressing Kennedy to investigate the rising influence of racketeers within the International Brotherhood of Teamsters. Kennedy resisted Mollenhoff's urgings on the grounds that the IBT had weathered two earlier Congressional investigations, the first led by Congressman Clare E. Hoffman of Michigan in 1953, the second by Congressman Wint Smith from Kansas, both of whom were Republicans. Alleged pressure on higher ranking politicians in the nation's capital had abruptly ended those investigations with no published findings or conclusions. McClellan's chief counsel also argued that the Senate's Labor Committee probably had a higher claim to jurisdiction on matters involving labor corruption. But Mollenhoff, ever the bulldog newspaperman, persisted. "Those other two ... investigations were fixed because of political pressure," he said, "and you do have jurisdiction because these unions are tax-exempt and are misusing their funds."[7]

Kennedy briefed McClellan on this growing evidence, and the latter agreed to launch a widespread investigation into labor corruption. His decision would unleash the most intense inquiry into US labor union practices ever undertaken by the federal government, before or since. Spreading across the country, the Senate's investigators would cross the political Rubicon that in the past had protected national labor leaders from attack by Washington's legionnaires. They would build fortresses of hard fact inside labor's territory which the union bosses' powerful friends in Congress, belatedly called into battle, would be unable to destroy.

The chief counsel's first step in this broad new sweep was to send his investigators to eastern and midwestern cities while he and staffer Carmine Bellino—a former policeman and FBI accountant whom Kennedy called an "investigative genius"—went to the West Coast. In Los Angeles they got first-hand exposure to the troubles besetting the labor movement: "We received reports of unsolved murders which appeared to be traceable to gangsters' muscling in on labor affairs. We studied reports of goons moving into the garment field. We learned of the attempt by gangsters and hoodlums to take over a local union of the Plumbers and Steamfitters with resulting shakedowns on new building projects."[8] Equally shocking was the story of a Los Angeles union representative who had returned to San Diego to organize juke-box operators despite a warning he would be killed if caught again in that area. Unknown assailants seized and beat him into unconsciousness. He awoke the next morning in blood-soaked clothes, badly bruised and with severe cramping in his lower abdomen. He set out for Los Angeles in his car but had gone only a few miles when mounting waves of pain became unbearable. Desperate for relief he managed to sight a hospital along his route and drive to its emergency room entrance where he collapsed in agony. Rushing the battered stranger into surgery, hospital doctors discovered and removed a large cucumber from his rectum. "Later he was told that if he ever returned to San Diego, it would be a watermelon. He never went back."[9]

Kennedy and Bellino went from Los Angeles to Portland, Oregon, where they learned of "a web of vice and corruption involving

Teamster officials" in that area.[10] Making notes of this information as the basis for a later investigation they moved on to Seattle, their main West Coast target. Acting on the advice of Eddie Cheyfitz, a well-known power broker and one of the Teamsters' Washington, D.C. lawyers, they sought out Frank Brewster, the head of the Western Conference of Teamsters. According to Cheyfitz, Brewster was *"the corrupt union figure on the West Coast."*[11] Brewster was out of town, however, and both his office and his lawyer professed not to know where he was or when he would return. Stymied in that direction, Kennedy met the next morning with some dissident members of Portland's local Teamsters union. Following that meeting, with a free afternoon on his hands, he decided to call a man whom a personal friend had described as knowledgeable about Teamster affairs in Seattle. That individual, never identified, turned out to be "a contact that changed the course of the entire investigation [and] perhaps the course of the entire labor movement in the United States."[12]

This knowledgeable informer identified IBT President David Beck, not Brewster, as the center of corruption within the Teamster union. The mystery man claimed to possess evidence that Beck secretly used $163,000 of union funds to build his family residence and then doubled his take by selling the house to the union for the same amount while continuing to live there rent-free. Kennedy's source also identified Nathan Shefferman, a self-styled "labor relations consultant" from Chicago, as the middleman in Beck's shady deals. According to the informant, Shefferman would charge the IBT grossly inflated fees for his consulting services, the bulk of which he then paid out to contractors and other providers of goods and services to Beck for the latter's personal use.

At this point a growing awareness of McClellan's broad inquiry was generating complaints from Beck and other labor leaders that the Senator's Subcommittee, an arm of the Senate's Government Operations Committee, lacked jurisdiction to probe union activity. The Labor Committee, they said, was where any such inquiry belonged— and where, they need not add, they had more friends. In a political compromise to enable its investigation to continue, the Senate formed a Select Committee on Improper Activities in the Labor or Management Field. The new Select Committee, chaired by McClellan, consisted of eight Senators, four from the Labor Committee and four from Government Operations, equally split between Democrats and Republicans with Kennedy remaining as the group's chief counsel.

For his new bosses Kennedy pursued the leads provided by his clandestine contact in Seattle. He met in Chicago with Shefferman, Dave Beck's bagman, who was initially evasive in his denials of wrong-doing but ended up supplying Kennedy and Bellino with voluminous records of his role as a conduit through which Teamster funds were laundered and redirected to the IBT president. By following further leads in Seattle, Committee investigators found that Beck had used union funds to purchase everything from motor launches and freezers for himself to diapers and nylon stockings for his family. Altogether he was shown to have misappropriated $370,000 of Teamster funds for his personal use, a significant sum in the mid–1950s.

Hearings before the recently established Select Committee got under way in March of 1957 with Dave Beck as its first witness. Pompous and confident when he first took the stand, the Teamster president responded with philosophical platitudes to softball questions from the Committee's Republicans. He managed to stay on the offensive with long-winded, rambling responses to the more direct questions of the Democrats, though in the end he refused to answer them, citing his right to avoid self-incrimination. But when Kennedy took over the questioning and offered concrete evidence of Beck's dishonest practices, the labor leader grew testy and less assured as he repeatedly "took the 5th." By the end of the second day, though still loudly proclaiming his innocence, most observers thought the Teamster president had been convincingly dis-credited. Loyal Beck insiders expressed their continued support but their voices would also fade as further evidence of his misconduct came to light.

The last straw on the pile of criticism against Beck was a disclosure made soon after his public questioning. Investigators from the Select Committee found that he had taken $71,000 from Teamster coffers and with it bought home mortgages, ostensibly as an investment for the union's pension fund but actually in the name of himself and a friend as their personal property. Some months later Beck sold the mortgages to a memorial fund established for the widow of one of his best Teamster friends, of which he was the sole Trustee, for $71,000, the same price he had paid for them. From that sum he refunded to the union only $60,000, the mortgages' reduced value at their then market price, keeping the $11,000 difference for himself and his friend. Disclosure of this unconscionable bilking of a trusting widow destroyed the last ounce of Beck's remaining goodwill among the Teamsters' rank and file. The announcement shortly thereafter that he would not seek reelection in September of that year as the International Teamsters' president was hardly surprising. Less than twelve months later he was twice convicted: of larceny in a state court in Seattle, and then in federal court for filing false income tax returns. For the latter crime Beck was sentenced to five years in a federal prison.

****

Waiting in the wings to succeed Beck was Jimmy Hoffa. The popular Detroit leader was a well-known figure within Teamster ranks but hardly a sure bet for the IBT's top job. In fact, when Beck made known his decision to retire, Hoffa was expecting trouble. Aware that along with Beck he was also under scrutiny by the McClellan Committee, he was anxious to learn what steps the senators were taking and what information they had accumulated. Hyman Fischbach, a Washington, D.C. attorney, was one of many Teamster-related agents, lawyers and consultants alerted by Hoffa to look for persons who might have a contact with someone on the Select Committee's staff. In early February, 1957, before the dates of Beck's public questioning, Fischbach asked his friend John Cye Cheasty, a New York-based private investigator, to meet with him in Washington. At the meeting the lawyer asked Cheasty if he knew anyone on the Committee's staff. When Cheasty replied that he knew one of Kennedy's New York investigators, Fischbach said he had a client who would pay good money to have an agent on McClellan's staff. When asked the name of his client, the lawyer used a technique acquired from years of dealing with closed-mouth clients of dubious character. Fischbach opened a black book, leaned toward Cheasty, and silently pointed to a name listed on the exposed page: Jimmy Hoffa.

Cheasty immediately understood the shady nature of Fischbach's proposal, but as a seasoned investigator his instinct was to follow a trail to see where it might lead. He asked to speak directly to Hoffa and within a matter of days he and the labor leader met in the latter's

Detroit office. There they agreed Cheasty would receive $1,000, with no strings attached, and then receive $2,000 per month if he got a job on the Senate Committee's staff. Returning to New York the next day the private eye contacted his friend on Kennedy's staff and told him of Hoffa's proposal. The aide immediately relayed this intriguing piece of information to Kennedy, who met with Cheasty on February 13, 1957 in Washington.

Cheasty impressed the chief counsel as both honest and courageous. He could have agreed to do Hoffa's dirty work in return for a salary well above his usual earnings. Or, he could have simply pocketed the $1,000 and bowed out with a story that he had been unable to make the connection. Instead, by disclosing Hoffa's offer to Kennedy, he had exposed himself to life-threatening retribution. While insulted by Fischbach's assumption he might consider the crooked proposal, he also struggled with the knowledge that his lawyer friend would be subject to criminal prosecution. In Kennedy's eyes Cheasty "was proud of his service in the Navy and the Secret Service, and … thought Hoffa's offer to him was on a par with attempts by the Russians to get US government employees to turn over secret information."[13] Out of the $1,000 received in cash from Hoffa, Cheasty reimbursed himself for his expenses and turned the balance over to the government, each bill dated and initialed "RFK" and "JCC" so as to be admissible into evidence when the proper time came. After a thorough interrogation by the FBI, the double agent was sworn in the next day as an assistant counsel to the McClellan Committee and went back to New York.

Calls from Hoffa and Fishbach greeted his return; both were pleased to learn he had been successful. A day or so later Cheasty called Hoffa to say that he had picked up some items of interest, and the two arranged to meet in Washington on February 19. Kennedy had given his new staffer a sheet of paper with the names of four men to be called as witnesses at the Committee's first hearing in March. This was part of the chief counsel's plan to give Hoffa material that was accurate but of insufficient importance to interfere with the Committee's work. On the afternoon of the scheduled meeting date Cheasty called Hoffa at the number he had been given. The Detroit Teamster told his spy to go to a specified corner of 17th and I Street in the heart of northwest

Washington's business district where he would be contacted. It was snowing hard when Cheasty arrived but he did not have long to wait. Hoffa walked up to him, took the folded paper, and after glancing at it said he knew three of the men listed. At that point a car pulled up, as if its driver had been observing them. Hoffa opened the door, took the seat beside the automobile's only occupant, and the two disappeared into the crawling rush-hour traffic.

Eddie Cheyfitz was a partner of the celebrated trial lawyer Edward Bennett Williams, the Teamsters' principal attorney in the nation's capital. Well before Cheasty's appearance, Kennedy had accepted an invitation to join Hoffa and Cheyfitz for dinner at the latter's home. The two adversaries would do well to meet informally, said his host, before they faced each other in the tense atmosphere of a public hearing. By one of those coincidences that sometimes seem more than accidental, Cheyfitz set the dinner date for February 19, the same day Hoffa later chose to meet with Cheasty. Hoffa was at his lawyers' office when Cheasty called him, and Cheyfitz had driven the car that whisked Hoffa away from his street-corner meeting. FBI agents had kept both Hoffa and Cheasty under close surveillance, and Kennedy was a bit late for dinner because he had waited in his office for a call from J. Edgar Hoover. Late that very afternoon the FBI chief reported that his agents had just filmed Hoffa receiving and reading the document handed to him by Cheasty. As he drove toward the meeting at Cheyfitz's house Kennedy felt sure that with this photographic evidence to back up Cheasty's sworn testimony he had Hoffa dead-to-rights on a charge of bribing a federal officer, a serious felony.

To his first face-to-face meeting with the bullying Teamster boss, Robert Kennedy brought an equal dose of testosterone. The young lawyer was in his prime—leaner and stronger, pound for pound, than either of his brothers. Still two inches short of six feet, he had gained weight since his college days, well proportioned and mostly muscle. Relatively short legs gave him a low center of gravity. His arms were long by comparison, with unusually large forearms that powered a vise-like grip. This bodily strength, coupled with an iron will and utter disdain for physical danger, heightened his capacity for hard work, hard play and fearless engagement with perceived enemies. His dinner partner that night was clearly one of the latter.

Both men wrote of their meeting and of the verbal sparring between them. Both mentioned only one particular exchange, however, each using exactly the same words. Defending the rough tactics he felt were necessary to deal with management goons and thugs hired by competing unions, Hoffa said, "I do to others what they do to me, only worse." To which Kennedy replied, "Maybe I should have worn my bullet-proof vest."[14] Hoffa then went so far as to claim he had accepted a challenge from Kennedy to Indian arm-wrestle and twice defeated the younger man, both times easily slamming his opponent's knuckles back onto the table. Kennedy made no mention of that but both men took pride in their own physical strength and courage; each wanting to show that he was as tough as the other. Hoffa's claim sounded more like bluster than fact, an effort to make the chief counsel appear juvenile. More likely was his assertion that Kennedy had asked him why he had not gone to college and how he had initially embarked on union work. Those questions, said the feisty Teamster, showed the young lawyer's unawareness of what it was like to come up the hard way, the immature curiosity of a "damn spoiled brat."[15]

Kennedy wrote nothing of these matters, describing only some of the issues they discussed, including Hoffa's reasons for having associated with Johnny Dio, the well-known racketeer from New York City, and others of like character. He learned little, however, concluding only that in describing these associations Hoffa was lying through his teeth. In sum, Cheyfitz's effort to soften Kennedy's attitude toward the Teamster boss was a failure, due in part to the chief counsel's belief that with the Cheasty bombshell about to burst he was looking down Hoffa's throat. Their dinner conversation more closely resembled a poorly performed Kabuki dance than a sparring match between middleweight champions. It was also the first and last meeting of these two adversaries involving even a trace of sociability.

Although the FBI now had Hoffa on film, Kennedy wanted to catch him red-handed in the possession of incriminating evidence. About three weeks following the Hoffa-Kennedy dinner, Cheasty told his FBI managers that he and the Detroit Teamster boss had arranged to meet that evening on a sidewalk near Washington's DuPont Plaza Hotel. On that day the chief counsel's staff gave their double agent a manila envelope containing several pages of additional Committee documents.

Cheasty duly delivered this envelope in exchange for his monthly salary of $2,000 in cash when he and Hoffa met in front of the hotel's entrance. Moments later, as the latter entered the hotel lobby with the documents in his possession, waiting FBI agents surrounded and arrested him, charging him with bribing a government employee and conspiring to obstruct justice.

Hustled off to the federal courthouse Hoffa was uncustomarily subdued, cold-eyed with anger, fear showing in his blanched lips. It was the first time he had been charged with a federal crime and his first arrest by the FBI. His disposition worsened at the sight of the horde of reporters awaiting him, alerted in advance that they would find a breaking news story at the courthouse by none other than Ethel Kennedy, the chief counsel's energetic and irrepressible wife. Her husband showed up a few minutes later, as did Ed Williams, the heaviest gun in Hoffa's legal arsenal. Amid the milling crowd a reporter yelled, "Hey, Bobby, what will you do if Hoffa is acquitted?" "I'll jump off the Capitol dome," replied a euphoric Kennedy.[16] And why not? A camera had captured Hoffa's payoff to the agent he had hired to steal Committee information, and the labor leader was in possession of the stolen documents when arrested. It seemed an airtight case.

But of course it was not. At Hoffa's trial in July the legendary defense counsel Edward B. Williams would play the race card for Hoffa as skillfully as Johnnie Cochran defending O. J. Simpson years later. Williams appeared in court accompanied by two African American attorneys as his assistants, one of whom was Martha Jefferson from California. During the selection of jurors Williams used peremptory challenges to exclude white panelists only, winding up with eight African Americans on the twelve-member jury. During the trial Williams posed for a photograph with Ms. Jefferson which appeared the next day as part of a front-page article in the *Afro-American*, a weekly newspaper published in Washington. The story described Williams as Hoffa's "White Knight," the "Sir Galahad" of the civil rights movement.[17] It praised Hoffa as "the hardest-hitting champion" of the Teamsters Union "which has 167,000 colored truck drivers." He was "a friend," it said, whom many "champions of Negro rights [felt] had been framed" by a vengeful government.[18] Hoffa's minions saw to it that copies of the newspaper were delivered to every juror's home doorstep. Judge Burnita Matthews denied the prosecutors' motion to declare a mistrial for this blatant ploy, deciding instead to sequester the jury for the rest of the trial. Plowing ahead, Hoffa's team brought former heavyweight boxing champion Joe Louis into the courtroom as a spectator. With all eyes on him the hugely popular Brown Bomber gave his "good friend" Jimmy a bear hug in the courtroom just to make sure his message was clear.[19] Perhaps these efforts succeeded in prejudicing jurors in the defendant's favor, perhaps not. But they surely injected racial issues into the heart of the proceeding.

Kennedy and Cheasty were the chief witnesses for the prosecution. Kennedy described his part in hiring Cheasty and supervising his actions. The forty-something, soft-spoken private investigator testified persuasively—and bravely—about his dealings with Hoffa and his motives for becoming a double agent for the Department of Justice. He weathered a stern cross-examination disrupted only when Williams asked if he had at one time investigated the National Association for the Advancement of Colored People. On the prosecutors' angry objection

Jimmy Hoffa testifying before Senate. Teamster President James R. Hoffa consults with his lawyer Edward Bennett Williams during Hoffa's testimony before Senate Labor Rackets Committee, August 5, 1958.

Williams withdrew the question, but the jury had heard it. All Cheasty could do on redirect examination was to steadfastly deny it. After FBI agents told of their role in handling Cheasty the government lawyers rested their case, satisfied they had made a compelling showing of the defendant's guilt. Their mistake, which would soon become evident, was their belief that Hoffa would not testify in his own defense.

Kennedy's prosecutors were caught flat-footed by the Teamster leader's decision to take the stand and brazenly contradict every material accusation in Cheasty's account of their dealings. Just days earlier Eddie Cheyfitz had confided to the chief counsel at a party that "Hoffa was sorry he had been stupid enough to be caught giving a bribe," and concerned that "the boys"—meaning his Teamster lackeys, many of whom were in daily attendance at the trial—"were laughing because he had handled it directly rather than through a third person."[20] Surely, thought Kennedy, Hoffa could not bluster his way out of this hole, and the more he tried to do so the deeper he would sink.

This was a costly underestimation of Hoffa's talent as a believable dissembler. Under oath he swore he had hired and paid Chesty $3,000 to act only as a lawyer who would keep his eyes and ears open for information of interest to his employer. When he received Committee documents from Cheasty, said the Detroit Teamster boss, he considered it none of his business how the papers were obtained. Further, he said, only after the FBI arrested him did he learn that his new lawyer was on Kennedy's staff. DOJ's prosecutors, deplorably under-prepared for Hoffa's surprise testimony, stumbled through a cross-examination that lasted only twenty minutes, sending the case to the jury as severely damaged goods. After deliberating only three-and-a half hours the jury returned a verdict of not guilty on all counts.

The bad news came in a note delivered to Kennedy by a Senate page during an open session of the McClellan Committee. Sitting at the press table, Clark Mollenhoff saw the chief counsel's jaw drop and his face turn gray. Without having to ask, he knew what had happened: Hoffa had beaten the rap. Outside the courthouse, the bantam labor leader crowed in victory. "[I]f you are honest and tell the truth," he shamelessly told reporters, "you have nothing to fear."[21] By his client's side and in a similarly buoyant mood, Ed Williams remarked that he planned to send Bob Kennedy a parachute for his promised leap from the Capitol dome. It was a hurtful defeat, but Kennedy shook it off like a bad fall on the ski slopes. His loyal staff stood behind him, as did his wife. "We're all sick to death about Hoffa," she wrote to her in-laws, "but we are relying on Carmine, Clark Mollenhoff, and Bobby and Jack to hit one for our team." [22] Even Kennedy's Republican adversaries on the Select Committee recognized that justice had miscarried. Knowing that the Teamsters had paid Joe Louis's hotel bills during his appearance at the trial, Barry Goldwater remarked: "Joe Louis makes a pretty good defense attorney. That's all I can say."[23]

Washington's Georgetown establishment of the late '50s was an exclusive club of politicians, lawyers and journalists, virtually all of them Democrats. Art Buchwald's wisecracks regularly broke up Ed Williams and the *Washington Post's* Ben Bradlee over lunch at Sans Souci, the in-crowd's favorite restaurant. Kennedy and *Post* columnist Roland "Rolie" Evans knew each other well enough to trade jibes, and their wives were close friends. *Washington Star* pundit Charlie Bartlett had been a grooms-man in Jack Kennedy's wedding. Lawyer-lobbyists Clark Clifford and Jim Rowe were the group's senior wise men. Kennedy had an open invitation from Cheyfitz to join the Williams' law firm should he decide to enter private practice. On any given day these men and a group of senators, congressmen and other notables could be seen rubbing elbows over short ribs and sauerkraut at another favorite watering hole, a large restaurant known as Duke Ziebert's. These regulars, in the words of the genial restaurateur, were "known from coast to coast like buttered toast."

In this club-like atmosphere, Cheyfitz told Kennedy of Hoffa's admission of having bribed Cheasty—thus conceding his client's guilt and his own knowledge of it. During their earlier dinner with Hoffa, Kennedy had argued that except in cases where the accused pleaded insanity or self-defense, lawyers should not represent clients who admitted to committing the deed charged. Nothing came of Cheyfitz's lawyer-to-lawyer statement, however, partly because he could not be forced to disclose it in open court but also because both participants tacitly acknowledged it was off the record. As Kennedy's prosecutorial pressure on Hoffa mounted, however, the relationship between the opposing legal teams changed radically. When the Teamster boss was in deep trouble four years later, none of his lawyers would have dared to disclose a similar admission to prosecutor Jim Neal.

Undaunted by the abortive ending of the Cheasty case, Kennedy's investigators continued their pursuit of Hoffa under an increased head of steam. In early August of 1957 the McClellan Committee called convicted felon Johnny Dio as a witness. From judicially authorized wiretaps made by New York City police the Committee staff had learned that Dio, at Hoffa's request, had formed "paper"—meaning nonexistent—Teamster unions composed of his gangster associates, a move obviously intended solely to get more votes for a Hoffa candidate in an upcoming IBT election. Dio and the Detroit Teamster boss had also been overheard discussing "Minifons," the trade name of tiny electronic "bugs" Hoffa wanted his union members to wear while appearing before grand juries. These devices would transmit to distant eavesdroppers every word of a witness's supposedly secret testimony. Pleading the Fifth Amendment, Dio refused to answer any of the one hundred and forty questions put to him during his day on the stand. Senator Irving Ives could no longer contain himself. Is "there anything [you] ever did from the time [you] were born to the present moment that would not incriminate [you]?" asked the frustrated Republican from New York. Dio's growled response came like a broken record: "I respectfully decline..." [to answer].[24]

Hoffa went before the McClellan Committee later that month. After debating with himself and his lawyers he had decided not to take the Fifth, and to answer all questions put to him in order to preserve his claim

Jimmy Hoffa clenching his fists while testifying before Senate Labor Rackets Committee, August 6, 1958.

he had nothing to hide. Pleading poor memory—and with a remarkable combination of verbal dexterity, mind-numbing repetition and his patented brand of confrontational bravado—he deflected questions from the senators and the Committee's chief counsel over four straight days of testimony. He swatted every ball thrown at him into foul territory, never getting a base hit but staying at the plate, ready for the next pitch.

Hoffa's responses to questions about his dealings with Johnny Dio showed him at his elusive best. Kennedy read to him parts of a taped telephone conversation between the two men in which the Detroit Teamster had asked the New York gangster to call strikes by several AFL unions under Dio's control. The strikes would occur prior to an upcoming meeting of labor leaders to demonstrate to Dave Beck, then the IBT's president, Hoffa's power among the Big Apple's labor leaders.

> Dio: "I think we're going to have twenty strikes before that meeting."
>
> Hoffa: "Well, that's good."
>
> Dio: "… Before I pulled it [off], I thought I'd consult with you on it."
>
> Hoffa: "I think that's [going to] show him who the fuck's got the people."[25]

When asked by Kennedy about this conversation, Hoffa replied, "I cannot hardly remember the meeting." And did they discuss Dio's bringing his men into the Teamsters? "I don't remember. I am trying to refresh my memory out of these conversations but they are such with other people that I don't know how I can do it."[26]

Hoffa and Dio had also been recorded while discussing the Minifons which Hoffa wanted Dio's men to use to record their grand jury questions and answers. At the hearing he was asked what use had he made of these listening devices.

> Hoffa: "What did I do with them? Well, what did I do with them?"
>
> Kennedy: "What did you do with them?"
>
> Hoffa: "I am trying to recall."
>
> Kennedy: "You could remember that."
>
> Hoffa: "When were they delivered …? That must have been quite a while.…"

Kennedy: "You know what you did with the Minifons. Don't ask me."

Hoffa: "What did I do with them?"

Kennedy: "What did you do with them?"

Hoffa: "Mr. Kennedy, I bought some Minifons …, but I cannot recall what became of them."[27]

The Chef Counsel then asked the reluctant witness if he had ever worn a Minifon himself. "You say 'wear,' replied Hoffa. "What do you mean by 'wear'? "[28] This empty rhetoric sometimes became more contorted. "To the best of my recollection I must recall on my memory I cannot remember." "I can say here to the Chair that I cannot recall, in answer to your question, other than to say I just don't recall my recollection."[29]

In another successful tactic Hoffa effectively designated others to take the Fifth Amendment for him. When asked a question involving himself and a subordinate—Bert Brennan, for example—he would plead loss of memory and suggest to the Committee they ask the other person. In due course, when Brennan and others named by Hoffa appeared as witnesses, they would dutifully invoke their rights against self-incrimination and remain silent. Like a football team with a commanding lead, Hoffa was also a master at eating up the clock to exasperate his interrogators. On the few occasions he was willing to answer a question directly, "it sometimes took him nine or ten hundred words to say 'yes' or 'no.' "[30]

The Committee's star witness used another ploy to gain even more time. Occasionally a senator or the chief counsel would summarize an earlier witness's derogatory statement as a predicate for a question to Hoffa. The wily Teamster would then dismissively claim, "That isn't in the record—I have read the record. Nothing like that is in the record." Twenty minutes later, with the hearing halted in its tracks, the clerk would read the record, confirming the accuracy of the questioner's summary. Unfazed, Hoffa would then "go off on a lengthy, uninformative tangent."[31]

And so it went for four days. At one point Committee Chairman McClellan accurately summarized the impact of Hoffa's devious manner on the average viewer among the millions following the hearings on television. "I have done as much to refresh your memory as I know how to do. If you cannot recall [whether or not you ever wore one of Dio's Minifon listening devices]—and if you want to think that [we] and the public [are] so stupid that we will believe you could not remember doing a thing like that—you leave the record that way."[32] And Hoffa was indeed content to leave it so. To most Teamster members he had given a virtuoso performance. He had survived a barrage of hostile questions from some of Washington's most powerful politicians without conceding error. He had not taken refuge in the legalisms of the Fifth Amendment. He had used memory loss to avoid the

Teamster President Jimmy Hoffa faces Chief Counsel Robert Kennedy at a meeting of the Senate Rackets Committee, September 17, 1958. Looking on is investigator Walter Sheridan (in bow tie).

kind of positive statements that could have brought charges of perjury. And unlike Beck, whose star was falling fast, Hoffa had preserved his image as a fighter for the interests of the Teamsters' rank and file. This army of supporters, amassed during his 25 years of union service, was composed of people he was counting on to elect him the IBT's next president.

Hoffa's opponents saw things differently. To them the McClellan Committee's hearings had exposed the Detroit labor boss's corrupt practices and close ties to the Mob. Taking the lead in the anti-Hoffa movement was George Meany, the outspoken, gravel-voiced Irish-American plumber who had risen through the ranks to become the president of the American Federation of Labor. In that role, Meany had spearheaded the merger of his union with the Congress of Industrial Organizations and now headed the AFL-CIO behemoth. In the early 1950s, as the AFL's president, he had supported Teamster dissidents who wanted none of Hoffa, and who were actively recruiting truck drivers and other transportation-related employees for membership in competing unions.

On September 25, 1957, at Meany's urging, the Ethical Practices Committee of the AFL-CIO voted 28-1 to approve a report charging that the "the Teamsters Union continues to be dominated, controlled, or substantially influenced by corrupt" forces.[33] Although former IBT President Dave Beck's corruption and numerous pleadings of the Fifth Amendment were the primary causes of Meany's ire, his organization's report also condemned Hoffa personally for committing "inherently evil" and "improper" actions, including the use of "union funds for personal purposes, and associating with ... notorious labor racketeers."[34] Just over two months later, at its convention in Atlantic City, the AFL-CIO took action based on this report. With Meany and the United Auto Workers' Walter Reuther leading the charge, eighty percent of the attending delegates voted to oust the Teamsters union from its umbrella organization. Condemned in this way by millions of its fellow unionists, the IBT was now strictly on its own.

The autumn of 1957 continued to bring bad news for the Detroit Teamster leader. Following an intense week of hearings at which some forty witnesses testified before his Committee, Senator McClellan released a document citing thirty-four instances of misconduct by

Hoffa in his capacity as a union official. Foremost among these was the misappropriation of $2 million from the union's coffers in the form of loans to businesses in which he had a personal interest, with kickbacks received from some of the borrowers. The Senate document also charged that Hoffa had rewarded "employers and convicted extortionists" with sweetheart deals harmful to the interests of rank and file workers and also helped his Teamster supporters arrange "improper business activities and ... collusive agreements with employers."[35]

Two seedlings among these allegations grew into the criminal charges that would eventually bear fruit. But for now, nothing could derail Hoffa's bandwagon on its way to the union's national convention in Miami. There, in early October of 1957, he was elected president of the International Brotherhood of Teamsters by almost three-quarters of the votes cast. In his acceptance speech, cloaked in the voice of reason, he laid the premise of his claim of innocence. "I have no fight with the McClellan Committee, nor ... any desire to obstruct a true and honest investigation. But when a congressional committee concentrates on a personal attack or misuses its power, it can be dangerous for all of us. ..."[36] Then, with a demagogic device as old as history, he equated himself and his fate with the Teamsters union and all of its members. By blackening his "reputation without the protection of judicial processes," the Senate investigators had done "a great injustice ... to the individual members of the Teamsters Union. You are the people whose good name has been smeared."[37] This quasi-religious theme—that he and his followers were one body, one blood—was a mantra Hoffa would steadfastly repeat over the years even as the evidence of his misdeeds mounted.

Undeterred by Hoffa's protestations, McClellan and Kennedy continued their inquiry into the corrupt practices of the Teamsters union. In late 1957, overlapping the dates of the AFL-CIO convention and Hoffa's perjury trial in New York (from which he escaped with a hung jury), the Senate Committee held nine consecutive days of open hearings in Washington focusing on union violence centered in the state of Tennessee and certain adjacent areas in Kentucky and Alabama. The length and intensity of the Committee's focus on this region was made possible by the abundance of raw material in John Seigenthaler's numerous articles in the Nashville *Tennessean*. As the hearings began, the Committee's staff summarized this information in a chart listing 178 labor-related criminal acts committed in this area during the preceding five years, 123 of them in Nashville alone. Teamster elements in Tennessee's capital city had sabotaged trucks by slashing tires and pouring syrup into motors, firing gunshots at non-union trucks, grabbing and severely beating the vehicles' drivers. In nighttime raids they had dynamited and burned the premises of non-union employers, shotgunning windows to bits in the places left standing. Noticeable among these reports were the infrequent arrests of participants in the violence, along with the high percentage of complaints withdrawn and the few cases in which known perpetrators were charged. In sum, the McClellan Committee reported in 1958, "Law enforcement agencies at every level in Tennessee have been shockingly derelict toward Teamster malefactors. Of 173 acts of violence ..., only eight were brought to a conclusion in a court of law."[38]

At Committee sessions in December of 1957 senators heard from some who had committed these acts and others who had been their targets, all of whom risked reprisals for going public with their testimony. Their willingness to speak out brought high praise from the Committee's chief counsel. "Tennessee people must be the most honest people in the world," said Kennedy. "I can't recall ever having as many people who sat down and just told the plain truth, regardless of whom it hurt—even their friends or themselves."[39]

One of the episodes he had in mind involved three men: Joseph Katz, president of Ace Highways Trucking Company of Atlanta; Frank Allen, the company's vice-president and the manager of Terminal Transport Company, its Nashville subsidiary; and W.A. Smith, a Teamster specialist in dynamiting. Smith, known as Hard of Hearing Smitty, was a hoodlum with a record of seventeen arrests which strangely lacked a charge of committing the crime that gave him his nickname. Appearing before the Committee, Allen testified that Smith had come into his office in April, 1955, demanding that he hire certain Teamster drivers whose job applications had been turned down because of past DWI convictions. When he refused, said Allen, Smith beat him senseless, sending him to a hospital for a week with nausea, a cut face needing stitches, a broken nose, and other fractured bones.[40] Identified by his victim, Smith had been indicted in Nashville for criminal assault with intent to kill. Knowing the vicious Teamster was represented by one of the union's local lawyers, and wanting to be sure Smith received the punishment he deserved, Allen's boss, Joseph Katz, prevailed upon the city's district attorney to appoint lawyer Jack Norman as a special prosecutor for the state. Alas, on the date set for trial, an embarrassed and frustrated Norman had to tell the judge that the state was dismissing the charge against Smith because Frank Allen, the victim and only witness to the crime, was refusing to testify against his assailant.[41]

At that time Nashville authorities could only speculate Allen had feared for his life and was apprehensive of further Teamster violence against Ace Highways' drivers and equipment. Almost three years later, in preparation for the hearings of December, 1957, Kennedy's investigators confirmed that suspicion when Allen disclosed the facts behind his unwillingness to testify at W.A. Smith's trial. Allen told his interrogators that while he was still in the hospital, "Joe Katz, my boss at Ace Highways, came into my room and said 'We've got to stop this sort of thing from happening again.' Several weeks later, however, he told me 'I've just come from Chicago and met with the man ... and it will be better for everyone if you don't press charges against Smith. So I'm asking you straight out, please don't testify at his trial.' "[42] Allen had reluctantly complied with his boss's request and agonized ever since at the resultant miscarriage of justice. Allen now told Kennedy he was ready to testify in an open hearing when called before the McClellan Committee.

Armed with this statement Kennedy subpoenaed Katz, the company president, to come before the Committee and give testimony. Talking with the chief counsel in the late afternoon of the day before his scheduled appearance Katz said he feared the consequences of confirming Allen's statement, and of disclosing what "the man" had said to him in Chicago. Therefore, to protect himself against a charge of withholding evidence, he planned to invoke the Fifth Amendment if asked about these events during his next morning's testimony. Empathizing with the obviously troubled witness, Kennedy acknowledged he could not force him to risk self-incrimination. He appealed, instead, to Katz's strong wish to come clean. "Frank Allen has agreed to testify," he explained, "and I'm going to ask you questions based on his testimony. You're an honest man, and you have nothing to hide. The best thing for you to do is to tell the truth, and I'm hoping you will do so."[43]

Kennedy's empathetic advice had the desired effect. The next day, after taking the oath as a witness, Katz responded to Kennedy's questions by telling the full story of his meeting with Hoffa and his later conversation with Frank Allen. Shortly after W.A. Smith's attack on Mr. Allen, Katz explained, he had been part of a team of trucking company representatives in Chicago to negotiate a regional agreement with a Teamster group that included James Hoffa. During the Chicago negotiations a Teamster agent had called Katz and said that Hoffa wanted to talk with him, one-on-one. He was surprised by this, he said, but agreed to the meeting. Later that day he sat with Hoffa at a table in the Pump Room of the Drake Hotel. Hoffa mentioned the case then pending against Smith for the assault on Allen, and said that "he would like to see the thing dropped." Katz replied that he was "deeply disturbed that a [Teamster] business agent … had beaten up one of my people." Hoffa agreed … and said, " 'Well, you know how the boys are sometimes. They will get into a hot-headed discussion.' "[44] The Detroit Teamster then told him, said Katz, that Frank Allen had recovered, that the union would take care of his medical expenses, and there was thus no good reason for him to press charges against Smith. And then came the clincher. " 'Joe,' Hoffa said to me, 'things will go easier for you *here* if you give me some help down *there.*' " Katz then regretfully concluded, "I wish I hadn't told Frank Allen not to testify in the Smith case, but I did."[45] This painful disclosure revealed the dark side of Hoffa's oft-repeated assertion: "I take care of my men." Katz—by admitting he had suppressed Frank Allen's testimony and cowardly submitted to Hoffa's high-pressure tactics—finally showed his adherence to the true meaning of the same motto.

Based on information set out in Seigenthaler's newspaper articles, McClellan Committee investigators also looked more closely into claims of Teamster corruption in Chattanooga. There they found numerous instances of violence, highlighted in a state indictment charging thirteen local Teamsters with criminal conspiracy to commit arson, tire-slashing, dynamiting and bodily assault on non-union truckers and trucking company facilities. Accompanying those charges was the startling allegation that Raulston Schoolfield, a Chattanooga criminal court judge assigned to try the conspiracy case, had accepted a $20,000 bribe to dismiss all charges against the "Teamster 13." To nail that down Committee investigator LaVerne Duffy produced a dated memorandum from the Internal Revenue Service stating that H.L. Boling, Local 515's secretary-treasurer, had confessed to the IRS that "this money" came from the union's treasury and "had been paid to [Judge Schoolfield] to quash the indictment."[46]

As a result of these disclosures, and at the urging of Tennessee Governor Frank Clement, the state's House of Representatives impeached Schoolfield for multiple violations of his judicial duties. He was tried by the Tennessee Senate, found guilty on four counts, and dismissed from office. One of the witnesses for the prosecution in the judge's impeachment trial was Robert Kennedy, whose visit to Nashville would introduce him to a coterie of the city's trial lawyers and set the stage for their involvement in his effort to send Jimmy Hoffa to jail.

****

In the spring of 1959, with a last bang of his gavel, Chairman John McClellan ended three years of hearings by his Select Committee. Kennedy went home to Hickory Hill to write his best-selling exposé, *The Enemy Within*. Along with Committee members and staff investigators, these two men could take well-deserved pride in their accomplishments. Corruption and violence in labor's hierarchy had been exposed not only in the Teamsters, but also in the Bakers, the Operating Engineers, the Textile Workers, and the Carpenters. Propelled toward action by the Committee's revelations, the US Congress passed the Landrum-Griffin Act of 1959 that set new standards in labor union management and the public reporting of their expenditures. It created a "Bill of Rights" for union members requiring secret ballots and fair procedures in union elections, and provided mechanisms for challenging violations. It criminalized the acceptance of bribes in labor-management relations and penalized the misappropriation of union funds. Landrum-Griffin also provided that a person convicted of committing any of several specified felonies would be ineligible for union office for five years after being found guilty.

This reform legislation was a hard-fought compromise between labor and anti-unionists. Its vague language and multiple loopholes left employers with considerable, often misused, power. It did bring greater democracy, however, to the process by which unions went about organizing employers' labor forces, and brought additional transparency to the process by which employers could legally resist unions' organizational efforts.

The Committee's prime target had unquestionably been Hoffa and the Teamsters. When Kennedy's book was published in 1960 his arch-enemy was hanging onto the IBT presidency but the Teamsters had been kicked out of the AFL-CIO and Hoffa's management of the union was under the scrutiny of a court-appointed Board of Monitors. Eight of Hoffa's closest associates were under indictment. And Kennedy correctly predicted that the IBT president's "days are numbered.... [A] man with Hoffa's power and position, and so corrupt, cannot survive in a democratic society if democracy itself is going to survive. I believe the country, not Hoffa, will triumph."[47]

By the time *The Enemy Within* showed up in bookstores Kennedy was a full-time manager of Senator John Kennedy's campaign for the presidency. On the surface it seemed ironic that the Democratic candidate—an outspoken critic of the practices revealed at the McClellan Committee hearings and the brother of its hard-nosed chief inquisitor—had across-the-board support within the labor movement. The Teamsters opposed him but George Meany of the AFL-CIO, Walter Reuther of the United Automobile Workers, and other labor leaders supported the dashing young Democrat. They, along with the rank and file members of most unions, saw in the senator from Massachusetts someone who understood that labor's rotten apples were relatively few and would be a steadfast friend to working men and women. Their support was crucial in an election where the overall margin of victory was less than one vote per voting precinct. Labor's friend got into the White House, but to the disappointment of some and the utter dismay of Jimmy Hoffa, the president-elect decided to name his brother the new administration's attorney general. Unofficially, Bob Kennedy would also be the president's personal adviser of last resort, a position which made him, in the eyes of some, the second most powerful man in the Western world. True or not, Hoffa could hardly have had a more formidable opponent.

CHAPTER 3

"Send a Reporter Down Here
if You Want a Story"

On the surface, Nashville of the mid-1950s seemed an unlikely place for a Kennedy-Hoffa showdown. The city sat placidly on the east and west banks of the Cumberland River amid the rolling green hills of middle-Tennessee. Its businesses were more white-collar commercial than blue-collar industrial. Its schools, public facilities and workplaces were fully segregated. Its airport was small and its rail and river commerce not large enough to make it a transportation center. To a city planner or casual observer, the state's capital seemed well out of the mainstream, a rather indolent southern city.

In fact, Nashville was on the brink of dynamic growth. In a short while, beginning in the latter years of the Eisenhower administration and on into the first year of John F. Kennedy's presidency, the state's capital began to expand and flourish. By the time Hoffa's criminal trial made the *Tennessean* newspaper's daily headlines in the early 1960s, Nashville had begun the vigorous growth that transformed it into one of the South's most vibrant metropolitan areas.

At the heart of the city's power structure in the mid-1950s were a few wealthy families dealing primarily in finance, insurance and transportation, along with a handful of well-connected, politically oriented lawyers. Also in this group were the owners and editors of the city's two daily newspapers. A few of the movers and shakers endorsed the liberal-leaning stance of the *Tennessean*, the morning paper, but a larger number embraced the conservative views of the evening *Banner*. In combination, they provided forward thinking, growth-minded leadership. World War II had ended a decade earlier. Small businesses formed since then were beginning to multiply. Entrepreneurs were turning the city's suburban thoroughfares into bustling franchise rows. Through its songwriters and performers—showcased at the Grand Ole Opry—Nashville would soon gain recognition as "Music City," the capital of American country music. Enhancing the city's quality of life were Vanderbilt University, Peabody College, and two of the country's leading traditionally black institutions of higher learning, Fisk University and the Meharry Medical College.

Nashville's labor unions were also growing in size and influence. Their leaders were engaged in legitimate struggles for higher pay and better working conditions for their members. Forsaking, for the most part, street brawls and under-the-table payoffs, a new generation of unionists was fighting for labor's goals with facts and figures in open debate. Its members were also begrudgingly getting behind the civil rights movement, recognizing that workplace equality held the potential for union growth and increased political power.

The major blot on this progressive labor movement was Teamster Local 327, a breeding ground of corruption led by Hoffa's Nashville loyalists. Like dictators they ruled by fear, smashing, burning, and bribing as necessary to perpetuate their power. They assaulted picket-crossing scabs and members of competing unions with brass knuckles, clubs and knives. In nighttime forays they destroyed opponents' property with shotguns, dynamite and torches. Non-union employers who refused to pay protection money for labor peace received similar treatment. With bribes and the dictated votes of its members, Local 327's leaders gained the friendship of elected officials and law enforcement officers. The city's police forces, understaffed and overworked, responded only to the Teamsters' most egregious law violations and then were slow to intervene. These sordid practices fostered conflict within the local union and periodic internal strife. Dissenting union members were threatened and in some cases beaten bloody. Representatives of these dissidents appealed for help directly to Hoffa, by calls and personal visits to his office, but their pleas went unanswered. It was a situation crying out for reform.

On the national level, reformative steps were under way. In 1951 the US Senate established a Special Committee to Investigate Crime in Interstate Commerce chaired by Estes Kefauver, a freshman Democratic senator from Tennessee. The grainy black-and-white images of Mob bosses testifying before the Kefauver Committee, broadcast live in daytime hours, attracted and held the rapt attention of millions of viewers. A vignette of one witness's testimony—the nervously twisting hands of Mafia boss Frank Costello, shown in close-up because the networks decided not to reveal the faces of alleged criminals—became a symbol of organized crime's sinister influence on the lives of ordinary Americans.

Kefauver, who had come to the Senate in 1948, was followed to Congress's upper house four years later by Albert Gore Sr., another Tennessee Democrat. Together they represented the coalition of labor, blacks and liberal whites who were gradually taking the reins of power in the Volunteer State. In this group were Nashville's left-of-center politicians and lawyers supportive of social change. Joining them were some of the city's more pragmatic business leaders and the influential owner and editors of the *Tennessean* newspaper. From this cast came the featured performers in Robert Kennedy's face-off with Jimmy Hoffa, each a character in his own right. Chief among them were John Seigenthaler, a tenacious investigative reporter, and Jim Neal, a skillful trial lawyer only a few years out of law school. Young and ambitious, both were at the beginning of careers that would take them to the top of their professions.

****

Published since 1937 by Silliman Evans and managed in the 1950s by Coleman Harwell, Nashville's *Tennessean* newspaper accurately reported the news. It also opposed union corruption, amplified the city's voices of reform, and supported proponents of a government more attuned to the needs of the people. Several *Tennessean* reporters of this era—including Tom Wicker, David Halberstam, Bill Kovach, and later Jim Squires and Wallace Westfeldt—went on to gain national recognition as journalists and authors. Future Vice-President Al Gore, fresh from army service and a tour of duty in Vietnam, got his start as a reporter at the *Tennessean*. Gore's wife Tipper, later known as the family's snapshot artist, learned her camera skills as a staff photographer for the same newspaper.

Among these journalists, John Seigenthaler was a true natural. "Sig"—his nickname since elementary school—was born July 27, 1927, the oldest child in a Catholic family of four boys and four girls. In 1947, after two years in the US Air Force, he enrolled at Nashville's Peabody Community College and spent the next two summers as a gofer and part-time reporter in the *Tennessean's* newsroom. At that point he decided a college degree was just a piece of paper while a bustling newsroom would give him all the further education he needed. Evans and Harwell welcomed Sig to the staff in 1949 as a full-fledged reporter and he never looked back—until, perhaps, the spring of 2003 when he received an honorary Doctor of Letters degree from Middle Tennessee State University.

During his first four years at the *Tennessean*, Seigenthaler developed his journalistic skills reporting police blotter crimes and writing obituaries, eventually moving on to cover the mayor's office, city hall and the state legislature. His first big opportunity came on a tip that Thomas C. Buntin, the scion of a prominent Nashville family who had mysteriously disappeared twenty-two years earlier, was alive and living in Texas under an assumed name. Sensing a blockbuster story, Sig convinced his bosses to send him there. Surely, thought Seigenthaler, if Stanley could find Livingstone in the vast tangle of the African jungle, a determined reporter could spot Buntin in the arid expanse of the Lone Star State.

After three discouraging months of interviews with hotel clerks, bartenders, sheriffs, police desk sergeants and department store sales people in one town after another, a dejected Seigenthaler was near the end of his tether. Finally a retired sheriff in Beaumont, Texas looked sympathetically at the dispirited young reporter. "Look for your man in a citrus city," the law enforcement officer said enigmatically. "A citrus city?" asked Seigenthaler, taken aback by the strange phrase. "Yes," said the sheriff, who then shook the weary searcher's hand and left the room. Puzzled, Sig pulled out his map and focused on the Beaumont area. "Eureka!" There, about twenty miles due east from where he sat, was the small town of Orange, close to the Texas-Louisiana border. He felt in his bones it was now or never.

With the help of a local lawyer who knew Evans, the *Tennessean's* publisher, Sig's dogged persistence and good luck finally paid off. He found Buntin in Orange, living under an assumed name but unmistakably identifiable by his distinguishing feature, a protruding right ear. Buntin was morosely un-talkative but his wife Betty spoke easily, asking about her family and disclosing that she and Tom had married after his Mexican divorce. Her only genuinely surprising news was that over the years she and Buntin had produced a total of six children.

Back in Nashville, Seigenthaler wrote up the tale of the missing socialites in a series of articles first published in the *Tennessean* on Thanksgiving morning, 1953. They were a sensation, a soap-opera in print, the talk of the town. For six consecutive days this was the story that sold thousands of extra copies, which everyone read first. In May of the following year the *Tennessean* received the "Headliner's Award" from the National Headliners Club for the "major domestic news story of 1953." In Chicago to receive it was the twenty-six-year-old Seigenthaler whose story, according to a Headliner official, was the "hands down" winner among the nine hundred entries.

Like his future boss Robert Kennedy, John Seigenthaler would not stand out in a crowd of strangers. About Kennedy's size, similarly stocky and well put together, Sig had an open and expressive face, piercing blue eyes, and a thick shock of sandy hair. Ever inquisitive and voluble, his soft southern accent had been slightly sharpened by two years in the military. His apt choice of words, the intonations of his voice, and the relaxed energy with which he spoke caught and held his listeners' attention as someone who had interesting things to say and knew his topics cold. His highly retentive memory could instantly recall past experiences with people, places and issues, which he described in compelling detail. Like Abe Lincoln, he amassed favorite stories told with infectious good humor, enjoying them as much as did his rapt audiences. If one word could describe Seigenthaler, "genuine" would come the closest.

Scarcely five months after the Buntin story came another opportunity which most reporters realize only in their dreams. Near noon on a clear

October morning Bill Maples, the *Tennessean's* city editor, answered the phone to hear a man's high-pitched voice saying he was tired of living and was headed for the Sparkman Street Bridge—a span high above the swirling waters of the Cumberland River—to put an end to it all. "Send a reporter down here if you want a story," the man yelled. Cupping his hand over the mouthpiece, Maples ordered Seigenthaler and a photographer to head for the bridge, and another newsman to call the police.

On arriving at the scene the breathless reporter saw the man standing on a girder outside a three-foot guardrail, screaming at several policemen to stay away from him or he would jump. Sig excitedly told the officers of the distraught man's call to the *Tennessean* and they let him pass. Hooking a leg around one of the guardrail's stanchions for security, the young journalist leaned toward the would-be jumper so they could hear each other amid the roar of the wind sweeping across the bridge's outer reaches. They talked for a few minutes as Seigenthaler waited anxiously for an opportunity to intervene. His story reported the conclusion of this real-life drama on the front page of the next day's paper.

> There was one split second when the little grey-haired man tensed up and looked down at the water and mumbled a few words. "So long," he muttered. "Good luck. God forgive me my sins." It was obvious he was going to jump.
>
> He dropped his hands to his side. I lunged down from where I was sitting astride the bridge railing and grabbed the back of his collar. I caught him tight and pulled hard. He started kicking and yelling, ... try[ing] to wriggle out of his shirt. But the police officers he had warned to keep back now rushed to help me. A dozen strong hands reached out, snatched him, [and] heaved his kicking form over to the safe side of the rail.

"He really wanted to die," mused police Sergeant J.D. Hall. "It's 100 feet down to the river."[1]

The *Tennessean's* enterprising reporter continued to uncover stories other newsmen might find once in a career if ever. A year or so later, Seigenthaler received a tip from Avon Williams, one of Nashville's few black lawyers. His informant told him that a recent episode in nearby

Benton County, Tennessee hinted strongly of injustice and flagrant racial bias. On looking into the tip Sig discovered that a grand jury had been hastily called to examine the death of a black man whose body had been found in a street near his home not long after the victim was let out of taxi at that location by a white driver. Based on brief testimony from the sheriff and the cabman, the grand jury decided not to issue an indictment. Among its members, Seigenthaler learned, was a well-to-do farmer who was the taxi driver's father-in-law. Upon the revelation in Seigenthaler's *Tennessean* story of this apparent cover-up, the county's newly installed district attorney reopened the investigation, which this time led to the cab driver's conviction as the black man's murderer. Thorough and fearless investigative journalism had done its job.

These stories did not fall like manna into Seigenthaler's lap. In recognition of his initiative, Evans, Harwell and Maples, his superiors at the *Tennessean,* chose him to seek out the long-lost Tom Buntin in Texas. They selected him to interview a distraught man on the edge of the Sparkman Avenue Bridge. Avon Williams, Nashville's leading black lawyer, chose to trust him, not his colleagues or bosses, with the story of racial injustice in Benton County. And only a few months after these events, dissident members of Local 327 would begin providing the enterprising young journalist with information about Teamster corruption in Tennessee that would help to fuel Kennedy's "Get Hoffa" campaign. Surprisingly, these local Teamster rebels allowed Sig to identify them as his sources. They believed this would help to protect them from retribution because, if harm later came to them, everyone would know why they had been mistreated and whom to suspect as their molesters—a wise and courageous decision by them and their young *Tennessean* ally.

After working closely with Kennedy in following up these leads, Sig became his administrative assistant in the 1960 presidential campaign and then went with Kennedy to the attorney general's office in the same capacity. Two years later he was called to become the *Tennessean's* Managing Editor and was ultimately named its Publisher, the first non-member of the Evans family to hold the latter position since Silliman Evans purchased the paper thirty-seven years earlier.

****

John Seigenthaler and US Attorney General Robert Kennedy in meeting at Department of Justice, 1961. Courtesy of John L. Seigenthaler.

James F. Neal was thirty-one years old when he went to work in 1961 as a special assistant to Attorney General Robert F. Kennedy. Born in Oak Grove, Tennessee, a small farming community forty miles northeast of Nashville, Neal came naturally by the swaggering walk and military bearing he maintained long after his hair turned a silvery gray. His grandfather, James Curran Clendenning, joined Lee's Army of Northern Virginia in 1860 and survived five major battles of the Civil War. When Clendenning's wife later gave birth to the daughter that would become Jim Neal's mother, the former Confederate soldier was well beyond his fiftieth birthday.

Young Jim graduated from Sumner County High School with honors. Only five-feet eight-inches tall but muscular, barrel-chested, and uncommonly agile for his stocky build, he went to the University of Wyoming on a football scholarship, played halfback on Wyoming's winning team in the 1951 Gator Bowl, and graduated in June of that year. With the Korean War then ongoing, he enlisted in the marines and went to Officer Candidate training at Paris Island, South Carolina.

There he took to the indignities and physical hardships of officers' boot camp like a bear to the woods, and for his overall performance was named "First Man" in his graduating class. As Neal remembered it, the only honor accompanying this award was the privilege of leading the parade of his fellow classmates, drawn sword glistening, on the day of their commissioning as marine corps officers.

The new second lieutenant went immediately to South Korea, ready to join his peers as a rifle platoon leader, the closest thing to cannon fodder on the American side of the front lines. On reading the young officer's record, however, his regimental commander abruptly ordered him to the Naval School of Justice at Newport, Rhode Island, the marine corps equivalent of law school. For two years Neal handled hundreds of cases and scores of trials, absorbing the fundamentals of courtroom conduct and whetting his interest for a career in the law. When honorably discharged in the late summer of 1954 he held the rank of captain and the title of regiment legal officer. He had also become a husband and father.

Free to leave California, Jim and his family moved back to Tennessee where he enrolled as a first-year student at Vanderbilt's School of Law in Nashville. From the outset he was a class leader in academics and moot court competition. In his senior year he was chosen editor-in-chief of the school's Law Review and noted on graduation day for having the highest three-year grade average in the class of 1957, a group often cited for the number of its members who went on to success in the law and politics.

After three years as a Nashville attorney, Neal joined Turney & Turney, a Washington D.C. law firm. A few months later he worked as a volunteer in northern Virginia for the election of the Kennedy-Johnson ticket in the presidential campaign of 1960. Neal had lately earned a masters degree in tax law, but John Kennedy's election gave him new options. Hoping to expand his horizons, he sought a position in the Department of Justice's Tax Division and for help called on his classmate John Jay Hooker Jr. Hooker had met Bob Kennedy when the latter came to Nashville two years earlier to testify in the impeachment trial of Judge Schoolfield, and had strengthened their friendship by working for him in the recent presidential campaign.

Hooker introduced Neal to Seigenthaler, who was then at the DOJ as the new attorney general's administrative assistant. Sig arranged a meeting between his boss and Neal in which Kennedy agreed to hire the ambitious young lawyer as a litigator in the Tax Division. Days after Jim reported for duty, however, Kennedy switched signals. "I offered you the job you wanted," he told him, "but now I'm asking you to work where I need you most, as a lawyer to help us try criminal cases against Hoffa's gang of Teamster cronies."[2] On the condition that he would work as Kennedy's "Special Assistant," Neal agreed. Neal felt confident his years as a marine corps litigator justified his request, but this was a bold demand by a young lawyer who had spent little time in federal courts. What mattered most to Kennedy, however, were intelligence, loyalty and solid work habits. He also liked Neal's direct manner. Shrugging off the applicant's limited trial experience, he said "That's all right. I don't have any experience as attorney general."[3]

Events validated Kennedy's judgment. After more than three years of government service, Neal was rewarded with an appointment as the US Attorney for the Middle District of Tennessee. In 1966 he returned to private practice in Nashville. Specializing in litigation, Neal began a career that would gain him national recognition.

Archibald Cox, the Solicitor General in RFK's Department of Justice, had worked with Neal during the Hoffa trials in the early '60s. A decade later, as the special prosecutor in the investigation of the Watergate burglaries, Cox invited Jim to join his prosecutorial team. Neal accepted the offer but after a few months felt he had made his contribution and returned to the more rewarding opportunities of private practice. Neal's reputation, along with his knowledge of the Watergate affair gained as a member of Cox's staff, soon brought him another offer to return to Washington. In 1973, Leon Jaworski, a prominent Texas lawyer and the new Watergate Special Prosecutor, asked Neal to be his chief counsel in the criminal trial of the infamous Watergate Seven, an invitation the Nashville lawyer was unable to resist. Among the indicted Nixon appointees were John Mitchell, the ex-attorney general, and former White House aides John Haldeman and John Ehrlichman. In a trial presided over by Judge John Sirica—featuring the missing seventeen minutes of Oval Office tapes and dominating the national news for many weeks—six of seven defendants were found guilty for their roles in a cover-up of the Watergate burglary. Neal returned to Nashville from this stunning victory, his star risen to a new height.

Among the major clients soon knocking on Neal's door was the Ford Motor Company. Several of its executives faced criminal charges of reckless homicide in the death of three teenage girls killed in a fiery explosion when a Chevrolet van rear-ended their subcompact Ford "Pinto" on an Indiana highway. It was a horrendous accident. The Pinto's three passengers had died at the scene, two burning to death inside their automobile and the third dying from multiple injuries after being thrown from the car. According to witnesses, the van was going 50 mph when it struck the girls' car, which was moving at 30 mph. Because the Pinto's gas tank had ruptured from an impact caused by a speed difference of only 20 mph, said the prosecutors, it must have had a dangerous design flaw which Ford's engineers knowingly and recklessly ignored.

Hired by Ford's management to head its legal defense team, Neal led an investigation into the facts of what became a highly publicized case. One thing was particularly puzzling: the Pinto, on its way westward toward Goshen, Indiana, was headed eastward at the time of the crash toward Elkhart, the girls' hometown, and no one knew why. Determined to find an eyewitness, Neal discovered a young man whose testimony would clarify that issue and contradict a key element of the prosecution's case. A trial lawyer's dream come true, the witness spoke forthrightly and told a compelling story.

Hailing from the upper Michigan peninsula, the youthful witness was a trained emergency medical technician. At the time of the accident he was driving eastward along the two-lane highway on which it occurred. Arriving on the scene moments after its occurrence, he stopped, went to the side of the young girl thrown from the Pinto and did his best to make her comfortable. Though she was dying, the witness continued, she was able to tell him what had happened. She had been the car's driver. She and her companions, after stopping for gas, had just pulled back onto the road to continue their westbound journey when she noticed in the rear-view mirror the cap from the Pinto's gas tank lying in the opposite lane. She made a U-turn and stopped in the eastbound lane directly behind the gas cap, the road having no shoulder at that point wide enough to accommodate her car. After stepping out to retrieve the cap, she got back into the driver's seat. At that moment, before she could engage the forward gear, she saw in the rear-view mirror a van closing in on them and moving fast. To her horror, she instantly realized that it was not going to stop.

The courtroom kept a hushed silence as the young man spoke. During a thorough cross-examination he stayed firm, leaving the witness stand with his testimony un-impeached. Now—on top of the van driver's concession that he was doing 50 mph at the time of impact— there was credible evidence that the Pinto was at a full stop. These were critical facts in Ford's defense, and Neal went on to show—by expert testimony supplemented with photos of rear-end crashes by similar vans traveling at 50 mph on Ford's test track—that under the same circumstances as in the fatal crash virtually any car's gas tank would explode on impact. The jury agreed and found the defendants innocent on all counts.

The victory in the Ford Pinto case brought a bigger stream of high-profile clients to Neal's Nashville office. These included one of Hollywood's leading directors, John Landis, who was charged with manslaughter in the deaths of three actors killed in a helicopter crash during the filming of *The Twilight Zone*. Neal immersed himself in the lore of movie making, talking at length with Billy Wilder, John Huston and other experienced directors on the nuts and bolts of their craft. After four weeks of testimony, *The Twilight Zone* director was not found guilty. Another client was Edwin "Fast Eddie" Edwards, the governor of Louisiana who was on trial in New Orleans for extorting money from building contractors to fund His Honor's well-known gambling trips to Las Vegas. Neal again submerged himself in the ways of the arena in which his client operated. By spending endless hours in Las Vegas learning the house rules of the casinos frequented by Edwards, and how his client's crap-shooting skills kept his losses to a mere three to four percent of the sums risked, Neal showed that although Edwards's credo was *laissez les bons temps roulez,* he did not have, and had no need for, the huge sums the government claimed he needed to cover his gambling losses. When the government failed to produce solid evidence of extortion, the jury found Edwards not guilty. Neal later conceded that if the feisty governor's trial had been held in Baton Rouge—the state capital where the citizens knew him better and accepted him less—the result might well have been different.

Also included among Neal's clients were high-ranking elected officials caught up in politically induced but substantively serious investigations of criminal violations within their administrations. Among these were two sitting governors of Kentucky, Wallace Wilkinson and Ernie Fletcher, both of whom, with Neal's help, escaped indictment. While Al Gore served as vice-president in the Clinton administration, he sought help from his friend and fellow Tennessean. Republicans were demanding the appointment of a special prosecutor to investigate charges that Gore had violated campaign finance laws by making fundraising calls to potential contributors using a White House telephone, and then gone so far as to hold a fund-raising session inside a Buddhist temple. Counseled by Neal, the vice-president beat down the charges of illegality, which evaporated when Gore lost the presidential race to George W. Bush.

These accomplishments lay well into the future when US Attorney General Robert Kennedy selected the thirty-one-year-old Tennessee lawyer as his special assistant. Most of Neal's future cases would have their share of dramatic moments, but his clearest memories were from the two trials of Jimmy Hoffa, the most unforgettable character ever to cross his path.

CHAPTER 4

"Will Someone Please Wipe Up
All That Blood"

The McClellan Committee hearings of 1957 put Hoffa on television screens and newspaper front pages nationwide. While most people saw him as labor's pit bull, opinions varied widely on the qualities of his character and leadership. To rank and file Teamsters he was a fearless protector, a tough nut who refused to crack as he battled for their interests. To them and many others, persuaded by his speeches and press conferences, he was big government's persecuted victim—a loud-mouth, perhaps, but someone who got things done and by no means a proven crook. Kennedy's investigators had a very different view, as did law enforcement officers in cities where the Teamsters held sway. To them Hoffa was more than corrupt; he was the main conduit for organized crime's growing influence within the labor movement, the personification of power gone astray.

In *Jimmy Hoffa's Hot*, author-journalist John Bartlow Martin speculated that the Senate hearings, despite their exposure of Hoffa's dark side, might be a blessing in disguise for the Teamster boss. "If he weathers the storms ahead, the [McClellan Committee] investigation, which has made him a national figure and … given him an identity few public men possess, may someday seem to him like an almost unmitigated blessing."[1] In other words, public relations mavens might be right: most people remember your name but soon forget the media's criticisms. Bob Kennedy saw Hoffa's survival in a different light. To him, the Teamster boss's ability to stay in office despite his pummeling by the Committee made him "the chief symbol [of labor corruption] in the minds of Congress," the main spur of their effort to draft corrective legislation.[2] The new laws, Kennedy felt, would either force Hoffa to mend his ways or send him to prison.

Fierce storms would ultimately surround the labor leader, but for the time being Martin's crystal ball seemed clearer than Kennedy's. Hoffa's only serious criminal conviction had come in 1946. Charged with extorting money from Detroit grocers in return for quelling dockworker strikes, he avoided jail by pleading guilty to the misdemeanor of violating state antitrust laws. For this he was fined $500 and ordered to return $7,000 to the offended grocery store owners, all of which came from the coffers of Teamster Local 299. For the next twenty-one tempestuous years, by fast footwork and artful dodging, Hoffa parried law enforcers' best punches. And when an occasional body blow landed in the form of an indictment, a shrill whistle brought a dozen lawyers scurrying to his side.

Three of Hoffa's narrow escapes had occurred in 1957 while the McClellan Committee was still in session. The first of these was the Cheasty bribery trial in which defense lawyers skillfully played the race card to gain their client's undeserved acquittal. Later that year Hoffa was tried in New York City for the federal crime of conspiring to tap the telephones of the Teamsters' Detroit employees suspected of disloyalty. Indicted along with him were his right-hand assistant, Bert Brennan, and Bernard Spindel, an electronics expert from mobster Johnny Dio's New York enclave. One of Spindel's men testified he had implanted the taps, working at night when the offices were empty. The tapper said he had also installed hidden microphones to pick up casual office dialogue, and then instructed Hoffa in the use of both systems. The Teamster boss admitted he had authorized the equipment's installation but claimed it allowed him to listen only to open discussions, not those that were wired. The case ended in a hung jury when eleven of the twelve jurors voted for conviction but could not change the mind of a lone holdout. Hoffa cited this "victory" as further evidence that he was a victim of a blood feud perpetrated by Robert Kennedy under the McClellan Committee's protective umbrella.

After having come so close to victory in that case, the prosecutors set a date for a new trial. Ironically, most of the government's evidence of the alleged telephone-tapping conspiracy had been collected through its own wiretaps of Teamster phone lines. Before the start of Hoffa's third trial of 1957, the US Supreme Court ruled that evidence obtained from wiretaps was inadmissible on the ground that electronic snooping without a warrant was unconstitutional. But the government's lawyers, showing more tenacity than good judgment, plowed ahead with a retrial. With the strength of the prosecution's case thus diluted, all three defendants were acquitted. Soon thereafter, and with this case as part of its motivation, the US Congress legalized telephone wiretaps that were first authorized by a judge's order.

The Senate's investigation put dark clouds over Hoffa's head for the next two years, but the McClellan Committee went out of business before the storm broke. Kennedy left his chief counsel position to write *The Enemy Within*, a narrative of the Committee's efforts and his role as its lead lawyer. A year later, in 1960, Hoffa and a local banker were indicted for mail fraud in Detroit, but his lawyers again got him out of trouble. The judge hearing the new charge voided the indictment for a flaw in the selection of the grand jurors who issued it, and the case never went to trial.[3] The labor movement's Houdini had once again wriggled free.

****

As 1960 drew to a close the public focused its attention on the nation's charismatic new president, his fashionable wife and his famous family. For all the Kennedys these were the heady days of the transition to Camelot, a time when a buoyant president-elect could say, with barely a ripple of criticism, that he was making "Bobby" the new attorney general to give his brother additional experience before having to practice law.

Seated behind a large partner's desk in his cavernous office, the somewhat smallish, thirty-six-year-old attorney general of the United States hardly looked the part. Across the expanse between the office doorway and his paper-laden desk—sleeves rolled up above the elbows, his tie loosened from an unbuttoned collar and a shock of brown hair perpetually draped across his forehead—the room's current occupant could easily have been mistaken for a young lawyer secretly trying out the boss's chair. It was only when a visitor drew close that Kennedy's weathered face, piercing gaze and heightened physical presence revealed a seasoned veteran of adversity and strife. When he rose and gracefully offered a strong hand in welcome he was clearly the man in charge, at ease with himself and his new responsibilities.

Bob Kennedy was a strong magnet for people who wanted to participate in government and who believed, as he did, that hard work and service to country were among life's more rewarding experiences. Once on the job, Kennedy's new hires saw firsthand his absolute dedication to each task, his courage to make the hard calls as he saw them. They felt included within his genuine concern for the well-being of his associates regardless of their status. These leadership qualities converted his co-workers into fiercely loyal compatriots ready to go the last mile to accomplish their joint mission. Together with others of like mind and heart, they would compose formidable teams whenever, and in whatever forum, Kennedy might call upon them to perform.

At the McClellan Committee and the Justice Department, the personal loyalty of Kennedy's staff members was as solid as the walls of the government buildings in which they worked. In return, they had his complete trust and real affection. Among these were his confidential assistant Angie Novello, her brother-in-law Carmine Bellino, the Senate Committee's senior investigator, and Walter Sheridan, "one of our best and most relentless investigators [whose] almost angelic appearance [hid] a core of toughness."[4] Pierre Salinger had been another trusted Committee staffer whom Kennedy remembered as always having a "briefcase in hand, the inevitable cigar in his mouth and an almost visible halo of excitement encircling his head."[5] The new AG would naturally have wanted the irrepressible former newsman with him at Justice, for leavening as well as investigative savvy, but Salinger had moved on to become JFK's press secretary.

John Seigenthaler, another trusted loyalist from the ranks of journalism, had helped Kennedy edit *The Enemy Within*, contributing to its success as a runaway best seller. He had then taken a leave of absence from his Nashville newspaper to be Kennedy's administrative assistant during the campaign against Nixon in 1960. Working together in the pressure-cooker of a tight presidential race the two men had developed a solid bond of friendship and respect. When RFK went to the Justice Department he asked his right-hand man to come with him in that same capacity, and without missing a beat the young journalist extended his leave of absence from the *Tennessean* to continue as the new attorney general's aide. In the course of these two jobs Seigenthaler came to know Kennedy as well or better than anyone outside the latter's immediate family. Only two years apart, the vibes between them were pitch- and note-perfect, even on sensitive subjects. "Bob, Senator so-and-so said today that you were a ruthless young autocrat," Sig would mischievously report. "Tell him I'm not so young," Kennedy would retort. In a variation on the same theme, when told someone thought him "considerate," his response would be "Tell him not to spread that around."

Including the president's brothers, Washington's most informed insiders numbered, at most, a baker's dozen: two or three members of JFK's cabinet, his national security advisor, a major newspaper editor, a couple of syndicated columnists, a well-placed lawyer, and one or two old friends.[6] This group soon learned that the second most powerful person in Washington was indeed JFK's brother Bob, whose duties extended well beyond the interpretation and application of federal law. When push came to shove in matters of state, defense, personnel appointments—and on any issue fraught with potentially explosive political consequences—the president wanted RFK's input. The first-brother also sat atop the Justice Department's organizational chart, a massive pyramid of divisions with separate responsibilities for criminal, civil, antitrust, tax, legislative and administrative matters, plus the FBI. His work-weeks of six long days and parts of some evenings left Sundays as the only regular opportunity for quality time with his family. The back-breaking duties of a department head and presidential confidant also meant that much of the department's workload rested on the shoulders of his assistant attorneys general and their staffs.

The busiest group in this beehive was a newly created investigative squad with a special mission: identifying union leaders who tolerated known criminals in their midst, followed by steps to erode and obliterate the influence of organized crime within labor's ranks. Kennedy built this new team because he was unwilling to rely solely on investigators from the FBI or prosecutors from the field offices of local US Attorneys. To say the least, J. Edgar Hoover did not have his complete trust. US Attorneys throughout the country—though appointed by JFK on brother Bobby's recommendation—had local fish to fry. So the new AG took a leaf from his thick political notebook. In Jack Kennedy's race for the presidency in 1960, Bob and Larry O'Brien, the campaign's titular manager, had assigned trusted workers to act as liaison to each of the specialized divisions of the Democratic National Committee. Their mandate was to make sure that the DNC's permanent staffers—whose allegiances to the party and their own livelihood sometimes strained a single-minded loyalty to the party's candidates—were going all out for the victory of the Kennedy-Johnson ticket.

Using this mold to form a group of lawyers and investigators to go after organized crime members, Kennedy hired men and women who shared his dedication, and in whom he sensed an unqualified loyalty. He was the team's general manager, Deputy Attorney General Nicholas Katzenbach its coach. Its captain was Jack Miller, Assistant Attorney General for the Criminal Division, Jim Neal its powerful young fullback among several other lawyers and investigators. They met in Kennedy's office also as necessary to deal with fast-breaking crises. Because the center of their attention was most often the Teamster president, the tightly knit group soon got the nickname that resonated with their colleagues, the press, the public, and, most of all, their main target. They became known as the "Get-Hoffa Squad," a title none of its members thought amiss.

Once handed the ball, Neal became the team's most reliable ground-gainer. His first assignment took him to Minneapolis in early 1961 to evaluate a case brought to light in the McClellan Committee hearings. The subject of his investigation was Benjamin Dranow, "a shadowy man whose fleeting tracks kept emerging on Hoffa's byways."[7] A fur merchant, Dranow had bought a controlling interest in the Thomas Department Store of Minneapolis at a fire sale price from owners worried they were sliding into bankruptcy. He then acquired, for little or no consideration, store assets worth more than $100,000. He next arranged, through a friend, for the Thomas store to receive a $1.2 million loan from the Teamsters' Central States Pension Fund.

Upon the loan's closing, the wives of all of Dranow's Teamster friends in Minneapolis and Detroit received expensive fur coats but the company itself was in serious financial trouble.

Upon his arrival in Minneapolis, Neal concluded that the strongest case against the crafty furrier was for criminal fraud in connection with the Thomas store's recent bankruptcy. Responding to Neal's presentation, a grand jury indicted Dranow for cheating the store's creditors by acquiring under-priced assets for himself, a felony charge under federal bankruptcy laws. On the day set for his trial the defendant failed to appear. His lawyer claimed his client was in a Miami hospital after suffering a heart attack. Smelling a wet mink, Neal flew to Florida and found his quarry's excuse a complete fabrication. Dranow's doctor refused to say that his patient had suffered a heart attack. Two nurses told Neal that their charge had offered them money to exaggerate the blood pressure and heart rate shown on his hospital charts. Armed with this evidence, Neal persuaded a Miami judge to order the stubborn indictee back to Minneapolis in the company of federal marshals. Prosecuted by Neal, Dranow was found guilty on eighteen counts of criminal fraud, fined $12,000, and sentenced to seven years in prison.

The Dranow conviction in mid–1961 was Neal's first victory as a Justice Department lawyer. Kennedy next sent him to Detroit to push for the indictment of the veteran secretary-treasurer of Teamster Local 299, Rolland McMaster. At six feet five inches, 245 pounds, McMaster had a long history of using his powerful frame to advance Teamster causes. He was a leader in his local union's wars with competing organizers from the CIO when baseball bats were the weapons of choice on both sides. He had fraternized in the late 1940s with the henchmen of Detroit's mobster boss Santo Perrone, and later served as Hoffa's bodyguard.[8] The newest evidence against him, which Neal presented to a federal grand jury, showed that McMaster had received regular under-the-table payments from a local non-union trucking company in return for his not trying to organize it.

Such payoffs had been made a federal crime with the passage of the Taft-Hartley Act in 1947. This law prohibited union officials from receiving, outside of ordinary business practices, money or other things of value from an employer or potential employer of their union's members. The reasons for outlawing these sweetheart deals, extortionate payments and other such transactions were clear: they sapped unions' strength in the fight for better contracts, and frustrated efforts to organize non-union companies. When union officials profited from hidden agreements with their members' actual or possible employers, rank and file workers ate leftovers from labor-management steak dinners.

As Neal prepared for his presentation to the McMaster grand jury he was mindful that the first rule on page one of a trial lawyer's manual was to be prepared—to know the facts of the case backward and forward and the law applicable to it. This was followed closely by a second rule: lawyers should always expect the unexpected, alert to the twists and turns common to most cases. Though fully attuned to these warnings, Neal could hardly foresee the surprise awaiting him in Detroit. The owner of the trucking company allegedly making payments to McMaster had recently died, leaving his widow, Elaine Mastow, as the company's owner and custodian of its files. These records, Neal had been advised, detailed numerous payments to McMaster with no written explanation for them. When subpoenaed to produce the documents Ms. Mastow refused to do so, announcing to the dumbfounded prosecutors that she had just become Mrs. McMaster and could not be forced to testify against her new husband. Her former spouse had died only forty-five days earlier, but no matter; her silence stopped the prosecution cold, ending the case against McMaster. But two years later, when Neal was occupied elsewhere, the Teamster extortionist showed he had learned nothing from his earlier experience. He and the president of Youngstown Cartage Company, another employer of Teamster members, were indicted and tried on a similar Taft-Hartley violation. Both were found guilty, with McMaster receiving a fine of $10,000 and an eighteen-month prison sentence.

Back in Washington from Detroit, and following a quick trip to Orlando to evaluate another pending trial, Neal went to work evaluating a set of potential charges against Hoffa that had first come to light several years earlier. "Test Fleet," as this case came to be known, would be for the Teamster boss the beginning of the end, the seeding ground of further illegal acts that would be his undoing.

****

Investigations by the McClellan Committee and earlier congressional committees had developed a wealth of material on the Test Fleet Corporation. The company had been formed in Tennessee in 1947 by Commercial Carriers, Inc. (CCI), a Flint, Michigan, trucking company. Test Fleet's business was to lease trucks to CCI, which had provided all of the new company's start-up capital and guaranteed its initial bank loans. All of Test Fleet's shares of stock went to the wives of Hoffa and Brennan under their maiden names of Josephine Poszywak and Alice Johnson, respectively. CCI filed Test Fleet's annual corporate reports in Tennessee, and paid all of the company's profits to its two owners until 1958 when Test Fleet went out of business. These recent activities eliminated any possible claim that the case was barred by the statute of limitations for staleness.

After three months of combing through Test Fleet documents Neal's review convinced him that Hoffa and CCI's management had violated the law, and that he could prove it in court. Kennedy agreed with Neal's assessment and the two of them talked about where the Test Fleet case should be tried. The company's business was in Detroit but it had been incorporated in Nashville under the laws of Tennessee. While indictments could be sought in either place, Detroit was Hoffa's fiefdom. His influence extended into the city's halls of government and the boardrooms of its largest businesses. The core members of the so-called Teamster Bar Association were also there, well-known to judges and local law enforcement officers. CCI, the other party to Hoffa's sweetheart deal, was an established Michigan business. Nashville, however, had no such connections. Its citizens knew of Hoffa and his union mostly through Seigenthaler's long-running series in the *Tennessean*. With Hoffa in town, the city's leading newspaper was sure to play up his trial to the hilt. Bob Kennedy's visit to Nashville as a witness in Judge Schoolfield's impeachment trial had introduced him to William Miller, a Nashville-based federal judge who seemed a man of unshakeable integrity. Jim Neal, the lawyer who would try the case, was of the same stuff as jurors to be called for duty in Tennessee's capital city. With these pluses all on Nashville's side the choice turned out to be a no-brainer. That settled, RFK's leading protégé headed south to seek Hoffa's indictment.

Only days later an unexpected event made their decision look even wiser. Silliman Evans Jr., the *Tennessean's* publisher since his father's death in 1955, had died suddenly a few years earlier of a heart attack at age thirty-six. Lucille Evans, the widow of Evans Sr., now controlled the newspaper and had mixed feelings about who should become its next publisher. Her younger and only remaining son, twenty-nine-year-old Amon Carter Evans, wanted the job but his mother had doubts about his maturity. To help persuade her that he could handle the position Amon called on his friend and counselor, John Jay Hooker Jr., only two years older. Brash and handsome, with a double dose of inherited charm and a natural story-teller's gift of words, the young Hooker was a persuasive advocate. Nowhere did his lawyer's skills and young male pheromones combine to better effect than on middle-aged members of the opposite sex. Mrs. Evans agreed to several meetings at her home with her son's emissary. These sessions turned into prolonged discussions at her kitchen table, the two chain smokers filling the air with a bluish haze as Hooker stressed her family's contribution to their state's progress and the need to keep the Evans name at the top of the *Tennessean's* masthead.[9] In the end Lucille agreed and chose her only surviving son as the newspaper's publisher.

Amon's first task in his new role was to name a replacement for Edward Ball, the paper's Managing Editor who had succeeded Coleman Harwell and was himself now ready to retire. Hooker urged Amon, who was also a friend and admirer of Seigenthaler, to contact Kennedy's assistant and offer him the job. Years earlier the *Tennessean's* star reporter had taken Silliman Evans's younger son Amon under his wings at the father's request, so the two men knew each other well. The new publisher and his mother agreed that Seigenthaler was the right choice, and Amon made the call. It was an offer impossible to turn down, though from Sig's perspective the timing was unfortunate. He had just agreed, at President Kennedy's request, to become the Democratic National Committee's liaison officer to the US Congress. The Kennedys were reluctant to let him go, but realized it was the opportunity of a lifetime for their friend and loyal ally. On March 21, 1962 Seigenthaler left Washington to take the editorial reins of the *Tennessean*, where fourteen years earlier he had been the newspaper's newest recruit.

Two months later, after a thorough review of Neal's evidence in the Test Fleet matter, a Nashville grand jury indicted Hoffa on two counts: conspiring with Bert Beveridge, CCI's president, to violate the

Taft-Hartley Act, and receiving over $1 million in illegal payments pursuant to a sweetheart deal between Test Fleet and CCI. Each was a misdemeanor with maximum penalties of one year in jail and a fine of $10,000. Beveridge was indicted on one count of conspiracy. The case came before Judge Miller, who set a trial date of October 22. This news made the *Tennessean's* front page, which, under Seigenthaler's supervision, would cover Hoffa's trial in detail on a daily basis.

The Teamster boss's greed was the source of most of his legal problems, but his volatile temper was often a contributing factor. At this moment both were causing him trouble. On the day before his Nashville indictment he was charged with assault and battery in Washington, D.C. The complainant was Sam Baron, an IBT officer whose loyal service to the Teamsters union went back to Dave Beck's presidency. At age fifty-nine Baron was ten years older than Hoffa and a devoted unionist. Except for two years spent fighting on the side of the Loyalists in the Spanish Civil War, he had been in the labor movement since his early twenties. As reported by Walter Sheridan, the diligent investigator who had followed Kennedy from the McClellan Committee to the DOJ, Baron had started out with the Ladies Garment Workers in New York and experienced firsthand the corrosive influence of Johnny Dio and other racketeers in the labor movement. Moving on to the IBT's national headquarters he had watched with increasing apprehension as Hoffa strengthened the Teamsters' ties to Dio and other members of organized crime.

In May of 1956 someone had thrown acid in the face of Victor Riesel, a nationally syndicated labor columnist for New York's *Daily Mirror* newspaper. Johnny Dio was indicted for conspiracy with an underling to commit this crime which had permanently blinded its victim. Prosecutors abandoned the case, however, when "someone" murdered the actual perpetrator and other suspects refused to talk. At IBT headquarters when the morning news of the attack on Riesel broke, Hoffa "walked up to Baron, poked [a] finger in his chest, and said 'Hey, Baron, a friend of yours got it this morning.' 'What do you mean, Jimmy?' 'That son of a bitch Victor Riesel. He just had some acid thrown on him. Too bad ... it ... [wasn't] thrown on the goddamn hands he types with.' "[10] At that point Baron's dislike of his boss, which had grown deeper over the years, turned to outright disgust. Hoffa was aware of his aide's feelings toward him but reluctant to fire such a respected member of his national staff. And Baron's commitment to the Teamsters and the labor movement kept the long-suffering employee from leaving voluntarily.

One morning, almost six years to the day following the Riesel incident, the tension between the two men finally boiled over. Hoffa yelled at his antagonist to come into his office. There, Baron found his boss shaking with anger, apparently upset by some aspect of contract negotiations then being supervised by his beleaguered employee. "What the hell do you do around here?" Hoffa barked. And, "If you don't know, why the hell don't you admit it?" "But Jimmy," said Baron, "I do know what I'm doing."[11] At that, Hoffa lost control. His face contorted with rage, he rushed at the older man and floored him with a looping right to the head. Shocked staffers grabbed their boss but he shook them off and, as Baron arose, once more knocked him to the ground. Looking his tormentor in the face, the abused victim spit out, "You bum, you would use your muscle."[12] Practically levitating with fury at Baron's cutting remark and level gaze, Hoffa shoved him violently over a chair and onto the office floor for the third time. Struggling to his feet again, with one eye turning black and his face cut and bleeding, the battered Teamster veteran managed to leave the office. By late afternoon he was in a D.C. police station filing his complaint.

Prosecutors in Washington later questioned six IBT employees who saw or heard Hoffa's attack. But like well-trained mobsters, all of them professed ignorance of the details or swore that Baron had landed the first punch. In the end, lawyers from the US Attorney's office conceded they had insufficient evidence to proceed to trial. Baron had taken and passed a lie detector test on what happened between him and Hoffa but the results of that test were not admissible in court. Though the Teamster boss and his lying toadies had risked turning a misdemeanor assault into a multi-party felony of obstructing justice, their fear-based silence, like the Mafia code of *omertà*, ultimately carried the day. But the war against Hoffa continued, with Nashville as the next battleground.

****

On October 22, 1962, President Kennedy startled the world by announcing that his administration had clear proof that Russian ballistic missiles had been installed on Cuban soil, poised to rain down destruction on major US cities. That morning, as Bob Kennedy huddled with his brother in the White House, the Test Fleet case—*United States v. James R. Hoffa and Bertram B. Beveridge*—went to trial in the federal district court in Nashville, Judge William E. Miller presiding. Some Teamster activists from Chicago had considered trying to bribe the judge, but in light of Miller's reputation for incorruptibility they could find no one willing to approach him. Representing Hoffa were four stalwarts of the Teamster Bar Association, two from Detroit and one each from Philadelphia and Washington, D.C. Joining them as the Teamster boss's local attorney was Zeno Thomas Osborn, a rising star from the top tier of Nashville's trial lawyers. Matched against this defense team of solid professionals were four lawyers from Kennedy's Get Hoffa Squad led by Jim Neal along with Charlie Shaffer, Jim Durkin and Nat Lewin. Supporting them was Walter Sheridan, the squad's top investigator, plus local FBI agents as needed for on-the-spot detective work.

The opening day of the Test Fleet trial set its highly contentious tone. Judge Miller began the proceedings with a surprising announcement. Kenneth Harwell, the US Attorney for Middle Tennessee, had just informed him of a disturbing telephone call received by Harwell the previous evening from a woman on the panel of prospective jurors. Miller directed the woman, who was in the courtroom, to take the stand. Under his questioning, she told of being called over the weekend by a man identifying himself as "Allen from the *Banner*," Nashville's evening newspaper, who claimed to be writing an article about the upcoming trial. After seeking her occupation and asking how long she had lived in Nashville he said, "How do you feel about Jimmy Hoffa and the Teamsters?"[13] By then, skeptical of her caller's intentions, she had broken off the conversation without a reply. That was enough for Judge Miller, who released her forthwith from jury duty. He then asked for a show of hands from others who might have received a call from the self-styled Mr. Allen. Several panelists responded affirmatively and they too were excused.

This troublesome start foreshadowed the rocky road ahead. Disturbed by the obvious attempt to influence jurors, Judge Miller warned the panel to avoid all media reports of the trial, and not to discuss the proceedings among themselves. James Stahlman, the *Banner's* publisher, reacted angrily. There was no "Mr. Allen" on the newspaper's staff he wrote in the next day's edition, offering a $5,000 reward for information leading to the caller's apprehension.

The next morning brought further evidence of the ordeal confronting Judge Miller. James Tippens, who had been accepted as a juror the preceding day, told the judge in chambers that a neighbor had come to his home that same afternoon and offered him "$10,000 in hundred dollar bills to vote for Hoffa's acquittal."[14] Shocked and struggling to keep his judicial calm, Miller called the parties and their lawyers to his chambers. Some person or group, he said, was clearly aware of what was transpiring in his courtroom and was attempting to put committed Hoffa supporters on the jury. Neal argued that the jury panelists should be sequestered—locked up at night without access to the media—to prevent further attempts to influence them. Tommy Osborn, Hoffa's Nashville lawyer, responded that "crackpots and do-gooders" were the likely culprits, or labor activists and other Hoffa champions misguidedly trying to help someone they admired.[15] That was a weak reed, particularly in light of Hoffa's public record of attempting to sway black jurors in the Cheasty trial and of secretly wiretapping the offices of his own employees. But there was no evidence, as yet, linking Hoffa to the advances made to Test Fleet jurors. Judge Miller was also reluctant to take such a drastic step so early in a case which, after all, did not involve a capital or even a felonious offense. He gave the parties a stern lecture and warned that any future reports of this kind would bring more serious consequences.

Thanks to the obstreperous behavior of Hoffa's lawyers it took four days to select a jury of twelve people plus four alternates. Announcing that the trial would begin the next morning, Judge Miller realized he held the reins of a fractious horse needing very tight control.

The lawyers' opening statements on both sides were relatively subdued given the palpable tension between them. For the government, Neal's assistant Charlie Shaffer stated that Hoffa and Bert Beveridge, CCI's president, had together violated federal labor laws by creating the Test Fleet Corporation as a payoff to Hoffa and Brennan for having ended a labor dispute on terms highly favorable to CCI. Over ten years, the prosecution would show, CCI had provided Test Fleet's day-by-day management and paid it over $1 million for leased trucks thereby producing $150,000 in net profits. In return, said Shaffer, Hoffa had approved a strike settlement highly favorable to Beveridge's trucking company. Having fired the striking workers, Beveridge then hired new drivers for the trucks leased from Test Fleet, paying them far less than the strikers had demanded and never rehiring the strike's leaders—all with Hoffa's explicit agreement.

For the defense, Osborn countered that his client had acted legally and without criminal intent. The facts of the case, he said, had been disclosed long ago to Congressional investigators. Hoffa's indictment was simply Kennedy's personal vendetta against his client, based wholly on "suspicion and insinuation."[16] Thus were the battle lines drawn.

To make the government's case Neal and his co-prosecutors presented a dozen witnesses to substantiate the claims of their opening statement. One of these was George Fitzgerald, Hoffa's personal lawyer for more than thirty years, to show that a substantial part of Test Fleet's profits had gone directly to Hoffa and Brennan through their wives, the company's owners. Fitzgerald testified that at one point he had given a personal check for $15,000 to Hoffa in exchange for a Test Fleet check in an equal amount, originally issued as a dividend to Josephine Poszywak and Alice Johnson but then endorsed over to Fitzgerald, ostensibly for legal services. Conceding that he had not provided services for the money received and did not expect Hoffa to repay the $15,000, the lawyer exposed a clear case of money laundering to hide the parties' real intent. Hoffa scowled and squirmed as his trusted confidant spotlighted one of the Teamster boss's favorite sleight-of-hand techniques. At the boiling point by the time the witness stepped down, Hoffa leapt from his chair, followed Fitzgerald into the hallway outside the courtroom and fired him on the spot.

The testimony of four more witnesses, unshaken by cross-examination, gave credible support to the prosecution's claim that Hoffa used Test Fleet profits as a source of funds for his personal investments. By the time these witnesses finished, the trial had been under way for six weeks. For health reasons Judge Miller had decided to limit his time on the bench to four hours daily, which was now being honored more in the breach than in practice. The two clumsy attempts to bribe or otherwise influence jurors at the trial's outset had prolonged its start. Six courtroom lawyers—two for the prosecution and four for the defense—had milked most witnesses dry before releasing them. Hoffa's attorneys had aggressively objected at every perceived opportunity, often, it seemed, not to suppress testimony but to provoke the judge into error. On Monday December 3, as the defense stood ready to offer its first witness, Miller asked both sides to move the case forward at a more efficient pace.

The defense's first two witnesses were lawyers, one of them the Chicago firebrand Jacques Schiffer, who would play a major role in Hoffa's later trials, the other Dave Previant, a Detroit labor lawyer. Both told of advising the Teamster boss that the Test Fleet arrangement was legal under the Taft-Hartley Act because it was an "ordinary way" of doing business. Neal decided not to question Schiffer, but did cross-examine Previant. This brought out the holes in the witness's analysis but also focused the jury's attention on the issue.

On the morning of December 5, in the absence of the jury, the patient judge sat listening to lawyers' arguments on one of the case's oft-recurring motions. Suddenly and without warning, like a bolt of lightning from a sunlit sky, a hatless young man in a tan raincoat entered the courtroom and strode rapidly up the aisle toward the judge's bench. Reaching the guardrail at the front of the spectators' section, he burst violently through its swinging doors and into the area reserved for the trial's active participants. Pulling out a pistol that to Neal "looked two feet long," the intruder frantically searched faces to identify his target among the men sitting at the counsel tables.[17] He pointed the gun tentatively at Neal and then, as heads turned, recognized Hoffa's face and began shooting at him within point blank range. As the horror of the moment registered, all began to duck and seek cover except Hoffa, who with indisputable courage lunged at his attacker. Raising his left arm instinctively to protect himself, he swung his right fist at the assailant but missed. Fortunately for everyone the man's weapon was an air-powered gun whose small pellets raised welts on Hoffa's face, arm, and upper body but did not strike an eye or penetrate his victim's tough hide. Simultaneously with Hoffa's charge Chuckie O'Brien, his personal aide and a front row spectator, leapt over the low wooden barrier onto the shooter's back. Together they fell to the floor, a berserk O'Brien furiously pounding his captive.

One of the bailiffs then smashed his pistol butt on the attacker's head, ending the struggle. Other courtroom officers pulled O'Brien away, confiscated the pellet gun and hustled the handcuffed intruder out of the courtroom through a side door.

The shooter was Warren Swanson, an itinerant vagrant and some-time dishwasher in his mid-twenties. The disturbed young man had come to Nashville on a mission from his native state of Nebraska. Several months before the shooting incident, while reading the Bible in a Cincinnati hotel room, Swanson had received a message from God telling him "to kill Jimmy Hoffa."[18] He decided immediately to do so but had trouble accumulating enough money to buy a gun. He finally read an ad in a pulp magazine for a gas-powered pistol that would "penetrate a one-inch board."[19] That was obvious hyperbole to most readers, but Swanson wanted to believe it and the price was right. He bought both the advertiser's false claim and the gun itself.

At the time of the assassination attempt defense lawyer William E, Bufalino had been speaking. As recorded by the court reporter Bufalino's argument broke off in mid-sentence, interrupted by Swanson's sudden appearance. Once order was restored the stenographer's notes took up again with a request by Judge Miller to the courtroom bailiffs: "Will someone please wipe up all that blood on the floor."[20] He then ordered the jury to be locked up overnight and adjourned court until the following day. He decided not to explain this decision to the jurors until the trial was over. Better to have them puzzled, he thought, than to tell them about the day's startling disruption and thereby risk having to declare a mistrial.

Reporters clamoring for a firsthand account greeted Hoffa as he left the courtroom. With his composure fully recovered he dismissed his assailant as "some jerk with a pellet gun."[21] Two years later, when Neal left the DOJ to accept a presidential appointment as US Attorney for Middle Tennessee, he learned the shooter had not been tried for his assault but remained under lock and key. He immediately obtained a court hearing on the prisoner's mental state, which found Swanson incompetent to stand trial and ordered his indefinite confinement to a mental health facility for treatment. In time the would-be assassin was released and never again entered Hoffa's life.

The day after this bizarre interruption defense lawyers moved for a mistrial on the ground that the episode had so unsettled Hoffa he was unable to receive and evaluate their counsel. Judge Miller, maintaining his own calmness with difficulty in the face of this ludicrous assertion, told them to put their motion in writing for his later consideration. Meanwhile the trial would continue. No sooner had the judge finished speaking than Neal tossed a new bombshell into the proceeding. Handing the judge a written motion backed by affidavits from FBI agents he asked for the removal of a second juror, a female, on the ground that certain specified individuals had approached her husband in an attempt to have him persuade his wife to vote for Hoffa's acquittal. Miller read the motion and forthwith ordered everyone from the courtroom except the lawyers, the defendants, and the court's bailiffs. When Neal said his witnesses were present and ready to testify, the judge decided to hold a hearing on the spot.

The details of the extraordinary conduct taking place outside the courtroom from the beginning of the trial to that moment would surface later. The upshot of the hearing was that the wife whose husband had been approached was excused from further duty and an alternate juror seated in her place. Adjourning court on that Thursday until the following Monday, Miller told the jury he was regretfully sequestering them for the rest of the trial. He knew that this announcement—coupled with the day's closed-door hearing on the heels of the unexplained interruption of the day before—had disturbed and confused the jurors. But their obvious discomfort, in his opinion, would not prevent them from judging the evidence impartially. Applying the same reasoning to the incident's impact on Hoffa, Judge Miller denied the defense lawyers' motion for a mistrial based on their client's alleged emotional state.

The following week brought to the stand the former Alice Johnson, Bert Brennan's widow and now Mrs. Peterson. Under cross-examination by Charles Shaffer she admitted having nothing to do with the organization or management of Test Fleet, and no knowledge of its original directors or of Commercial Carriers' participation in its creation.[22] She had never attended a stockholders meeting and was also unaware of why Test Fleet had gone out of business in 1958 or what had become of its assets. Rather than risk similar admissions from her co-owner, the defense lawyers did not call Hoffa's wife as a witness.

On Friday of the following week Hoffa took the stand in his own defense. Questioned by his local counsel Tommy Osborn—who had replaced Detroit lawyer William Bufalino as the defense team's courtroom leader—the Teamster boss made an effective witness. By turns voluble, glib, testy and self-righteous, he claimed to have had no connection with Test Fleet. Brazenly contradicting several prosecution witnesses, he denied ever having received anything of value from the company. When his wife occasionally loaned him money, he said, he always paid her back. His former attorney George Fitzgerald had lied about laundering Test Fleet profits. Moreover, said Hoffa, his lawyers had advised him from the beginning that the ownership of Test Fleet— originally by him and Brennan and later by their wives—was legal. He could not come up, however, with a plausible reason for having put the new company's ownership in the maiden names of the two men's wives.

On Neal's cross-examination Hoffa shamelessly stuck to his version of the facts: the prosecution's witnesses who testified against him were liars. When his testimony contradicted several sworn statements he had formerly made to the McClellan Committee he claimed his earlier assertions were mistaken. Subjected to redirect and recross-examination, Hoffa was on the stand for the better part of three days.

Following his testimony, both sides quickly wrapped up their sides of the case. Closing arguments produced nothing new and neither side could confidently predict success. Both felt that Hoffa's fate would turn on two things: how much doubt he had managed to sow in the minds and hearts of the jury members, and whether their long ordeal—with the trial's numerous interruptions, juror substitutions and their own sequestration—had confused jurors to a degree that would influence their decision. At that point, with nothing left but the judge's instructions on the applicable law, the jury was again unsettled when Neal asked once more that the courtroom be cleared for a closed hearing. That done, he announced that an attempt had been made to influence yet another juror, a retired railroad employee named Gratin Fields, to vote for Hoffa's acquittal. He handed to Judge Miller and Hoffa's lawyers the prosecution's written motion with attached FBI affidavits, this time supplemented by a sealed envelope containing a document which Neal asked the judge to read and then reseal without disclosing its contents. Infuriated by this attempt to hide evidence, defense lawyers rose in unison with shrill objections to their being denied access to a potentially harmful statement by an unknown witness. Following an hour of tumultuous wrangling, Miller granted the prosecution's motion, resealed the envelope without revealing its contents and ordered Fields's replacement by the third alternate juror.

On the morning of the next day, Friday, December 21, Judge Miller charged the jury and sent them off to begin their deliberations. Unable to reach agreement by late that afternoon the jurors returned on Saturday for an all-day session that brought no consensus. After meeting briefly on Sunday morning and telling the judge they were stalemated, they were directed to make one last try for a unanimous decision. Around noon the jury foreman returned to report that despite their best efforts they were "hopelessly deadlocked" with no room for compromise. Disappointed and bone tired, the judge realized the case was over but did not bang his gavel to formalize his decision. Without a pause he told the packed courtroom he was about to make a statement and cautioned everyone to remain seated until he had finished.

A grim-faced Judge Miller found renewed energy to speak from a prepared text intended for delivery regardless of the trial's outcome. "It is my duty," he intoned, to disclose "some of the unfortunate events which have marked the trial from its inception." He then made clear that he was not questioning the honesty or integrity of any of the persons called for jury duty, or of those who had made such "tireless efforts and ... sacrifices" while serving as jurors. He then explained that he had removed one prospective juror and two seated jurors based on evidence presented in closed hearings that "illegal ... attempts were made by close labor associates of the defendant to contact and influence" the dismissed jurors. Accordingly, he was ordering the US Attorney in Nashville to present evidence to a new grand jury concerning charges of jury tampering. Next, he was immediately unsealing the records of the closed sessions (except for the sealed envelope presented during the last hearing) for filing in the court clerk's office as public documents. "The right of a defendant in a criminal case to be tried by a jury of his peers," Judge Miller concluded, "is one of the most sacred of our Constitutional guarantees. ... [T]rial by jury, however, becomes a mockery if unscrupulous persons are allowed to subvert it by improper and unlawful means.... [S]uch shameful acts to corrupt our jury system shall [not] go unnoticed by this Court."[23]

Jurors and spectators sat in silence as Judge Miller spoke. After finishing his prepared statement he told them of the gunman's attack on Hoffa that had caused Miller to order the jury's sequestration. He also told them that he had heard evidence, on the day following the attack, of a third attempt to influence a juror, leading him to continue their isolation. Then, after again thanking the jury, he excused them from further service, declared a mistrial, and adjourned court. The tension finally broken, Hoffa and his lawyers leapt to their feet with smiles, handshakes and bear hugs all around. They were joined immediately by Chuckie O'Brien and three or four Teamster cronies who had faithfully attended each day's session. Downcast, Neal and his associates gathered up their papers and walked to the prosecution's temporary courthouse office. Equally dejected was Walter Sheridan, Bob Kennedy's eyes and ears throughout the two-month trial. Sheridan had played a key role in the FBI's uncovering of jury tampering by Teamster agents in the Nashville case. This would come fully to light later as the Get Hoffa Squad continued its relentless pursuit of the elusive Teamster boss.

For the moment, Hoffa was in a celebratory mood. After all, it was the government's fourth failure in five years to gain his criminal conviction. He was "naturally disappointed" not to have been acquitted, but "cheerfully wished everybody connected with the trial a Merry Christmas" as he left for the airport to board a flight home. The Teamster Bar Association's William Bufalino was similarly upbeat: "In 1962, Santa Claus has simply refused to put Jimmy Hoffa in Bobby Kennedy's stocking."[24]

By the next afternoon Hoffa's mood had soured as the realization sunk in that a Nashville grand jury was about to indict him for jury tampering, a much more serious charge than the one he had just dodged in the Test Fleet trial. In an interview taped at Detroit's WWJ-TV on Christmas Eve day for broadcast that night and the following evening, he accused Judge Miller of being prejudiced against him and called Jim Neal "one of the most vicious prosecutors whoever handled a criminal case for the Department of Justice." It was "a disgrace," he continued, "for anyone to make a statement that this jury was tampered with."[25]

In the light of later events this statement put into clear focus the degree to which Hoffa's creed of belligerent denial had come to dominate his public persona. Not only proclaiming his innocence, he was also dismissing the possibility that anyone else had unlawfully tried to help him during the Test Fleet trial. Perhaps he had become truly paranoid, believing in his heart things he knew or should have known to be false. But in any case, why change the brazen style that had served him so well for as long as he could remember? And as to substance, why defend himself by struggling along a narrow path when dynamite could quickly clear the way? Why worry about observing the law if every breach of its constraints could be nullified by a combination of smart lawyers and payoffs to enemies who seemed always to have a price for their cooperation? The cynical assumptions underlying Hoffa's attitude and tactics would again be tested in only a few months. His trial for jury tampering, conducted in a different venue, would bring challenges and confrontations of a magnitude he had never before faced.

CHAPTER 5

"They're Fixin' to Get at the Jury"

Though intended as preventive medicine, Hoffa's attempt to fix the Test Fleet jury produced side effects worse than the underlying ailment. Charged with a misdemeanor the Teamster boss sought to avoid his conviction by committing a felony. Ironically, his efforts to buy jury votes were unnecessary. Post-trial reports of individual juror's views were sketchy, but the consensus was that as many doubted his guilt as wanted to convict him. Though the reasons for the split decision never came fully to light, the jury did not learn the facts behind the removal of three jurors until after the case ended. Even if some felt that attempts had been made to influence the jury in Hoffa's favor, as was probably the case, their suspicions seemed not to have affected the trial's outcome.

Judge Miller's concluding words left no doubt that the feds had solid information on attempts to influence the Test Fleet jury and were closer than ever on Hoffa's trail. Fully aware of his increasing jeopardy the Teamster boss and his sycophants turned up the volume of the party line: "Victimized by Bob Kennedy, Jimmy Hoffa cannot get a fair trial in a federal courtroom." This oft-repeated plaint by the president of one of the nation's most politically powerful unions resonated with a number of Washington's more conservative politicians. Even before Test Fleet got under way, Senator Homer Capehart of Indiana, along with a group of other Republican congressmen, had accused the Justice Department of treating Hoffa unfairly. The DOJ was intentionally delaying Hoffa's trial in Orlando on various criminal charges where, the senators claimed, the government had a weak case. Following the hung jury vote in Nashville, Democratic Senator Edward Long of Louisiana and maverick Wayne Morse of Oregon joined the chorus of those paying tribute to the IBT and its bellicose leader. Another critical voice was that of William Loeb, the troglodyte publisher of the *Manchester Union Leader* in New Hampshire. With typically harsh rhetoric, Loeb declared that the tactics of Kennedy's Justice Department were no different than the merciless campaigns of Julius Caesar and his Roman legionnaires. Loeb and Hoffa agreed in principle: the bigger the lie, the better the chances of its acceptance as truth.

In the days immediately following his Test Fleet "victory," Hoffa's motor-mouth again ran at full speed, sometimes making sense but occasionally drifting into paranoid fantasy. FBI agents, he argued soberly enough, pull some "creepy stuff. [They] investigate my kid" at his school. They order "every airline office in the country" to let them know "when Hoffa makes a reservation [and report] the time he takes off and the time he arrives. Our phones are tapped and our hotel rooms are bugged. [We] make remarks ... and the government attorneys [know] next morning what [we] said." But he then went off the deep end: "FBI agents are ... a bunch of rats and stool pigeons. You're walking on a picket line and an FBI agent comes up and rubs this white chemical on you and you're wired from then on. They can pick up everything you say until the suit is cleaned."[1]

From temporary offices in Nashville's federal courthouse on Broadway at Eighth Avenue Walter Sheridan had been RFK's alter ego in Nashville during the Test Fleet trial. Sheridan was the government's only link to a clandestine informer within the Hoffa camp, the sole conduit to FBI agents of leads on suspected jury tampering. In Washington, Kennedy learned the story of Hoffa's efforts to fix the Test Fleet jury from the regular firsthand reports of his tireless chief investigator.

In late September of 1962, about three weeks before the start of the Test Fleet trial, Sheridan had received a call in his Washington office from Frank Grimsley, the newest member of the attorney general's legal team. Based in Atlanta, Grimsley said that Sargent Pitcher, the district attorney in Baton Rouge, Louisiana, had called him to pass along a startling piece of information. The DA's chief investigator, Billy Daniels, had reported to his boss a conversation with Edward Partin, the president of Teamsters Local 5 in Baton Rouge. Partin was in the county's jail on a charge of helping in the kidnapping a fellow Teamster's children. According to Daniels, Partin claimed that in a meeting with Hoffa some months earlier the Teamster boss "had talked to him about killing Bob Kennedy."[2]

Though somewhat skeptical of Partin's motivation and truthfulness, Grimsley felt duty bound to pursue the informer's frightening accusation. Through Pitcher he arranged to meet with Partin along with the Baton Rouge DA and the latter's investigator Daniels. To assure the secrecy of Grimsley's mission they interviewed the tipster in his jail cell at 3:00 a.m. on October 1. In a meeting lasting three hours the man whom Hoffa would later consider the ultimate stool pigeon told a story sounding more like pulp fiction than fact.

Partin had met with Hoffa in the Teamster boss's Washington office the preceding June. He had gone there to solicit Hoffa's support for a battle Partin was fighting within his local union. He had been disappointed, he added frankly, by Hoffa's noncommittal response. Though unaware of the specific pressures on the Teamster boss—from the upcoming Test Fleet trial, Sam Baron's pending assault charge and a variety of internal union issues—Partin sensed that his host was too stressed out to focus on anything but his own problems.

At one point during their meeting, said Partin, Hoffa laid bare the root cause of his anxiety. Going to the window of his Pennsylvania Avenue office and looking toward the Department of Justice just up the street, he motioned for his guest to join him. As Partin came forward, his host growled, "I've got to do something about that son-of-a-bitch Bobby Kennedy. He's got to go."[3] In checking up on Kennedy's habits, the Teamster boss continued, he had learned that the AG rode around town in an open convertible accompanied only by a big black dog, and swam alone in his home pool unprotected by guards. The little shit had guts, Hoffa admitted, but was a constant irritant. After asking whether Partin knew anything about plastic bombs, Hoffa said that someone could throw such a device into Kennedy's car or his house. He also claimed to know where he could get a silencer for a gun.

In Partin's jail cell Grimsley listened intently to the Louisiana Teamster's story, asking him to repeat some details and to explain why he had waited until four months after the fact to tell his bizarre tale. The burly Teamster said he had been deeply shaken by the intensity of Hoffa's remarks, and though no stranger to labor violence, he considered his leader's murderous threats beyond the pale. Finally, he said, he had grown highly uncomfortable keeping them to himself. But, Grimsley asked, was he not motivated partly by the hope of getting the US government's help in resolving Louisiana's kidnapping charge? No, said Partin, he had committed no crime. He had acted only to help a friend mired in a messy divorce proceeding who feared the loss of his children. Leaving the informer's cell Grimsley realized that whatever the reasons behind his informer's decision to talk, the only issue that finally mattered was whether or not he was telling the truth.

Partin put his statement in the form of a sworn affidavit. He also made the unusual offer of voluntarily taking a lie detector test to prove he was telling the truth. Though the test results would not be admissible in court, Sheridan wanted confirmations of the Louisiana Teamster's credibility wherever he could find them. He also felt that the FBI should consider taking additional steps to protect the attorney general, particularly if the informer was honestly reporting what he had seen and heard. Moreover, the value of a Teamster insider acting as a government ally could hardly be overestimated. In a follow-up meeting at DOJ headquarters among Kennedy, Jack Miller and Sheridan, they decided to take advantage of Partin's willingness to put his veracity on the line. That evening, on their separate ways home, Sheridan and the AG crossed paths in the Department's parking garage. "What do we do if that fellow passes the test? asked [Kennedy] with a wry smile." "I don't know, but I think he might," Sheridan replied. In response his boss simply "shrugged and climbed into his car." Two days later, in unusually categorical language, the FBI's report on the lie detector test stated that "from all indications" Partin's description of his meeting with Hoffa was true.[4]

Things then moved swiftly. In return for Partin's promise to help return his friend's children to their mother, his bail was reduced to an affordable level and on its payment he was released from jail. The

Louisiana Teamster also agreed to cooperate with DOJ investigators by staying in touch with Grimsley.

On October 8, soon after his release from prison and still seeking his boss's support in his fight to retain control of Teamster Local 5, Partin called Hoffa to ask for another meeting. Their conversation was inconclusive so he called again ten days later. This time Hoffa said he was planning to arrive in Nashville on the 21st and could meet with the Louisiana Teamster then. Who said what to whom in this latter conversation, which Partin recorded with equipment given him by Baton Rouge investigator Daniels, would become a critical issue in Hoffa's jury tampering trial. For now, however, Partin told the DOJ's Grimsley only that the Teamster boss had agreed to meet him in Nashville, which information the Atlanta lawyer passed on to Sheridan. "Tell him," said Kennedy's chief investigator, "to be on the lookout for any indication of jury tampering or other illegal activity, [and] if he calls me he should use the name 'Andy Anderson.' "[5]

Grimsley did as instructed and the leading players now began taking their places for the drama about to unfold on the Nashville stage. Was Partin a government mole, planted and controlled by Kennedy's agents, or had he volunteered for duty with the understanding that he would act on his own? That issue would loom large in the days ahead.

Two days before Test Fleet's scheduled start on October 22, Hoffa sycophants began their migration to his Nashville headquarters. Nicholas Tweel, a cigarette vending machine distributor from Huntington, West Virginia, came to town seeking a loan for his business from the Teamster pension fund. Tweel was a friend of Allen Dorfman, Hoffa's go-to guy on such matters, who would also be in Nashville. Another toadie on his way to join Hoffa's defense forces was Larry Campbell, a black Teamster business agent. Though he lived in Louisville, Kentucky, Campbell was assigned to Detroit's Local 299. His uncle, Tom Parks, lived in Nashville and might know people through whom black members of Test Fleet's jury panel could be contacted.

On Sunday afternoon, October 21, Hoffa flew into Tennessee's capital city in his sleek-bodied twin-engine Lockheed Lodestar, the latest word in luxurious private air transport. On hand to meet him were several local Teamsters and other hangers-on led by Ewing King, the president of Nashville's Local 327. King was "a tall, lanky, chinless man" in his fifties who looked like a farmer from Middle Tennessee's fertile fields but drove a sporty red Thunderbird to display his flashier self-image.[6] Indebted to Hoffa for recently helping him put down a rank-and-file revolt, King proudly drove his boss downtown to the Andrew Jackson Hotel, not far from the federal courthouse. The hotel's entire seventh floor would be the Teamsters' trial headquarters with a large space for Hoffa's office, bedroom suites for him and his lawyers, and single rooms for a few select assistants.

Edward Partin arrived in town the next day and went straight to the Andrew Jackson's lobby, which gave every appearance of housing a Teamster convention. In the coffee shop he joined Allen Dorfman, whom he had met before, along with Dorfman's swarthy companion who introduced himself as Anthony Quinn. As the three men left the restaurant together, "Mr. Quinn" invited his new acquaintance to continue their conversation in his hotel room. Thinking Partin might be of help to him, Quinn confessed that his real name was Nick Tweel. Of Lebanese extraction, Tweel probably enjoyed playing on his resemblance to the famous actor but now got down to business. Arriving soon to assist him, he confided, were some friends from his hometown, including a private eye who was an officer in Huntington, West Virginia's Fraternal Order of Police, along with two specialists in photographic and electronic surveillance who hoped that Hoffa's fear of government bugs and listening devices would bring them some counter-spy business. Their joint mission, he told Partin, was "to help Dorfman with the [Test Fleet] jury."[7]

Returning to the lobby, Partin used an adjacent pay telephone booth to make his first call to Walter Sheridan. In a rich southern accent with Cajun overtones he introduced himself as "Andy Anderson." The next words out of his mouth, though spoken matter-of-factly, electrified his listener. "They're fixin' to get at the jury," said the Louisiana Teamster. "Who are *they*?" asked Sheridan. "Allen Dorfman and a man named Tweel," came the reply.[8] The two men agreed to meet right away in Sheridan's room at the Noel Hotel where they could talk privately. Answering the knock on his door the DOJ investigator found "a big man with brown wavy hair" in a tight-fitting suit with a monogrammed handkerchief protruding from the breast pocket of his jacket. To Sheridan, Partin resembled a friendly

Portrait of Teamster official Edward Grady Partin, after testifying before East Baton Rouge Parish grand jury, October 26, 1967.

grizzly bear squeezed into a businessman's uniform, a blue-collar worker who would have preferred jeans and an open-collared shirt.

The thirty-eight-year-old Louisiana Teamster was surprisingly soft spoken for a man of his bulk. He showed some emotional scars but lacked the hard edges of many of his colleagues. Sitting on one of the room's twin beds as Sheridan made notes, Partin talked openly in a pleasant drawl with no visible suspicion or discomfort. He had just met with Hoffa in the latter's hotel suite, he said, and told him he had talked with Dorfman and Tweel. "I know Tweel," the IBT boss had replied, and "he's all right, he's up here to help me." And then, in the first of many shocking disclosures Partin would make as a matter of course, he said that Hoffa had asked him to "stick around for a day or two to make some calls ... We're going to try to get a juror—or a few scattered jurors—and take our chances."[9]

Before leaving for Baton Rouge the next afternoon Partin made another call to Sheridan. He had seen Tweel again, this time in the company of the latter's vigilante friends from Huntington. He had also paid a second visit to the Andrew Jackson's seventh floor. There the Teamster boss had said to him that when he returned to Nashville, " 'I might want you to pass something for me,' hit[ting] his hip pocket as he said it."[10] Partin understood clearly what that meant; the only thing Hoffa carried in his back pocket was his wallet. That conversation took place on the day before Judge Miller dismissed James Tippens from the Test Fleet jury after Tippens's disclosure of an offer to pay him $10,000 to vote for Hoffa's acquittal.

Three days later Sheridan heard again from Partin, who had returned to Nashville late the night before and gone to Hoffa's hotel suite early the next morning. The jury had been selected, and Tommy Osborn was to make his opening statement for the defense when court began that day. A harassed Hoffa appeared distracted and angry. When Partin asked if he could be of service, Hoffa abruptly replied "No, that dirty bastard went in and told the judge that a neighbor had offered him $10,000. We're going to have to lay low for a few days."[11] Thinking later about this conversation Sheridan realized that his informer had been in Baton Rouge when the bribery offer to juror Tippens had been reported to Judge Miller. Tippens's disclosure had taken place in a closed hearing in the judge's chambers so there had been no news of it in the *Tennessean* or the *Banner*. Since Hoffa was Partin's first contact with anyone on his first morning back in Nashville, he could have learned of the Tippens incident only from the Teamster boss. Clearly, thought Sheridan, my informer is telling the truth.

After Judge Miller's court adjourned on the Friday of its first week, Partin called Sheridan at his courthouse office to report a conversation with Ewing King. Local 327's president, said the informer, had spoken of a plan to make contact with a woman on the Test Fleet jury who was married to a Tennessee highway patrolman. No names were mentioned; King had said only that the couple's home was outside the city and that he knew one of their friends who lived nearby. He planned to try to talk with that friend before the weekend was over. In the next few days, King added, he expected to get a complete jury list "to show to people they could trust."[12] Sheridan thanked Partin for the call and asked him to stay in touch.

My God, thought Sheridan as he went down the hallway to talk to Neal, these people are serious. Partin could not have known the occupation of a juror's spouse without hearing it from someone within Hoffa's camp. "Andy Anderson" was the prosecution's only insider and Sheridan was the only government agent in touch with him. Again the informer's message sounded unarguably truthful. As Sheridan and Neal together scanned the jurors' names and résumés, one name immediately caught their attention: Mrs. James Paschal, whose husband was a "Tennessee highway patrolman." The two men decided that the FBI should put a tail on King and watch him closely until further notice. Ed Steele, chief of the Bureau's Nashville office, agreed. Within hours his agents had King's red Thunderbird in their sights.

This decision could not have been timelier. Shortly before noon the next day King walked out of his house, climbed into his car and drove southeast along the state Route 1. With enough traffic on the road to protect their anonymity, two FBI agents followed in an unmarked car, easily keeping their subject's conspicuous vehicle in sight. At Murfreesboro he turned due east, finally stopping in front of a modest home near the town of Woodbury. The unsuspecting Teamster parked in the driveway and went inside. This turned out to be the residence of Oscar "Mutt" Pitts, a truck-driving member of King's union who was indeed a friend of James Paschal, the state patrol officer and juror Paschal's spouse. After ninety minutes or so inside Pitts's house, King returned to his automobile and drove back to the city, again with the FBI close behind. Reading the agents' reports the following Monday, Sheridan marveled at how closely King had followed the scenario he had described to Partin three days earlier. So far, Andy Anderson was batting a thousand.

Most of the time Sheridan and his informer talked in telephone calls initiated by Partin, though occasionally they would go for a drive in the countryside in Sheridan's car. After each conversation Kennedy's investigator would advise local FBI agents of what he had learned. Tracking Sheridan's leads but not knowing his source they could only suspect it came from a well-placed mole. Under strict orders from the attorney general, the agents did not survey Hoffa, his lawyers or the jurors by any means, electronic or physical. Partin would go back and forth to Baton Rouge but had continual access to Hoffa's headquarters, readily accepted as a fellow conspirator by the many Teamster associates in town to do their leader's bidding. Hoffa would sometimes assign Partin the job of guard and doorman at the Andrew Jackson suite, a sure sign he had the boss's confidence.

On Wednesday, November 7, in the trial's third week, Partin met once more with Sheridan. The Louisiana Teamster said he needed to return to Baton Rouge for a week and wanted to relay one new piece of information before he left. Hoffa had just told him that Larry Campbell, the Teamster business agent from Detroit, had contacted the only "Negro male" on the jury. As a result, Hoffa said, he had the juror safely "in his pocket. He wouldn't take any money, but … [agreed he] wouldn't vote against his people," apparently meaning anyone his black brother Campbell was working for. [13] This juror, Sheridan knew, was Gratin Fields, a retired railway worker and the jury's only African American male. The business agent's presence in Nashville was news to Sheridan and the FBI, and they now realized he too would require close observation.

Following Partin's latest report, Sheridan called Jack Miller—the DOJ's Criminal Division head and no relation to the Nashville judge—to update him on the expanding scope of Hoffa's efforts to fix the Test Fleet jury. Based on Sheridan's summary, Miller asked Kennedy's chief investigator to come to Washington. The two of them met with the attorney general on the night of Sheridan's arrival and again the following morning. Kennedy agreed that the FBI should expand its coverage of Hoffa's team as necessary to stay abreast of their jury tampering efforts, continuing to avoid surveillance of Hoffa himself, his lawyers and the jurors. They should also advise Judge Miller of the subjects they were monitoring and seek his approval of their actions. On Friday of that week Judge Miller met with Neal's prosecution team and approved the DOJ's proposed plan.

Meanwhile King was proceeding with his intention to talk to James Paschal, the highway patrolman and husband of a Test Fleet juror. His visit with Paschal would be arranged by local Teamster Mutt Pitts and take place at the latter's rural home. More like Inspector Clouseau than James Bond, Local 327's president would pose as a raccoon hunter using borrowed hounds as his cover. He would meet with Paschal in a remote area around midnight, coon hunting's prime time. Telling Partin of his scheme, King said that to make sure he wasn't being followed, on his way out of town he would at some point swap cars with one of his local

Teamster friends, exchanging King's Thunderbird for the friend's less noticeable sedan.

King's journey to his planned meeting with Paschal got under way on Saturday, November 17. Around seven o'clock that evening the radio in Ed Steele's FBI office crackled with a message from one of his agents keeping Local 327's president under round-the-clock observation. Through the static came three words: "Topcat is moving," enough to let his boss know that King, *a/k/a* "Topcat," was leaving home in his red car. Followed by Steele's two-man team in an unmarked gray car, King drove along the same route toward Woodbury he had taken a week earlier. Just outside the city limits he turned into the parking lot of a large suburban restaurant. Not long after, a blue Chevrolet pulled into the same lot and its lone male driver also went inside. A few minutes later the two came out together. King got into the humble Chevrolet as the other man took the wheel of the racy sports car. The two then drove off in opposite directions, the Chevrolet now taking the road to Woodbury. King's co-conspirator that night was George Broda, a business agent of Local 327. Broda was a man Partin had met with several days earlier and described to Sheridan as a Teamster "named George" who spoke with a "Slavic" accent and carried a pistol.

Knowing from Sheridan that this exchange might take place, Steele had assigned four agents in two cars to cover King that night, who now split up to follow their respective targets. Broda took the Thunderbird on a meandering route to his own home while King proceeded on his mission. To make sure that King and the blue Chevrolet stayed in sight, Steele put another two-man team on its track, with the double-coverage vehicles sufficiently separated to avoid attracting attention. As expected, the Chevrolet went straight to the home of Mutt Pitts where it sat, parked and empty, when an FBI team passed by at 9:30 p.m. Later, at 1:25 a.m., FBI agents observed Broda's Chevrolet parked in front of the Paschal residence with a uniformed patrolman standing next to the car and talking to king, its only occupant.

Early the following week the FBI agents assigned to tail King confirmed Broda's ownership of the Chevrolet and Paschal's identity as the patrolman seen standing alongside it. They had done a good night's work and could now say with certainty that King had undertaken a hundred-mile round trip to a secret rendezvous in the middle of the night to meet with the husband of a Test Fleet juror. At his next meeting with Partin, King confessed that Hoffa was angry at him for being unable, thus far, to convince Paschal to accept a payoff. Thinking also of James Tippens, the juror who had refused the offer of $10,000, and of Mutt Pitts, who had dallied for weeks before contacting his friend Paschal, the Teamster boss also scorned the local populace's timidity: "These god-damn people don't have any guts!"[14]

Hoffa's feeling of anguished impotence grew steadily as his attempts to fix the Test Fleet jury seemed to go nowhere. The case Neal was steadily building against him in court added to his frustration. Showing some of his anger in public, he referred scathingly to the attorney general as "Bobby Boy." He castigated the press for its "barrage of filth and slime" about him, particularly in the *Tennessean*. Privately he raged against trusted associates he now believed had turned against him. It was in late November, during the trial's sixth week, that George Fitzgerald, Hoffa's lawyer for thirty years, confessed to receiving $15,000 of Test Fleet dividends from the Hoffa/Brennan wives and then issuing his personal check for that amount to the Teamster boss. Hoffa's frustration at this damning testimony lasted well into the evening. As reported by Partin, he paced frantically about his Andrew Jackson headquarters, screaming obscenities at Allen Dorfman for not convincing Fitzgerald to take the Fifth. In Hoffa's distraught mind, Dorfman's ineptitude was compounded by outright disloyalty.

On Wednesday, December 5, in the middle of the trial's seventh week, the deranged gunman Warren Swanson made his abortive attempt to assassinate Hoffa. The day after that, Neal asked Judge Miller to remove Mrs. Paschal from the jury. Supporting his motion were written affidavits from FBI agents who had tracked King to his meeting with patrolman Paschal and observed their midnight conversation. The judge ordered an immediate hearing on the motion in a closed courtroom. Bailiffs taped newspaper sheets over the two small glass panels in the courtroom doors to avoid observation by excluded spectators and the press. Through a cordoned-off rear entrance, Officer Paschal and Teamsters King, Pitts and Broda were brought in to the courthouse and put into separate rooms to await their appearances before the judge.

The attesting FBI agents were the hearing's first witnesses. As they told of observing King's and Broda's nocturnal car-swapping followed by King's visit to the Pitts house and his subsequent meeting with Paschal, Hoffa listened in stony silence. The next witness was King, Local 327's president. As he entered the courtroom and glanced at Hoffa, the Teamster boss flashed his well-known signal of five fingers held close to his right cheek. Obligingly, like a well-trained performing seal, his underling took the Fifth, as did Pitts and Broda when they were called to testify.

Patrolman Paschal then came into court through a side door. On edge as he nervously swore to tell the truth, it was clear he wished fervently to be somewhere else. Testifying haltingly the patrolman first denied having talked to King but then changed his story when questioned directly by the judge. At the suggestion of his friend Pitts, he confessed, he had met and spoken with the local Teamster president. But, he said, they had not discussed the Test Fleet trial or his wife's position as a juror. His midnight visitor had said only that since Paschal was a friend of Pitts, King would like to help him get a promotion within the highway department. When asked why the local Teamster president had singled him out and met with him in a secret midnight rendezvous, Paschal had no answer. After four hours, Judge Miller had heard enough. He ordered that Mrs. Paschal be replaced by an alternate juror and that the jury be sequestered every night until the trial was over.

That Thursday afternoon, after ordering Mrs. Paschal's dismissal, a tired Judge Miller adjourned court until the following Monday morning. Sheridan spoke with Partin early that evening. Hoffa was now convinced, the informer reported, that someone on the defense team was leaking information to the FBI. He had told Chuckie O'Brien to stay in Nashville and work with private detectives over the weekend to try to ferret out the mole. He had also instructed lawyer Tommy Osborn to interview King, Broda and Pitts to see if they might have a clue as to the leaker's identity. What this trio told Osborn never came to light. However, Partin's disclosure that Hoffa's local lawyer was directly contacting these jury-fixers was a red flag to those who believed the defense lawyers must have been exposed to Hoffa's jury-tampering efforts. Common sense led in that direction, and here was evidence that the respected Nashville lawyer might also be drifting into the magnetic field of corruption surrounding the Teamster leader. But that was not Sheridan's immediate concern, and if Osborn was ever to face a day of reckoning it would have to come later with much stronger evidence.

At this point, with the case winding down and the government's lawyers fully occupied in court, Sheridan worried that Gratin Fields, the jury's only black male, might have been influenced to vote for acquittal. Hoffa had said as much to Partin when he claimed, some five weeks earlier, that "the male Negro juror" had been contacted by Teamster agent Larry Campbell and was safely "in his pocket." King had made a similar statement to Partin. Sheridan knew it took only one "not guilty" vote to hang the jury.

The government had only a few telephone calls and other bits of circumstantial evidence pointing to efforts by Campbell to persuade his uncle, Tom Parks, to contact juror Fields. These alone were unlikely to support a charge of jury tampering. What was needed, Sheridan thought, was direct testimony from Partin of Hoffa's incriminating statement, later confirmed by King, that Campbell had spoken with Fields and believed he would not vote against anyone who had the support of "his people." The difficult question, however, was how to get that statement into the record without identifying Partin as the government's informer. Such disclosure would destroy the prosecution's only valuable source of information from inside the enemy's camp. Sheridan discussed the issue with Jack Miller by telephone on the Friday morning Hoffa took the witness stand. Miller decided to send two of his DOJ peers—department heads like himself—to Nashville that afternoon. They would meet with Neal and Sheridan over the coming weekend and offer their assistance in the selection and evaluation of the FBI's voluminous data. They could also offer advice concerning the prosecution's ongoing strategy.

One of Miller's colleagues was Assistant Attorney General Burke Marshall, head of the DOJ's Civil Rights Division. A brilliant lawyer, Marshall had left the prestigious D.C. law firm of Covington & Burling in 1961 to join Bob Kennedy's Justice Department. He would later serve as IBM's general counsel and then move on to become Dean of the Yale Law School. The other was Howard Willens, Miller's deputy, a successful criminal lawyer who had come to the DOJ with his boss from the D.C. office of Kirkland Ellis, a Chicago law firm highly respected for the quality of its litigators. Out of this four-man meeting came a daring decision: Sheridan would prepare an affidavit for Partin's signature, fully disclosing the statements by Hoffa and King that the black juror had been approached by Campbell and was in Hoffa's "pocket." Kennedy's chief investigator, still the only person aware of Andy Anderson's true identity, would meet with Partin alone and attempt to get his signature on the document, a delicate task to say the least. The affidavit, if made public, would throw Partin's life into turmoil. It might also be considered, by some of the Teamsters' more unsavory elements, a warrant for the Louisiana Teamster's death. Jim Neal's daunting task was to prepare an argument that would persuade Judge Miller to hold a hearing on a motion to oust juror Fields and, most importantly, to convince Miller to keep Partin's affidavit under seal to preserve the informer's anonymity.

Sheridan struggled for two days drafting Partin's proposed affidavit, a volatile narrative that would explode upon contact with the open air of publicity. He was also concerned with how to overcome the informer's reluctance to sign a sworn statement whose exposure would assure Hoffa's permanent hatred. On Wednesday night, with only the defense's closing argument and the prosecution's summation remaining to be given the next day, Sheridan met with Partin and handed him a final draft of the unsigned affidavit. The document, he explained, would supplement the FBI's information on Campbell's travels, statements and phone calls. Because it was only a part of the cumulative evidence to be offered on the attempt to influence Mr. Fields, the government's lawyers believed—though they could not guarantee—Judge Miller would honor their request not to disclose the affidavit's contents or its author.

Sheridan's task, once he and his informer agreed on the affidavit's language, was not as difficult as he had imagined. Partin had known from the beginning that the information he was passing on to the DOJ investigator was prosecutorial dynamite, almost certain at some point to be used as evidence in open court. He no doubt wished the risk of his exposure could be delayed to a time more of his choosing, but he understood the reasons behind Sheridan's current request and his mind was made up. As Sheridan succinctly noted, "Partin knew ... he was taking an irrevocable step but agreed to give the affidavit."[15] That done, the FBI's Ed Steele provided a trusted notary public to attest to the signing of the document. With that, Partin put himself into the hands of Judge Miller.

The lawyers completed their final arguments on schedule the next morning. When the judge took his seat following the luncheon recess, but before the jury had been recalled, Neal announced his intention to make another motion and again asked that the courtroom be cleared. As before, newspapers over the door panels blocked the efforts of the press and spectators to see what was going on. With bailiffs guarding the entrances the chief prosecutor handed his written motion to Judge Miller and to opposing counsel, simultaneously stating as its purpose the removal of Gratin Fields from the jury. Neal's motion was based on the appended affidavits of several FBI agents then assembled in adjacent witness rooms and ready to testify if summoned. Their statements described Larry Campbell's telephone calls to Nashville and Detroit, and two women's allegations that Campbell had told them that he had come to Nashville to help Hoffa with the trial. Also attached, under seal, was Partin's latent bombshell which the judge read and then resealed.

Quickly getting the gist of the unsealed sworn statements supporting Neal's motion, Hoffa's lawyers claimed surprise and their right to confront all of the witnesses who had made statements to the FBI. Outraged at Judge Miller's refusal to allow them to read the sealed affidavit they compared themselves and their client to the victims of the Spanish Inquisition and Hitler's Gestapo. The judge abruptly dismissed those arguments. Defense counsel's shrill histrionics throughout the Test Fleet trial had worn his patience paper thin. As far as he was concerned the FBI statements, made under oath, were adequate to sustain Neal's motion without further testimony. The prosecution's burden was not to show jury tampering beyond a reasonable doubt, only that it was likely to have taken place. Any reservation about that was removed by Partin's sworn statement, whose desire to remain incognito Judge Miller understood and agreed with. The hearing ended in just over an hour with an order from the bench that Mr. Fields be removed from the jury and replaced by an alternate.

The harassed judge had kept his feelings under control up to this point, but Partin's disclosure of Hoffa's leadership role in the jury-tampering scheme poured gasoline on the embers of his frustration and anger. Miller's statements at the trial's end—caustically criticizing the "close labor associates of the defendant" for their "illegal and improper" efforts to influence the jury—showed little doubt that he wanted indictments for tampering to be brought as soon as possible. As Sheridan, Neal and their teammates headed home for the year-end holidays they knew his words were their orders. Like General MacArthur leaving the Philippines, they would return.

CHAPTER 6

"Bobby Kennedy's Just Another Lawyer Now"

Test Fleet's mistrial dampened the Christmas celebration at the home of Bob and Ethel Kennedy. As predicted by Teamster lawyer Bufalino, Hoffa was not found in RFK's stocking. Nor was his image among the avalanche of presents under the tree at Hickory Hill. Had the IBT president been convicted, effervescent Ethel would surely have found a bobblehead or some equally frivolous trinket to put there as a symbol of her husband's courtroom victory. Such tokens would remain in the closet for now. The only bright spot in Test Fleet's disappointing outcome was Judge Miller's call for an investigation into the "shameful" attempts to influence the jury that had recently come to his attention. Though he pointed to no one by name, the obvious target of his scorn was Hoffa. Neal's post-trial report to the attorney general left no doubts that jury-tampering indictments were imminent, with real meat on their bones. Kennedy thus looked forward to 1963 as the year in which his prime target might finally be brought to account.

Thanks to Test Fleet's temporary reprieve, Hoffa enjoyed his Christmas. He and wife Jo spent the day at home with their son James P., a first-year student at Michigan Law School, along with their daughter Barbara and her new husband, Robert Crancer. Chuckie O'Brien, Hoffa's protégé and the son of Jo's closest friend, shared in the family's holiday cheer along with Chuckie's wife. The next day, however, the Teamster boss went back to work. The pleasant family gathering had not decreased his growing discomfort from government attacks pressuring him on several fronts. His indictment in Nashville for jury tampering seemed a sure thing, carrying with it the threat of serious jail time. A fraudulent loan charge, known as the "Sun Valley" case and pending in Orlando since 1960, was showing new life. Adding to his problems was a midwestern grand jury investigation of kickbacks to him and his cronies from other loans and investments by Teamster pension funds. Back east in Washington, IRS agents were examining Hoffa's personal income tax returns and the US Congress was considering legislation to impose further constraints on labor union officials by broadening the Landrum-Griffin Act. Hoffa "knew, and told intimates, that his worst days were in front of him."[1]

****

Back in Nashville on January 3, Neal and his associates met with Sheridan to organize and assess the material they would submit to a new grand jury looking into charges of jury tampering during the Test Fleet trial. Sheridan summarized the way things were shaping up.

> It was a slow, day-by-day, piece-by-piece process. A telephone record would lead to another person, and one person would lead to another. Some people told the truth, others lied, and some … would not say anything. Some … were … simply scared to death. Some of the pieces were still missing but the ones we had were all fitting together into a fabric of corruption. By the time we finished, we [were] confident … that it was one of the most massive attempts to corrupt a jury in the history of the federal judiciary.[2]

It took Sheridan, Neal and associate lawyers Shaffer and Nat Lewin three months to gather the information necessary to persuade a Nashville grand jury to indict Hoffa and his associates for jury tampering. Their next step was to seek the approval of Bob Kennedy and his Department of Justice colleagues. On Thursday morning, April 11, the foursome met in Washington with Assistant Attorney General Jack Miller to review their voluminous materials. The

Nashville team requested authority to seek an indictment of Hoffa and his henchmen Larry Campbell, Allen Dorfman, Ewing King and Nick Tweel, along with Tom Parks, Campbell's uncle, for attempting to influence the Test Fleet jury. Miller responded positively and arranged for all of them to meet with the attorney general.

After discussion but before making a decision, Kennedy told them he wanted to add a Nashville lawyer to the prosecution's team for increased local flavor and greater depth. He had talked about this with Seigenthaler whose choices were Jack Norman or John Hooker Sr., the twin lions of the Tennessee trial lawyers' bar. But, Sig added, Norman might be reluctant to enter the lists against Tommy Osborn, his close friend and protégé who would surely continue to represent Hoffa in a second trial. Kennedy noted he felt closer to Hooker Sr. through his friendship with John Hooker Jr. The younger Hooker, when consulted, recommended his father without reservation, settling the matter in Kennedy's mind. Neal easily accepted the AG's decision, assuring his boss that he and the seasoned older lawyer would work well together. He was given little choice, of course, but the comforting thought of teaming with a co-prosecutor of Hooker's stature quickly overcame the disappointment of having to share the spotlight.

****

John Hooker Sr. was among the top two or three litigators in the state of Tennessee. As a respected member of the American Bar Association and a Fellow of the American Trial Lawyers Association he was widely known in national legal circles. He was friendly with many legal luminaries including Supreme Court Justice William O. Douglas. "Sr." was appended to Hooker's name in his later years to distinguish him from his son, John Jay Hooker Jr., Bob Kennedy's confidant and a popular political figure who would twice seek election, unsucessfuly, as the state's governor.

The elder Hooker was born in 1903 to middle-class parents in Lebanon, Tennessee, a rural community located in Wilson County about twenty miles east of Nashville. After graduation from high school at Castle Heights Military Academy he earned both a bachelor of arts and a bachelor of law degrees from Lebanon's Cumberland College. Gregarious and well-liked, with a keen mind and sense of humor to match, Hooker entered politics a few years later and in 1927 was elected to the Tennessee House of Representatives. After serving a two-year term, during which he married and had the first of his three children, he did not seek reelection. A serious student of the law, he viewed elective office as a distraction from the practice of his profession, a higher and more rewarding calling in his view. He was a civic activist in the heyday of local service organizations and was twice elected president of the Tennessee Bar Association. He was a lifelong member of First Presbyterian Church, one of Nashville's largest church congregations and its most establishment-oriented house of worship.

A dapper dresser, Hooker favored hand-made Sulka ties and three-piece suits of dark blue with a gold chain and watch fob artfully draped across the vest covering his ample paunch. In the summer he shifted to seersucker suits and a beribboned straw boater. His transportation for a journey of more than a few city blocks was a chauffeured black sedan. Many of his cases took him to rural county courtrooms throughout Middle Tennessee, most often to defend the L&N Railroad Company against personal injury claims ranging from fractured limbs to wrongful death. On his arrival in those towns in a shiny limousine he would emerge in full city attire through a rear door held open by his uniformed driver. He would then walk grandly into the courthouse shaking hands with the court's male employees and tipping his hat to their female colleagues. With a gently protruding belly, a slightly bulbous nose, and a face becoming a bit fleshy, he resembled their favorite uncle. But his self-confident bearing, slicked-back hair, and penetrating gaze gave him an air of authority appealing to men and women alike. Gracious of manner, he exuded genuine warmth and was a recognizable figure wherever he went.

In the courtroom, thoroughly versed in the facts of the case and the law applicable to it, Hooker took command. Having established by his appearance that he was a wealthy and successful lawyer he would then earn a jury's confidence with his down-home style, colloquial speech and a patient but incisive questioning of witnesses to draw testimony favorable to his clients. When a witness turned hostile or evasive the gentle interrogator became indignant, his eyes glaring, his voice scornful, his tone sharp and probing. His rapport with judges, with whom he was deferential in attitude but forceful in argument, was equally strong. Some called him a "walking book of law."[3] On the rare occasions when his objections were overruled Hooker usually managed a look or an offhand comment to help jurors understand that sometimes judges could be wrong. From the beginning of a trial to its end he was unyielding in his theory of the case and the presentation of his client's point of view.

The stories illustrating Hooker's legal skills were legion. In the early days of his practice he and his brother-in-law and partner Seth Walker successfully defended Lem Motlow—the proprietor of Tennessee's iconic Jack Daniel Distillery, a company passed on to him by his deceased uncle Jasper N. Daniel—on a charge of murder. Motlow had shot an L&N railroad conductor at point blank range on a moving train. The defendant described the shooting as accidental when the train lurched while rounding a sharp corner, but admitted to drawing his pistol in anger and to sampling some of his own product not long before firing the fatal shot. Walker and Hooker artfully persuaded the jury that the testimony of the sole eyewitness, a circuit-riding preacher, could not be trusted because the L&N Railroad Company let him ride for free as a wearer of the cloth. Motlow paid their fee with shares of stock in his distillery, worth several million dollars when Brown-Forman bought the Jack Daniel distillery many years later.

Several years thereafter Hooker demonstrated his enormously persuasive powers by talking the Davidson County district attorney into dropping the charges against his client, a wealthy Nashville socialite accused of murdering of her husband. The DA agreed with Hooker that his client had acted only in self-defense when thrusting a souvenir Samurai sword through her husband during an overheated, post-party quarrel in the bedroom of their spacious home—a spat, some said, that included a bouncing chase across their oversized bed.

As Hooker grew older the stories of his courtroom prowess expanded to match his increasingly colorful character. One such account involved his representation of a young man sued for alienation of affection by a husband whose wife had allegedly been seduced by the defendant. Hooker's opening statement explained that his client and the wayward spouse were good friends who saw each other often. Meeting by chance early one evening in the small town in which they lived they decided to walk awhile together. As they strolled along the bank of a nearby stream the plaintiff's wife spoke of a deeply troubled and essentially loveless marriage. At one point, having reached a more secluded area, she broke into tears and threw herself into her friend's arms for comfort. This physical intimacy, initiated by the wife, should have stopped there. Instead, Hooker conceded, it was consummated in the heat of a shared passion for which the lonely wife was equally if not primarily responsible.

As occasionally happened in rural courtrooms, one of the men allowed to remain on the jury was a friend of Hooker's who might be sympathetic to his client's plight. The trial did not go as well as expected; the all-male jury seemed uneasy as Hooker began his closing summary. After casting the facts in the light most favorable to the defendant, and now hoping to stir the jurors' hearts, his rhetoric soared. "My client was trying his best to comfort and reassure a friend when suddenly she was in his arms, looking at him with tearful eyes, seeking his understanding, silently inviting his affection. The night was clear, willow trees along the bank swayed gently in a warm breeze; moonlight sparkled on the waters of the bubbling stream. Like all of us my client is only human and sometimes the devil gets his way. But gentlemen of the jury, should you punish and humiliate this decent young man for surrendering to temptation in these surroundings under such unsolicited and powerful provocation?" After a pause, gazing directly at the juror friend he hoped might influence the latter's unsympathetic peers, Hooker said, "I ask each of you: Can you honestly say that you might have not acted just as my client did in these circumstances?" Enthralled by the story and mesmerized by his questioner's intense stare, the juror jumped to his feet and blurted "For God's sake, Mr. Hooker, don't ask me. I'm on the jury!"

Whether this brash tactic caused a mistrial, influenced a verdict, or was only something from Hooker's storybook, its effect has been lost in time and lapsed memory. Among the trial lawyers of the Nashville Bar Association, however, it was remembered as a testament to the wily charm of their distinguished colleague. Like many stories that swell to mythic proportions, factual or not, it spoke truthfully of Hooker's persuasive powers.

****

As Seigenthaler remembers it, when he told his boss some of these anecdotes, Kennedy laughingly remarked that any lawyer who could convince a district attorney not to prosecute a woman for fatally stabbing her husband while the two were alone in the privacy of their bedroom had to be right for the job. At the attorney general's invitation, Hooker flew immediately to Washington, met with Kennedy and Miller, and received from Sheridan and Neal a full briefing on the facts of the jury tampering case. The Nashville trial lawyer said he would consider join-ing the prosecution's team only after talking with Partin, the man on whose testimony the case against Hoffa would succeed or fail. On the following Monday, Sheridan joined Hooker in Nashville and the two of them flew to Atlanta for an airport meeting with the man they hoped would be the prosecution's star witness. Off by themselves, the Louisiana Teamster and the distinguished Nashville barrister talked one-on-one for the better part of two hours, each evaluating the other. According to Sheridan, "Hooker ... thought the evidence was strong and Partin would make an excellent witness."[4] But Hooker was not yet ready to make a final decision. He was much in demand and at the top of his earning power. He knew a commitment to prosecute the country's most powerful union boss would require an enormous sacrifice of time and money not to mention the intense emotional pressure which trial lawyers often referred to as a piece of one's stomach. He would return to Nashville to decide whether the game was worth the candle.

The attorney general himself was also wrestling with the question whether the government's evidence was strong enough to convict Hoffa. The so-called Sun Valley case, a pending loan fraud case, might be a better vehicle. In addition, one more hung jury would fan the flames of anti-Kennedy criticism in the national press and the nation's capital. Several persistent issues were still open for investigation and debate. Had Partin been present at Hoffa's meetings with defense counsel during the Test Fleet trial? If so, was this a violation of Hoffa's constitutional rights, under either the Sixth Amendment's guarantee of lawyer-client confidentiality or the Fifth Amendment's protection against self-incrimination? Was the Louisiana Teamster in Nashville of his own accord during this period, voluntarily advising Sheridan of what he learned? Or was he acting as a secret government agent, thereby violating the Fourth Amendment's prohibition of unreason-able searches and seizures? Any one of these violations would prevent acceptance of Partin's courtroom's testimony.

Kennedy saw to it that his chief investigator Sheridan got a third-degree grilling from the DOJ's senior lawyers, beginning with Jack Miller. Under Miller's questioning, Sheridan confirmed that he had passed on to the prosecution lawyers information relating only to attempts at influencing the jury. He next had a day-long session with John Douglas, head of the DOJ's Civil Division, who reviewed in detail the investigator's copious notes on conversations with Partin during the Test Fleet trial. Douglas concluded that Sheridan and his informer had spoken of only two things: actions Partin had seen or heard that were intended to influence the jury, and the movements of various people within the Hoffa camp. Nothing in the investigator's notes referred to an overheard conversation between the Teamster boss and his lawyers.

Encouraged by reports of these interviews, Kennedy summoned the DOJ's top-level lawyers to his office to hear a full-blown presentation by Neal, Shaffer and Sheridan. Gathered there were Jack Miller and his assistant Bill Hundley, head of the Organized Crime Section of the Criminal Division. Also attending were the Department's four other division chiefs, each an assistant attorney general appointed by the president—John Douglas (Civil), Burke Marshall (Civil Rights), Ramsey Clark (Lands), and Lou Oberdorfer (Tax). Rounding out the group were its two heaviest hitters, Deputy Attorney General Nicholas Katzenbach and Solicitor General Archibald Cox. Kennedy hoped they would all agree but in any event wanted the decision-making process to include all of his principal advisors.

He should have known better than to expect anything approaching unanimity from eight high-powered lawyers. As the old saw had it, the tendency of legal experts to disagree was the reason they were rarely, in those days, called for jury duty. Not only were they quarrelsome; a lawyer-dominated jury might spend a day or two just choosing a foreman. But on this occasion the DOJ's senior attorneys reached a consensus on one point: the evidence against the Teamster boss's henchmen was solid, and they should all be indicted along the lines proposed by Neal.

Kennedy's advisers differed, however, on whether to indict the Teamster boss himself, which was of course the heart of the matter. Ramsey Clark argued that the trial judge would probably bar Partin's testimony, which all agreed was the key to Hoffa's conviction. Clark reasoned that the Louisiana Teamster's mere presence in the Teamster boss's Nashville headquarters had infringed on Hoffa's Sixth Amendment right to speak confidentially with his lawyers. Further, said Clark, if the judge allowed Partin to take the stand his ruling would likely be overturned on appeal. Bill Hundley, the organized crime specialist, opposed Hoffa's indictment on a more pragmatic level. Viewing the evidence from a trial-lawyer's perspective he thought the jury would be reluctant to give full credence to Partin's testimony. The defense would characterize him as a secret government informer, trading lies about Hoffa for leniency in the handling of the kidnapping charge then pending against him. Furthermore, Partin was a Teamster turncoat with a criminal record and a history of physical violence and ugly marital discord. Hoffa would vigorously deny the Louisiana Teamster's allegations against him, portraying himself as an innocent, hard-working man of the people, persecuted by big government and outraged at being falsely charged with criminal conduct. To be acquitted the IBT boss need only plant the seed of reasonable doubt, and at that task, in front of several earlier juries, he had proved to be an expert.

Solicitor General Cox, the refined but tough-minded professor on leave from Harvard Law School, countered Clark's fear that Partin's activities had violated Hoffa's confidential relationship with his lawyers. Cox said that he was "firmly convinced of both the propriety and necessity of going forward, and that he would have no compunctions about arguing the case before the Supreme Court if and when the time came."[5] Neal and Sheridan, conceding that Hoffa would testify forcefully in his own defense, stuck to their view that Partin's testimony would hold up under rigorous cross-examination because it had the ring of truth and common sense. It would be buttressed by the fact that his predictions of jury tampering, some of which he could have learned only from Hoffa, had all come true. Neal also believed the jury would see the Teamster boss as a micro-manager who, on important matters, demanded full knowledge in advance of what underlings were doing on his behalf.

In the end, the latter arguments carried the day. No one doubted that Hoffa had captained the entire operation. Kennedy also believed that the magnitude and flagrance of the attempt to fix the Test Fleet jury threatened the administration of justice in the nation's federal and state courts alike. He thus felt obligated, despite the risks, to indict and try Hoffa as the episode's guiding force. When the meeting broke up he called Hooker, who was still on the fence, and asked him to come to Washington for a conference. The senior lawyer did so, and after talking with Kennedy agreed to take the co-prosecutor's job. Less than three weeks later, on May 9, 1963, the Nashville grand jury indicted Hoffa and the others for jury tampering.

Hoffa was named in all of the indictment's five counts: one for conspiracy to influence the jury, and four for attempting to influence specific jurors. Threatening Hoffa with imprisonment for up to twenty-five years and his co-defendants to five years each, these charges comprised the broadest sweep of any indictment yet brought against the Teamster president and his cronies. Kennedy was determined that its accusations would reflect the magnitude of the crimes he was convinced they had committed.

Upon reading and digesting the indictment's contents Hoffa and his lawyers exhaled a collective breath of cautious but genuine relief. They felt he might once again be able to avoid the government's best shot. None of the counts accused Hoffa of contacting any of the jurors, but rather of "commanding … inducing … and aiding" others to do so. Nothing in the recitation of the charges hinted that the DOJ had a secret source of evidence connecting him to the alleged crimes of other defendants. Seeing this as a wide gap in the case against him, Hoffa climbed on his high horse and whipped it forward with renewed rhetorical dash. Kennedy was on "a personal vendetta" against him. As usual, the attorney general was "trying to convict me on planted stories in the press. Of course I'm not guilty, but I can't get a fair trial in Nashville. This indictment talks about ten people and I know only three of them. Two of them worked for me as Teamster officials and the other is an insurance agent who represents our Central Teamster Conference. Outside of that I wouldn't know the other seven persons if they walked down the corridor of the courtroom."[6]

It was a smokescreen, of course, but his words had their desired effect. William Loeb III, the outspoken owner and publisher of the influential *Union Leader* newspaper in Manchester New Hampshire, was Hoffa's perennial mouthpiece. An arch-conservative, Loeb held an intense hatred of the Kennedy clan. On May 12, only three days after Hoffa's indictment and five weeks after the newspaper mogul's receipt of a $500,000 loan from a Teamster pension fund, Loeb again spat his poison, this time in an editorial on his paper's front page. "Under any just and fair system of government, it would seem that [Kennedy's] persecution of Hoffa should cease…. [T]he only crime [he] seems to be guilty of is that he will not knuckle under to the Kennedys and give them the slavish obedience that other labor unions … do."[7] Like the politicians who had supported the Teamster boss during his past trials, Loeb spurned any suggestion that he look for supporting facts before rising to Hoffa's defense.

Such protestations had no apparent effect on Kennedy's Get Hoffa campaign. DOJ lawyers carried the fight to Chicago where, on June 4, a federal grand jury indicted the Teamster boss and seven of his business associates. It accused them of illegally receiving $1 million in kickbacks on loans from Teamster pension funds, and of fraudulently inducing those loans by lying to the trustees who authorized them. These offenses carried potential penalties even greater than those Hoffa faced for jury tampering. But the tampering indictment had a head start, and a week later the IBT boss was arraigned on its charges in Nashville.

With the passage of time a growing number of Hoffa's Teamster colleagues had been convicted and sentenced to prison. The day after the IBT boss's arraignment, Anthony ("Tony Pro") Provenzano, a Mafia capo and president of the Teamsters' Joint Council 73 in New Jersey, was convicted of extortion by a jury in Newark and sentenced to seven years in jail. Some of Hoffa's oldest and closest associates—muscleman and former bodyguard Barney Baker, Ohio's Teamster chief Bill Presser, and Frank Collins, one of the "Strawberry Boys" from the 1930s — were in jail or fighting to overturn criminal convictions.[8] The hard facts of these DOJ victories, coupled with Hoffa's obsessive belief that he was under constant FBI surveillance, began to erode his outward bluster of invulnerability. Indeed, when his jury tampering trial later turned ominous, his inner strife would overflow like molten lava.

Early that summer Judge Miller recused himself. He felt his exposure to the evidence of jury tampering brought out in the Test Fleet trial, and his rulings on the issues raised, would subject him to charges of bias at every stage of the upcoming trial. These claims, he believed, would unnecessarily complicate and prolong the new proceeding. And in his heart of hearts he knew they had merit. Miller's withdrawal put the case in the capable hands of Judge Frank Gray, Nashville's other federal judge.

For several months now, two trains had been speeding toward the point where Hoffa stood. The Nashville's jury tampering trial was coming at him from the south. Chicago's loan-fraud indictment headed toward him from the west, moving more slowly but steadily gaining ground. Targeted by both, Hoffa began to make more strident public comments. In late September he spoke to a crowd of two thousand at a meeting of the Kiwanis Club in his hometown of Detroit. He told the business audience that an upcoming congressional hearing on organized crime would be a "radio and television circus, designed to serve as a propaganda campaign for new wiretap legislation."[9] Embellishing his oft-repeated claim that the nation was becoming a police state under the Kennedys and a hostile Congress, he warned that "You're no longer in a neutral corner. When you walk into a federal court building … you don't appear as an American citizen, innocent until proven guilty. [You are] a … citizen guilty until proven innocent." In an October speech in Indianapolis, Hoffa again called the attorney general "a spoiled brat who never had to work for a living and who never tried a case in court."[10] Both trains steadily got closer as he spoke.

In late November, 1963, Hoffa's upcoming jury tampering trial was put on hold pending an appellate court's decision on defense motions to quash the indictments. In Nashville, Neal, Sheridan and other members of the DOJ's team impatiently awaited a judicial green light for their case to proceed. Around eleven-thirty on the morning of November 22 their focus on the case was engulfed by the tidal wave of grief that swept the nation. Nowhere did news of John Kennedy's assassination create greater emotional trauma than among Hoffa's prosecutors at the federal courthouse. Unable to reach Bob Kennedy, Sheridan called Seigenthaler, who invited him, Neal and the others to come over to the *Tennessean's* offices. Soon after their arrival official word came that the president was dead. Like most of the country they sat like zombies watching television, transfixed by the ongoing story. Still in their thirties, younger than the nation's youthful president, it was the saddest day of their lives.

At the time of Kennedy's assassination Hoffa was in Miami negotiating a national trucking contract. The ranking official at the union's Washington, D.C. headquarters that day was Harold Gibbons, the IBT's first vice-president and Hoffa's top administrative assistant. Not long past the noon hour he was lunching at Duke Zeibert's high-testosterone eatery with Ed Williams, the Teamsters' general counsel. On hearing the news Gibbons joined the exodus of grim-faced diners and headed back to his office at 25 Louisiana Avenue, NW. There he huddled with Larry Steinberg, former head of the Toledo, Ohio Teamsters and now the IBT's office manager. Steinberg was a long-serving, loyal aide to the IBT boss but cut from a different cloth, a hard worker untainted by any hint of physical or financial wrongdoing. Among the first to learn of the president's death he had already ordered the American flag on the Teamster building's rooftop lowered to half-mast and sent all headquarters employees home. Gibbons agreed with Steinberg's decisions and put in a call to Hoffa to report their action. On hearing what his top assistants had done Hoffa went berserk. In a frenzied, oath-laden tirade he blasted his hapless vice-president for approving Steinberg's decision and then growled, "Which one of you thinks he's the General President?"[11] There would be no further acknowledgments or expressions of condolences from his office, period. "I'm no hypocrite. I hope the worms eat his eyes out." Ordered to re-hoist the flag, Gibbons said it was too late for that. Hoffa then hung up but Gibbons's words left him steaming. He called back to repeat his outrage to both assistants, managing also to chastise a secretary "for crying instead of rejoicing."[12]

In stark contrast, the president's assassination sent a dispirited Bob Kennedy into deep mourning. "On the night JFK died a friend heard RFK, alone in the White House bedroom, cry out [in anguish] 'Why, God?'"[13] For many days the younger brother's internal pain was also visible, "like a man on the rack" said another of his friends.[14] His faith shaken—in God and in himself—it took months of prayer, introspection, reading and consultation with many friends for him to climb from the depths of despair and regain his sense of mission and purpose.

When Hoffa returned to work the following Monday Gibbons told him "he could get himself a new boy" and quit his job as the boss's executive assistant. Steinberg followed suit, as did three other headquarters' workers. Gibbons told reporters that through all of Hoffa's foul moods and his own ill-treatment, he had "stuck with the little guy … who had been through a lot of trouble without deserving it."[15] But Hoffa's verbal attack on him the day of the assassination was too much. The resignation of the IBT's second in command was a heavy blow to an already bruised and buffeted Hoffa fighting for survival among his many legal problems. Uncharacteristically the IBT boss swallowed his pride and urged his second in command to stay on the job, at least until the intense pressures of the day began to dissipate. Ever the loyal trouper, Gibbons agreed to do so but relinquished his job as Hoffa's executive assistant, along with its accompanying salary. He remained a paid IBT vice president and fully exploited huge expense account that went with it. This arrangement kept him at Hoffa's side for the next two years.

On his way back to Washington from Florida on the Sunday of that fateful weekend Hoffa diverted his private plane to Nashville to address a Teamster rally for Ewing King, Local 327's president. As a prime suspect in the jury-tampering indictment King faced opposition within his own union, and Hoffa was there to lend him support. Leaving the speaker's platform, the IBT boss went to a local television station for an interview. The softball questions seeking his opinion of the attorney general generated typical vituperative responses that disappeared forever into the airwaves, with one exception. When asked what the assassination of President Kennedy meant to him, his answer was memorable. "Bobby Kennedy," he snarled, "is just another lawyer now."[16]

In early December the Sixth Circuit Court of Appeals denied Hoffa's intermediate appeal of his jury-tampering indictment. Nashville's Judge Gray, having been involved in a peripheral but closely related matter, withdrew as presiding judge at Hoffa's upcoming trial. At Gray's request the Court of Appeals then assigned the case to Judge Frank Wilson of Chattanooga. Several days later, on Christmas Eve, Judge Wilson moved the case to Chattanooga and reset it to begin on January 20.

****

During this second year-end holiday season following Test Fleet's hung jury the turmoil of Hoffa's life continued unabated. In three weeks he would face a new judge and jury that could send him to jail for twenty years. Two of his top IBT staffers, with a few others, had quit in disgust at what they viewed as his loathsome reaction to the murder of the country's chief executive. Word was spreading that other union officials, including several directors of the IBT board, were fed up with Hoffa's autocratic rule and angered by his continued immersion in troubles of his own making. They were outraged at the rise of organized crime's influence within the union, and the extortionate feathering of gangsters' nests at the expense of the rank and file. And they were frustrated by the inability of the Teamsters' leadership to identify and support someone to replace their tyrannical leader.

Nothing of substance came from their concern. Undermining the IBT's inability to clean its own house was a pervasive sense of fear among its members. Ordinary workers knew that protests sparked threats of physical violence which sometimes escalated to the real thing. Business agents, organizers and other middle-managers worried about losing their jobs. Members of the IBT's executive board, aware of Hoffa's Mafia support, had a deeper apprehension. As one of them put it, he "did not want to go out feet first in a box."[17] For the time being, therefore, they passed the buck, rationalizing that the government might do the job for them. "If the feds put ol' Jimmy in jail," said many of his followers, "that's when we'll give him the bum's rush." This, they thought, would not happen soon, and they were right.

CHAPTER 7

"My God, It's Partin"

At the beginning of 1964 Lyndon B. Johnson had been the nation's chief executive for just over one month. With the country still in shock from the assassination of its youthful president, Johnson had promised to continue the programs and goals of the Kennedy administration. But no CEO wants to linger long in the shadow of his predecessor. In politics, especially at the presidential level, new personalities inevitably bring new policies. And no member of the Johnson administration had a more forceful temperament—or was more adept at using it to get his way—than the arm-twisting, back-slapping, workaholic former Senate Majority Leader from Texas. Beneath his hearty exterior, however, the new president was a man of many moods and striking contradictions. He was now the most powerful political leader in the free world, but an assassin's bullets, not the people's votes, had put him in the Oval Office. Born and raised on the plains of the American Southwest, he was transparently conscious of his humble origins. Among the Ivy League academics, business school graduates and eastern socialites his administration had inherited, he felt deeply insecure.

Like every modern president, Johnson wanted senior aides he could trust, people whose foremost concern would be the welfare of his administration. Among a president's cabinet officers the one traditionally chosen for unquestionable loyalty, the one who would squarely face political opponents when the long knives came out, was the attorney general. Despite Hoffa's bravado claim that Bob Kennedy was now just another lawyer, the Teamster boss's nemesis was still the nation's chief legal officer. But there were questions. How long would Johnson accept in that position the coolly self-confident, flinty son of privilege from Massachusetts? And when would the new president want to reevaluate the financial and political costs of the DOJ's various programs, including its relentless pursuit of the country's most popular union boss?

Neal, Sheridan and other stalwarts of Kennedy's team pondered these questions as they reassembled in Chattanooga in early January to prepare for Hoffa's jury-tampering trial. Uppermost in their thoughts was whether Robert Kennedy's diminished power would cause Grady Partin, their star witness, to lose heart. Partin was familiar with the ruined lives of other Teamsters who had challenged their vindictive boss. He knew that on hearing his testimony an enraged Hoffa would come at him like a wounded bull, horns lowered, lusting for blood. Sheridan had assured the Louisiana Teamster that the FBI would protect him against threats and harassment. Now, with the trial set to begin in less than three weeks, it was time to renew that pledge.

On January 6, at a Holiday Inn in Columbia, Tennessee, about forty miles south of Nashville, Sheridan, Neal and Hooker met secretly with their star witness to confirm their appreciation for the risk he was taking, and to reassure him of their continued support. Unexpectedly Partin turned the tables and became the comfort-giver. Without commenting on Kennedy's new situation he calmly confirmed his willingness to go forward as planned. Relieved, Neal said they would notify him when they were ready for his testimony and asked that when the time came, he make his own arrangements to travel from Baton Rouge to Chattanooga.

Sheridan persuaded the FBI to send Nashville agents Steele and Sheets to Chattanooga for the duration of the trial. With their experience of the Test Fleet case still fresh they could hit the ground running. As in the former trial the Bureau would not put the accused or their lawyers under surveillance of any kind. They decided to "follow" only three people during the course of the trial: George Hicks, the president of Chattanooga's Teamster Local 515; William Test, its former president; and John Cleveland, an IBT official from Washington, D.C. They would keep an eye on these men because the FBI did not want to be caught napping if jury-fixing attempts similar to those made in the Test Fleet case were repeated in Chattanooga.

Judge Wilson joined in the precautions being taken to avoid a repetition of the jury tampering that had occurred in Nashville. And well he might. Nine days before the trial's scheduled start one of Wilson's former law partners reported that a well-known Tennessee politician, never publicly identified, offered him "$5,000 if he could influence the judge to postpone the Hoffa case for sixty days."[1] With that kind of money being offered merely for delaying the trial there must have been a mountain of cash available for those willing to perform acts of more serious misconduct. Wilson ordered that the two hundred names on the jury panel be kept secret until the day the selection process began, and prospective jurors then be identified only by their last

Cameraman capturing James Neal outside at Hoffa hearing. Walking by Neal's television interview, Hoffa (over cameraman's left shoulder) yells, "Yeah! The marines are here!" January 22, 1964.

names and first initials. He also asked Harry Mansfield, the area's chief US marshal, to increase by severalfold the number of marshals assigned to keep order at the trial. Knowing these imported peace-keepers would need close supervision, the judge told Mansfield to be on his toes. "Harry," he said, "don't let the marshal service cause a mistrial."[2]

Hoffa's trial opened on the morning of January 20 to a packed house. Jury panelists and spectators filled every available seat, with some turned away for lack of space. At counsel tables in front of the bar—the railing separating the trial's participants from its observers—sat eight lawyers for the defense and three for the prosecution, Jim Neal, John Hooker Sr. and Jack Reddy, the US attorney in Chattanooga. Also assigned to assist the chief prosecutors were Test Fleet veterans Jim Durkin and "Instant Law" Nat Lewin, the latter so named for his ability to dash from the courtroom and return momentarily with case precedents to support his colleagues' arguments.

The eight defense lawyers sat cheek by jowl at two tables. Seated behind them were their six clients. Representing Hoffa was his Test Fleet counselor James Haggerty along with Chattanooga attorney Harry Berke. Berke had formerly been censured by the Tennessee Bar Association for questionable practices and would later be disbarred. Cecil Brandstetter, a Nashville lawyer who had occasionally represented a few local Teamsters, defended Larry Campbell. Harvey Silets represented his fellow Chicagoan Allen Dorfman. Ewing King had a single local lawyer; Nicholas Tweel had two.

The oddest twosome in the courtroom was Jacques Schiffer, a New York labor lawyer, and his client Tom Parks, Larry Campbell's uncle. Obviously chosen by Hoffa, the strident Schiffer had little in common with his taciturn client. A vociferous flame-thrower, he was perpetually on the attack at the top of his voice. He had come to Hoffa's attention a decade earlier when as a lawyer for three Teamsters on trial in Chicago he held daily press conferences on the courthouse steps, harshly condemning Bob Kennedy as the source of his clients' problems. Julius Miner, the presiding federal judge at that Chicago trial, finally decided he'd had enough of Schiffer's diatribes. After threatening Schiffer with "severe disciplinary measures" if his antics continued, the judge castigated the brash lawyer for his "vile soap box oratory, obnoxious to this court and degrading to the legal profession."[3] Just the man, thought the present-day Hoffa, to test the limits of Judge Wilson's patience in Hoffa's own trial ten years later.

Additional Teamster lawyers occupied specially assigned seats in the front row of the spectators' section of the Chattanooga courtroom. Their presence, along with a crowd of unpaid Hoffa lackeys sprinkled throughout the audience, lent a carnival air to the proceeding. Had the scene been captured on film, the setting would appear to have been planned by an old-line Hollywood director intent on showing, by exaggeration, the wealth and influence of the trial's principal defendant. Leading the cohort of hired legal guns was Jacob Kossman, a "rumpled, street-wise lawyer from Philadelphia" who had represented Hoffa for many years and been part of his back-up team at the Test Fleet trial. With him was Frank Ragano of Tampa, later to become a self-styled "Mob lawyer" who would spend thirty years "working for Mafia bosses Santo Trafficante of Florida and Carlos Marcello of New Orleans."[4] Joining them was Harry Berke Jr., a son of Hoffa's new local counsel. Also among the front-line soldiers was William Bufalino, the Detroit lawyer-Teamster official who had co-captained Hoffa's squad of lawyers in the Test Fleet case. Bufalino had come to give counsel and to manage Hoffa's field headquarters in Chattanooga's Patten Hotel. Rounding out the front-row gang was Daniel Maher, a former US Attorney and current Hoffa friend unable to resist the labor boss's magnetic pull.

Volunteer supporters added to the ranks of Teamster loyalists attending his trial. They swarmed like groupies around a rock star, hoping their solicitude would one day be rewarded. Among these "helpers" were Ewing King's car-swapping buddy George Broda and Hoffa's protégé Chuckie O'Brien. Also hanging around were Frank Chavez, the tough Puerto Rican Teamster boss from San Juan, and Morris Shenker, a noted gangsters' lawyer from St. Louis. A Mafia godfather at a Mob gathering could hardly have mounted a more ostentatious and menacing display of power than Jimmy Hoffa on trial at the pinnacle of his career.

Frank W. Wilson, the presiding judge, had been appointed to the federal bench in 1961 by President Kennedy on the recommendation of Democratic Senator Estes Kefauver, Wilson's political mentor. The forty-seven-year-old judge was known for fairness and legal scholarship, attention to detail and the same high standards of behavior he demanded of those appearing before him. He had become a seasoned trial lawyer as a city and county attorney in rural east Tennessee. He had also worked in the state's political vineyards, including the management of Kefauver's successful campaign for the US Senate in 1948. With his appointment to the federal bench Wilson's legal skills and political savvy served him well. On the trial's first day his crowded courtroom more closely resembled a cattle call than a formal legal proceeding, but the judge appeared unintimidated and firmly in control.

The trial's first day began with Judge Wilson's announcement that members of the jury would be sequestered from the day they were chosen. This would elicit formal complaints from the defense, but for now the lawyers went forward with the voir dire selection of prospective jurors. With so many cooks stirring the pot, the jury selection process barely simmered. Despite the judge's warning that he would query the jurors himself unless the tempo picked up, only six had been tentatively selected by the end of the second day. The next morning, true to his promise, Wilson took over the job. This brought Schiffer to his feet, spewing angry words as he rose. First pointing his finger accusingly at the prosecution's lawyers and then turning toward the defendants he said heatedly, "There seems to be an undue rush to force these defendants to trial. This is not Russia. These men have a constitutional right to due process of law." A few moments later he was again the provocateur. "Federal agents," he claimed, "were tapping his telephone and surveilling the defendants and their lawyers." Neal rose immediately with a flat denial. "The government states categorically, without any reservation, that no phone is being tapped and no counsel or defendant is being surveilled." "I don't believe it," Schiffer snarled.[5] These relatively moderate outbursts were but a foretaste of coming tirades from the defendants' designated gadfly.

Judge Wilson's tactic worked. What he had said would take three weeks at the voir dire's original pace was completed in three more days. By the end of the week eight men and four women had been unconditionally accepted on the jury. Four alternates were chosen on the following Monday morning and the prosecution began its presentation. For the next six days, taking turns at questioning twenty-two witnesses, Neal and Hooker methodically built the cases against the five men on trial with Hoffa. Their witnesses repeated in open court the same descriptions and reports they had given to Sheridan and the FBI of the ways Hoffa's indicted underlings had tried to influence several Test Fleet jurors.

During this early testimony Teamster lawyers maintained a staccato volley of objections and motions, mostly on frivolous grounds, to strike from the record statements that truly hurt. A witness's statement would often bring one or more of them—usually the clamorous Schiffer—screaming to their feet. At one point in the trial a reporter wrote that the New York lawyer interrupted the testimony of a prosecution witness fifty times in one hour. Each time Judge Wilson allowed a particularly harmful statement to stand, defense lawyers moved for a mistrial. Shooting randomly in the dark they hoped one stray bullet would hit its target. Mind-numbing arguments on these motions occupied a substantial portion of the nine thousand pages of the trial's written transcript.

It was now time for the prosecution to call its star witness, Grady Partin. On instructions from Neal and Hooker, Sheridan called Partin in Baton Rouge and arranged to meet him at a spot in the Chattanooga suburbs near Lookout Mountain. Partin's agreement to testify had been guarded so closely that the DOJ's Frank Grimsley—who accompanied the Louisiana Teamster on the drive to the rendezvous with Sheridan—did not know the purpose of their trip to Nashville until it was under way. Arriving on schedule the trial's two prosecuting lawyers followed Sheridan's car up the mountain to a rented cabin. There they were welcomed by two FBI agents on assignment to provide Partin around-the-clock protection. It was Sunday afternoon, February 2, two days before the witness's planned appearance on the following Tuesday. Neal and Hooker joined the group at sundown for a final review of Partin's testimony. Like a brave soldier on the eve of battle their subject was nervous but fully resigned to carrying out his dangerous mission.

On Tuesday morning Sheridan and Grimsley left the federal building soon after the opening of court and drove to join Partin at his mountain hideaway. The three men left the cabin around 11:30, timing their departure to arrive back at the federal courthouse during the luncheon break. Sheridan pulled up to the back of the building where steps led down to the basement. By prearrangement a deputy marshal was there to park his car. Two others stood inside the basement door ready to whisk the trio along the underground corridor to an elevator holding on that level at the front of the courthouse. Occupied only by a DOJ associate lawyer, the elevator took them to the fifth floor. From there they walked down the stairs to the third floor. Sheridan emerged first from the stairwell alone, where another waiting associate signaled that the coast was clear. Joined then by Partin and Grimsley the three-some hurried down the hallway and into the offices of Jack Reddy, the US Attorney, immediately opposite the courtroom. Bypassing the reception area they went directly into Reddy's inner sanctum. Closing the door behind them they slumped into chairs, relieved that Partin had not been seen by anyone who would have recognized him.

Judge Wilson re-opened court that afternoon about two o'clock. Hooker then rose and called to the bailiffs to bring in the next witness. In those days the government was not required to give a defendant advance notice of witnesses the prosecution planned to call. All was quiet as a side door opened and the bulky Louisiana Teamster came into the courtroom. A few front-row spectators were looking at Hoffa as the realization hit him that one of his trusted aides was appearing as a witness for the prosecution. "My God, it's Partin," he said in a shocked whisper as his face went ashen.[6] Though not fully aware of the coming explosion, he knew he was in danger. His mouth tightened and turned downward, his steady gaze focused on the witness with incin-erating ferocity. This was Hoffa's "deep, strange, penetrating expression of intense hatred" Kennedy had felt when it was directed at him during the McClellan Committee hearings.[7] Now, with disaster looming, the Teamster boss's supremely malevolent stare also showed a hint of fear. Like a cornered animal, he was a textbook victim of legal ambush.

Partin's testimony began routinely. He identified himself by saying he had known Hoffa since 1957 and met with him on union business several times since then. The latest such occasion, he continued, was two years earlier when he sought the IBT boss's help on a local union matter. With Hoffa's concurrence he had gone to Nashville in the fall of 1962 on the day before the start of the Test Fleet trial. On walking into the lobby of the Andrew Jackson Hotel, he had bumped into Messrs. Dorfman and Tweel. Later that day he had met with Hoffa, who said that Dorfman was a friend who had come to Nashville "to help him."

The defense lawyers listened attentively to this testimony. Tense and ready to pounce, they had made no objections to that point. Then Partin casually tossed his first bombshell. In a follow-up meeting with Tweel in the latter's hotel room, he said, Hoffa's West Virginia "friend" told him that Dorfman had called Tweel and said "it would be a personal favor … if he would come down to Nashville and help him set up a method to get to the jury."[8] A nanosecond later three defense lawyers leapt to their feet, simultaneously shouting demands for a mistrial, a separate trial for each client, and other means of relief undecipherable in the bedlam created by Partin's shocking statement.

Hoffa's lead counsel James Haggerty alone kept his composure. He asked Judge Wilson to excuse the jury so he could make a motion. In the defense team's most understated remark during the long trial, Haggerty then said that Partin's appearance had taken him "completely … by surprise."[9] The witness should not be allowed to testify, he argued, because the Louisiana Teamster was "an undercover agent for the government" whose presence in the Teamsters' hotel suite fatally infringed on Hoffa's legal rights.[10] Wilson called a recess but soon decided to say he would hold a hearing then and there on Haggerty's motion. This was the issue Assistant Attorney General Ramsey Clark had raised and though none knew it at the time, would, as Clark predicted, be decided ultimately by the justices of the US Supreme Court.

Judge Wilson's hearing lasted four hours. Harvey Silets, counsel for Tweel, the man to whom Partin had just attributed the startling incrimination of Hoffa, bored into Partin's history as a government witness. How had he become a spy for the prosecution? Had he been present when Hoffa's Test Fleet lawyers discussed their strategy? What information did he pass on to Sheridan? What had he been promised in return for his testimony? Partin explained how he had first spoken with William "Billy" Daniels, an investigator in the Baton Rouge DA's office, who had put him in touch with Frank Grimsley, a DOJ lawyer based in Atlanta. Grimsley, he said, asked him to be alert to any signs of jury tampering or other illegal activity when he went to Nashville to meet with Hoffa. From Grimsley he also learned Sheridan's name and telephone number as his government contact. Partin denied having heard any strategy discussions between Hoffa and the Test Fleet defense lawyers. The information he had voluntarily passed on to Sheridan concerned only jury tampering and nothing else.

Sheridan testified next, confirming Partin's version of how their contact had come about and emphasizing the limited nature of the information provided by the Louisiana Teamster. The DOJ investigator was followed by five Teamster lawyers who had been in Hoffa's hotel suite during the Test Fleet trial. They all swore that Partin had been regularly among them during that time, with ample opportunity to overhear their discussions with Hoffa. None, however, could pinpoint Partin's exposure to any specific confidential information.

Wilson took the matter under advisement and the next morning announced he would allow Partin to testify. "The government did not place Mr. Partin in the defendants' midst. ... Rather, he was knowingly and voluntarily placed there by one of the defendants," an obvious reference to Hoffa.[11]

Answering questions then put to him by Hooker, Partin described the acts of jury tampering he had secretly conveyed to Sheridan during the Test Fleet trial. One by one he told how each of Hoffa's accused minions had tried to influence a juror's vote, and how each had reported his actions to the IBT president. He also threw back into the Teamster boss's face some of the colorful remarks Hoffa had made to him, incriminating words having a distinct ring of authenticity. Regarding Test Fleet juror Tippens, Hoffa had said to Partin: "The dirty bastard went in and told the judge that his neighbor had offered him $10,000." Then referring to juryman Fields: "I've got the male colored juror in my hip pocket." On strategy, "I would pay $15,000, $20,000 ... whatever it costs to get to the jury. ... Our best bet is a hung jury unless we can get to the foreman. If the jury does deadlock, it will be the same as an acquittal because they will never try it again."[12]

Partin thus nailed Hoffa as the jury-tampering ringleader, the man who gave the orders and controlled the money to be paid to receptive jurors. His testimony meshed perfectly with the statements of the prosecution's witnesses who had preceded him. By the end of the day, Partin's stunning revelations had put the defendants into a deep pit from which they could emerge only by attacking their accuser's credibility. Their lawyers would have to keep the lights burning, all night if necessary, to prepare for the pile-on when Partin's cross-examination began the next morning.

The defense lawyers' reaction to Partin's surprise appearance was a sea breeze compared to the hurricane force of Hoffa's fury. In front of the judge and jury the Teamster boss could only squirm and mutter, but in the privacy of the defense's courthouse lounge area during breaks his pent-up rage burst forth. He paced around the room flailing his arms, roaring like a mortally wounded bear. He picked up a heavy chair and hurled it several feet against a wall. He cursed Partin for disloyalty and himself for stupidly trusting someone who, in hindsight, had been so obviously upset by the denial of his request for help. He remembered their meeting in December, 1961, at which Partin complained of charges filed against him at the Southern Regional Council by "stooges" from his Baton Rouge union. Instead of promising to quell those dissident voices Hoffa had told the man now turned traitor to "keep his mouth shut" and it would all work out.[13] It had *not* worked out, and the seed of Partin's animosity toward Hoffa, surely sown that day, had become a determination to get even.

Hoffa's reaction to Partin's testimony reflected an awareness of how deeply it had hurt the Teamster boss's case. In the parade of witnesses during the preceding week his name had hardly been mentioned. Now an eyewitness had placed him squarely at the center of the jury-tampering effort. One of the defense lawyers could not help acknowledging the Perry Mason quality of the prosecution's accomplishment. "I've seen some great coups in my time," he confided to Sheridan, "but that was the greatest" of them all.[14] The coup had also taken its toll on Partin, who returned exhausted to his mountain retreat. Unable to relax, he knew that his ordeal had been only a warm-up for a grueling interrogation by the defense.

Hoffa's local lawyer Harry Berke led off Partin's cross-examination when court reopened the next day. The defense team's strategy became clear with Berke's first few questions. Instead of challenging the witness's memory or the substance of his charges they would concentrate on destroying his character and credibility. They had much to work with. The Louisiana Teamster's record of misconduct began when he was a teenager. During the next twenty years he had been "convicted of breaking and entering, [given] a bad conduct discharge from the US Marines, and indicted for rape, forgery and first-degree manslaughter"[15] In 1962 he had been charged with stealing money from the treasury of Teamster Local 5 and then falsifying its books in an attempt to cover up the theft. Now pending against him as he spoke was a charge of assisting in the kidnapping of a friend's children. By the end of the day this barrage of questions had undercut Partin's credibility and weakened his confidence. The defense, however, felt the witness was only wounded and they wanted him dead. They would continue their cross-examination of the turncoat for three more days.

As Partin's interrogation dragged on with little added effect, the witness's confidence returned and he gave as good as he got. One of his questioner's attempts to use sarcasm backfired abruptly. "You had your story pretty well rehearsed, didn't you?" asked Berke. "If I had it rehearsed," Partin replied, "you would have heard a lot more than you did. I *forgot* some things!"[16] The heavyset Teamster had also learned to speak directly to the jury in his soft cajun drawl. During the afternoon break Bill French, a DOJ lawyer, overheard evidence of Partin's increasing effectiveness. French was in the men's room as Hoffa and two of his lawyers came striding through the door. The IBT boss was complaining loudly, "He's killing us with those asides to the jury. You've got to get him off that stand."[17] He then saw French and lapsed into a grim silence.

Prior to the Louisiana Teamster's appearance Schiffer's histrionics had created most of the trial's acrimonious moments. When Partin took the stand, however, an aura of bitterness and anger rose across the width of the defense table that would permeate the courtroom until the trial's end. Feeling the heat directly, Hoffa grew more agitated and defensive. He sent scribbled notes to defense lawyers or tugged on their clothes to have them bend down for a few whispered words of advice. When Partin made a particularly telling point the IBT boss spat a muttered curse toward Neal or looked toward Sheridan in the first row of spectators and did the same. In the courthouse hallways Hoffa was more openly belligerent. Walking by the prosecutors or standing aside when they passed he would obscenely tell them where to go and what to do when they got there, usually flipping them a quick salute with his middle finger.

The Louisiana Teamster ended his third day of cross-examination on Friday, February 7. Hoffa went home that night but flew back to Chattanooga the following Sunday morning. At a rally held that afternoon in his honor by Local 515 he was disappointed that only ten to fifteen percent of the local union's members showed up. But they were enough to warm him to his subject: Washington was now considering anti-union legislation and union members needed to get politically engaged in the fight to block it. He also played his favorite card as the victim of a government juggernaut to remove him from power, citing the "hundreds" of FBI agents and US Marshals in Chattanooga as part of Bobby Kennedy's gestapo. That night, as if to echo Hoffa's thoughts, unknown provocateurs fired shotguns at the house of Donnice Bennet, the man who had succeeded Partin as the president of Teamster Local 5 in Baton Rouge.

The trial's surprise witness finally left the stand near noon on Wednesday, February 12. The remaining bits and pieces of the prosecution's evidence were put into the record during the next forty-eight hours and at noon the following Friday, three weeks into the trial, Neal announced that the government rested its case. During the following week each of the five other defendants testified individually in his own behalf. All denied attempting to influence Test Fleet jurors and took issue, individually, with the incriminating statements made by prosecution witnesses against them.

Ewing King fared worst of all. His excuses for late night meetings with Mutt Pitts and patrolman Paschal were lame at best, and Hooker's cross-examination provided the coup de grâce. At one point, King said that it was "not uncommon for country people to meet at a spring, or around some hill, or someplace by the side of a road." "What kind of country people do you know who meet by a spring after midnight on a rainy night?" Said King, "The best kind of people I know, country people. ... Do I look stupid enough to ask a highway patrolman I don't know about his wife on a jury?" "Don't ask me that question," said Hooker, his tone clearly implying what his response would be, and perhaps remembering the juror who had responded to him in a similar fashion years earlier. King went on to deny having talked to Pitts about meeting with Paschal, adding that they were talking only about buying a "rabbit dog." With that, Hooker pounced on King like a wrestler determined to pin his careless opponent's shoulders to the mat. "But you weren't hunting rabbits that night, were you?" he bellowed. "You were hunting jurors!"[18]

On Friday, February 21, at the end of the trial's fifth week, Hoffa took the stand in a crowded courtroom. Radiating confidence under questioning by Harry Berke he began by telling his life's story—his father's early death, his mother's struggle to keep the family fed and clothed, leaving school at age fourteen to help with the family's finances, and his rise through the Teamster ranks to its presidency. He said Partin had invited himself to Nashville to ask for help with his troubles at Baton Rouge's Local 5, and in their initial discussion had seemed nervous and ill at ease. When he told Partin he would have to "straighten out" or risk having his local put into trusteeship, the Louisiana Teamster got angry and "stormed out the door."[19] After that they saw little of each other during the Test Fleet trial. The Louisiana Teamster occasionally brought him a newspaper and guarded the door to the IBT's hotel suite on one brief occasion, but they never discussed any efforts by anyone to contact Test Fleet jurors. He then denied, in detail, having any such discussions with any of his five co-defendants.

John Hooker was the natural choice to conduct Hoffa's cross-examination. He and Neal were an efficient team, each putting his individual talents to their best uses. The hard-driving, sharp-witted younger man set the prosecution's pace. He kept its case moving forward and took the lead in counterattacking the defense through its continuous barrage of outlandish motions and strident complaints. He argued against the defendants' lawyers in court and masterminded the government's responses to the defense lawyers' written pleadings. He also handled his share of witness interrogations. But his co-counsel took on the heavyweights. A generation ahead of Neal and ten years older than Hoffa, Hooker was the maestro of the prosecution's effort to win the hearts and minds of the jury. He was scheduled to make the prosecution's final closing argument. He had led the preparation of Partin as a witness and conducted his direct examination. He had cross-examined Ewing King, the president of Nashville's Local 327, and was now ready to probe the Teamster boss himself.

Though unknown at the beginning it gradually became apparent that Hooker, like a boxer with a long reach, had an advantage over his tough but short-armed opponent. Hoffa was convinced that the FBI had bugged his hotel suite during the Test Fleet trial, thus possibly overhearing some of his conversations with the jury tamperers. This fear caused many of his answers on cross-examination to be uncharacteristically tentative and equivocal. He conceded knowing that Test Fleet juror Paschal "was the wife of a highway patrolman."[20] He "might well have discussed [with Ewing King] the matter of a man named Pitts." He "might have rode" with King "in [George Broda's] Ford one day,"[21] and "might have discussed somewhere" the government's charge that King was involved in Mrs. Paschal's departure from the jury."[22] Individually these admissions rocked Hoffa's boat only slightly, but taken together created a sizeable wave.

Hoffa also allowed Hooker to get under his skin. When the lawyer raised his voice, Hoffa said "I cannot hear you the way you holler. ... It just gets in my ear [and] I can't understand the words. ... I am not used to people hollering at me."[23] "You're used to doing the hollering yourself at people, aren't you?" Hooker shot back. As the questioning went on, the Teamster boss became more rambling, more agitated and argumentative. When his cross-examination ended, Hoffa spoke up spontaneously. "Mr. Hooker, may I apologize to you if I was too aggressive or too loud in my debate. It is my natural habit. If I offended you, I apologize."[24]

As Neal listened to Hoffa's testimony he silently chuckled at the memory of how he had played on the Teamster boss's paranoid suspicion of being electronically bugged. A few days earlier, the young prosecutor had collected some discarded metal boxes looking as if they had once been part of a dismantled electrical system. He had then connected them with strands of old wires of various colors from the closet of the courthouse electrician. After attaching knobs and a bare metallic wire resembling an antenna, Neal put the Rube Goldberg device on a wheeled cart. He gave this assembly to his assistant Jim Durkin and told him to wait at one end of the corridor leading to the defense counsels' assigned room. Then, when Hoffa emerged from court and headed in that direction, Durkin was to wheel the cart past him in a furtive but not overly dramatic manner.

Listening to Hoffa now, Neal suspected his quarry had taken the bait and was wriggling as a result. Long afterward he wondered whether he or Hoffa would have been more embarrassed if his ploy had been discovered. Of one thing, however, Neal felt certain. He had strengthened the Teamster boss's fear that the FBI was electronically eavesdropping on his telephone calls and tracking his every move. On cross-examination Hoffa spoke with far less confidence than the prosecutors had expected. Also lacking were the bluster and aggressive posturing that usually accompanied his denials of wrongdoing and protestations of innocence.

The Teamster boss was on the stand for less than a full day. Though the trial was now winding down it took another week for the defense to complete its case. Much of the time was absorbed not by the presentation of additional evidence by either side but by the defense lawyers' desperate attempts to provoke a mistrial. The most blatant example of their efforts occurred during the cross-examination of a character witness for Partin. When defense lawyer Berke's questions became unduly repetitive, Judge Wilson stopped him and temporarily took over the questioning. Schiffer, reactively wielding his sledgehammer to kill a fly, sprang to his feet and demanded a mistrial. Stunned by the lawyer's hostility, Wilson told him to sit down. At that point, Harvey Silets, defendant Dorfman's lawyer, accused the judge of using a "vicious" tone when speaking to Schiffer. When Wilson replied that he was trying to be "fair and impartial," Schiffer scoffed at the suggestion.

Spectators in the courtroom squirmed in obvious discomfort at the ferocity of the defense lawyers' attack on the presiding judge. Swept away by his own angry rhetoric, Schiffer ignored the effect he was producing. "I say this," he shouted, "the net effect to this jury"—who were not present as he spoke—"is that all defendants' counsel … are charlatans; that we are tricksters; that we are trying to fool the court. …"[25] Wilson let him finish and then, in a voice sounding barely under control, denied the motion for a mistrial. Though it failed to do so, the New York lawyer's performance was clearly designed to provoke Judge Wilson into a careless mistake.

Tampa lawyer Frank Ragano, still insinuating himself into Hoffa's gang of loyalists, thought he saw a way to capitalize on his colleague's bombast. As Schiffer continued at full volume Ragano left the courtroom and went down the hall toward the room occupied by the jury when they were outside the courtroom. Standing at their door he could still hear Schiffer's high, penetrating voice. With one ear against the door and his hand covering the other, he listened in the hope of overhearing a juror make reference to Schiffer's argument. Sure enough, next morning the defense team sought a mistrial, attaching to their motion Ragano's affidavit that he had overheard a juror commenting on Schiffer's outburst. Again containing his anger, Judge Wilson brushed aside the defense team's latest ploy. The attempt to turn Schiffer's unrestrained argument into grounds for a mistrial, he said, had only compounded the defense team's misconduct. Ragano should simply have suggested to his irascible co-counsel that he tone down his remarks. "The defendants cannot create such a situation as this and seek to take advantage of their own actions."[26]

In the perspective of time, Ragano's performance was only one of several moments that could have eased the high tension of this courtroom drama. Kossman, Maher and Bufalino were Hollywood stereotypes of mobster defense lawyers with Ragano as their buffoon. Sidling up to the jury room door, he might have been compared to a jealous lover hoping to hear incriminating utterances by an unfaithful mate. And because Schiffer's shouting and flailing went so far over the line, someone might have seen his performance as a parody, almost a caricature, of an aggressive trial lawyer gone completely haywire.

But the atmosphere of the Chattanooga courtroom was irrevocably poisoned. Both sides had too much at stake. A jail sentence would end Hoffa's union leadership at the peak of his power. His acquittal, or another hung jury, would dispirit Kennedy's Get Hoffa team, already concerned about their viability within a new administration. Failure to gain a conviction would also energize the Teamsters' public relations team in pursuit of their twin goals—additional support for Hoffa at the highest political levels and the further demonizing of Kennedy as a weakened attorney general in malicious pursuit of an enemy which no jury would ever convict. There was no comic relief to be had from the unremitting intensity of every trial moment.

Back in their seats following the latest uproar the jurors listened to a rebuttal witness attesting to Partin's good character. That testimony ended the presentation of evidence by both sides.

Final arguments to the jury began on Monday morning, March 2, 1964, following the classic model by which the law attempts to balance, as evenly as possible, the interests of the government and the accused. The prosecution would make the first and last arguments. Each of the defendants would have only one say, in the middle, but in return could claim protection behind the high wall of reasonable doubt. If the government did not prove guilt *beyond* such doubt, the law required an acquittal.

Jim Neal led off for the prosecution with the statement that this case involved "one of the greatest assaults on the jury system the country has ever known."[27] He took the jury step-by-step through the activities of the defendants, from their arrivals in Nashville and their meetings and conversations with Hoffa to their attempts to contact Test Fleet jurors directly or through family and friends. He reviewed Partin's testimony at length, emphasizing that whenever the Louisiana Teamster reported that something was about to happen, it actually took place as he had said it would. He reminded them, "The government does not contend that Mr. Partin has led a perfect life. The government does contend that he is telling the truth."[28] He described Hoffa as a hands-on leader insistent on knowing what his subordinates were up to. In turn these Teamster minions were careful to see that their boss was informed, particularly when their actions might earn his praise. It was unthinkable, Neal argued, that they would keep their leader in the dark during the Test Fleet case on something that affected him, and only him, so deeply and directly. Were it not so serious a matter it would be laughable for Hoffa to claim otherwise.

Five defense lawyers then had their say. Harry Berke, after professing Hoffa's innocence, led the charge against the Louisiana Teamster. Partin was a thief of his own union's money, a disgruntled traitor, a paid government spy and a depraved human being unworthy of belief. After that, it was all about Kennedy's vendetta. The government's case was a "foul and filthy frame-up." Walter Sheridan was "the architect of [a] diabolical plot [in] service [to] his master, Robert Kennedy."[29] Jacques Schiffer, true to form, provided the defense's harshest and most emotional argument. Kennedy was the villain of the piece and Sheridan his "axeman."[30] Ending his trademarked tirade with a flourish, Schiffer took a handful of coins from his pocket and flung them toward Neal and Hooker seated at the government's table. "I say to the Washington prosecutors, including Mr. Sheridan: take these thirty pieces of silver and share them—you've earned [every penny]!" Scattered about the floor, the coins lay untouched until reporters gathered them up when court adjourned. Falling far short of the present value of Judas Iscariot's reward there were only twenty-one "pieces" with a total value of $2.50.

Hooker made the prosecution's closing argument the following morning. For a few moments he paced slowly before the jury box, looking at the floor and stroking his chin as if to gather his thoughts. He began by reminding the jury that the case had been started in Nashville by Judge Miller immediately after the hung jury's vote in the Test Fleet case, and not by Robert Kennedy or the Department of Justice in Washington. Later, in the hushed courtroom, he had the jurors' full attention. "With all the sincerity at my command, I say to you that Chattanooga, after a hundred years, has survived a Chickamauga and a Missionary Ridge, but Chattanooga can never survive the acquittal of those who have been proven ... guilty of contaminating, tampering with and fixing a jury in the courts of justice in this state."[31]

That afternoon Judge Wilson gave the jurors a summary of the law applicable to the case. At seven thirty that night, after a light supper, they went to the jury room to begin their deliberations. When they left Sheridan went by himself to the courthouse steps for some fresh air and a momentary break from the tension of a long day. A few moments later Hoffa emerged, accompanied by the ever-present Chuckie O'Brien. Never willing to miss a chance to vent his anger the Teamster boss glared at his tormentor. "Sheridan," he growled, "you don't have an ounce of guts in your body."[32] No rest for the weary, thought the DOJ investigator as he silently turned and went back inside. Hoffa's tortured utterance was unjustified and misdirected. Over the years, from the McClellan Committee forward, Sheridan had proven his grit and courage time and again as he searched for information in the hostile presence of Teamster strongmen. The IBT boss had simply shown, once again, his inner turmoil and his compulsion to blame others for his troubles.

The jurors returned to the courthouse the next morning, March 4, to resume their deliberations. At two o'clock that afternoon word came they had reached verdicts on all of the charges. Surprisingly, they had debated for less than six hours, a brief time for a case involving five defendants and lasting more than six weeks. Dorfman and Tweel were acquitted. King, Campbell, and Parks were each found guilty on one count of jury tampering. Hoffa, said the jury, was guilty on two counts—of working with Campbell and Parks to get the vote of juror Gratin Fields, and with King to influence juror Betty Paschal.

At last! After the better part of a decade the Get Hoffa team finally felt the elation of victory. For the first time in his life, Hoffa had been unable to threaten, negotiate or buy his way out of a guilty verdict. The laconic but now excited Sheridan rushed to a telephone and gave his boss the good news in three words he had long been hoping to say: "We made it!" "Nice work," came Kennedy's understated but heartfelt reply.[33] Neal and Hooker basked in the congratulations of friends and supporters, knowing that the verdict could have gone either way and particularly thankful the jury had accepted the testimony of their maligned key witness. Partin himself had mixed feelings: satisfaction that he had done the right thing by telling the truth, but apprehension regarding Hoffa's anticipated onslaught to discredit him.

Upon dismissing the jurors Judge Wilson thanked them sincerely for their attention during the trial, for their patience during its numerous interruptions, and for enduring sequestered lives for over six long weeks. Life for the confined jurors had indeed been lonely. Semi-isolated in the Read House Hotel, they had been the tenth floor's only occupants. Marshals and other court officers were on the floors above and below. All tenth-floor exits and entrances were guarded to prevent unauthorized visits, even by wives or other relatives. The jury gave their personal guards high marks for their conduct. All of them were "good guys, careful and polite, as well as firm"—particularly Marshal Mansfield's deputy and the jurors' chief caretaker, Mr. Sertell, familiarly known to his charges as "shirttail."[34]

Jurors could watch TV only in one room on their floor set aside for that purpose, with a marshal always present to keep local and national news—including the weather channel—off the screen. Discussion of trial matters was strictly forbidden and there was almost no private visiting among jurors. Jurors could leave the hotel to attend church or synagogue, but only in a marshal's company and able to wave or say hello to friends only if they kept moving. They went once to a theater for a memorable performance by Liberace. At all times marshals walked ahead and behind, stopping traffic at signal lights and stop signs to permit their passage without a halt. One marshal stayed well out front to avoid unwanted contacts such as coin boxes showing newspaper front pages, which were turned aside as the group went past.

The conscientious jurors believed Partin for a number of reasons. The first of these was his demeanor. As one juror remembered the trial, the star witness "droned on in such a soft Cajun accent that he soon became boring. We hated to see him come back on the stand day after day, but we had to listen carefully. He said what he wanted to say and wouldn't change his story."[35] Partin's testimony was also consistent with the jury's belief that he and the other Teamster underlings on trial were acting on Hoffa's orders. "Hoffa was the boss and Partin was his right-hand man. He did what he was told and had the guts" to say what he did. There was no bargaining among jurors due to differences of opinion. They convicted Hoffa, King, Parks and Campbell because they were all "in the loop," and acquitted Dorfman and Tweel who were perceived as "visitors." Dorfman came from Chicago to Nashville "just to sell insurance." Tweel, the West Virginian businessman, was out of his element and "didn't belong there."[36] A naive analysis, perhaps, but it was the judgment of those who saw and heard the out-of-towners in the flesh.

Because Hoffa kept his temper tantrums out of their sight, jurors saw the Teamster boss as calm and "quiet, except when Partin walked in." Judge Wilson was "dignified, cautious and never raised his voice." Hooker "demanded respect, just by standing up." Neal "talked faster" in a style that suggested "you'd better listen to me." Hoffa's local lawyer Harry Berke was remembered as a lawyer "who must have handled a million divorce cases, and who was the 'go-to guy' in Chattanooga if you got in trouble." Defense counsel Schiffer was a loudmouth. "When he threw those coins on the counsel table we laughed and I crossed him off of my list."[37]

On the day of her husband's conviction Hoffa's wife was in a Miami hospital with a recurrent heart ailment but their children and son-in-law were on hand to lend support. On leaving the courtroom the newly convicted felon responded to reporters' questions as they milled around him. Yes, he would appeal. His conviction had been "a railroad job …, a farce of American justice." He would fight to overturn the verdict, not letting it interfere with Teamster business, or his position as its leader. "You can rest assured of one thing. The entire membership of the Teamsters Union is behind Hoffa in this fight."[38] With those comments he left for the Chattanooga airport and his private plane that would take him to Miami to be with Josephine.

Wasting no time Judge Wilson set March 12 as Hoffa's sentencing date. Far from intimidated by what they saw as only a temporary setback, and moving equally fast, the gang of Teamster supporters that couldn't shoot straight again went into action. Chattanooga's Read House Hotel had been the sequestered jury's home throughout the trial. This gave someone the bright idea that one or more of the hotel's bellmen might have noticed juror misbehavior which might taint the jury's verdict. With money as their means, Hoffa's henchmen persuaded four of these employees to sign affidavits saying they had regularly delivered liquor to several jurors' rooms and seen some of them intoxicated during that period. On March 10, two days before the sentencing date, defense lawyers filed yet another mistrial motion, this one claiming ninety-four fatal errors including the drunkenness of the trial's jurors.

As even the most amateurish would-be fixer might have suspected, the jurors were aghast. H.E. Bullen, their foreman, spoke for them all. "I am flabbergasted. It is ridiculous. We were most circumspect because we realized the importance of our assignment ... I am willing to testify anytime" to the falsity of the defendants' allegations.[39] And of course the Get Hoffa Squad was able to get contrary affidavits from other bellmen. These latter employees denied having supplied liquor to jurors or seen any of them intoxicated, adding that they, the employees, had been offered bribes to give false statements and had refused. One of them told of having been shown an open briefcase full of cash. Judge Wilson needed no live testimony to decide that the defense's claim of juror misconduct was completely unfounded.

In the aftermath of this fiasco the Read House fired the perjurious bellmen. Ironically they immediately got job offers from the Cabana Motor Hotel in Atlanta, a new motel financed with loans from the Teamsters' Pension Fund. This completed a circle of malfeasance that never should have begun. The defense lawyers who vetted the bellmen as witnesses and prepared their affidavits had surely smelled a rat. But they and their bribed witnesses were part of a society in which everyone seemed to have his price, a group whose members believed that the government was as corrupt as the individuals it called criminals. It was a culture of cynicism, greed, dishonesty and fear that began and ended with the man who created it, Jimmy Hoffa.

The sentencing of the four convicted defendants took place on March 12. Professing his innocence, an unrepentant Teamster boss predicted that "when the evidence has been sifted calmly and coolly" he would be found innocent. Speaking more to his union's rank and file than to the judge, he bragged that he would be vindicated on appeal, at which time "the working people will know … that I have not betrayed their trust."[40] Judge Wilson then finally got his say. He began with a finding that the evidence in the case supported the jury's decision that Hoffa had "knowingly and … corruptly" attempted to bribe Test Fleet jurors.[41]

> It is difficult … to imagine … a more willful violation of the law. … Most defendants that stand before this court for sentencing have … violated the property … or personal rights of other individuals. You stand here convicted of seeking to corrupt the administration of justice itself, … of having tampered, really, with the very soul of this nation. …

Judge Wilson ended with a summation, dated somewhat, perhaps, by events unimaginable at the time he spoke:

> You hav[e] struck at the very foundation upon which everything else in this nation depends, the very basis of civilization itself. … [W]ithout a fair, proper, and a lawful administration of justice, nothing else would be possible in this country. … [I]f a conviction of such an offense were to go unpunished, … it would surely destroy this country more quickly and more surely than any combination of any foreign foes that we could ever possibly have. [42]

The most jail time Hoffa could receive was five years for each of the two counts on which the jury had found him guilty. Wilson sentenced him to a prison term of eight years and ordered him to pay $10,000 in fines, the maximum financial penalty. When asked if he had any questions, a stone-faced Hoffa replied, "I understand my sentence perfectly and I will take my appeals."[43] The other convicted defendants—King, Parks and Campbell—received jail terms of three years each.

At the sentencing hearing Judge Wilson also dealt with Jacques Schiffer, the most belligerent of the defense lawyers. Finding him in contempt of court for his over-the-top histrionics, Wilson sentenced the voluble New York lawyer to sixty days in jail. To be sure that Schiffer could not talk his way out of this decision Judge Wilson detailed the reasons for putting him behind bars. Reading aloud from a lengthy citation of contempt, he listed seventeen instances of flagrant misconduct. As he recounted Schiffer's misdeeds the judge spoke with resignation and relief in a voice reflecting the physical and mental toll his long ordeal had taken. Years later Wilson's son noted his father's belief that "the Hoffa trial took several years off of his life."[44]

Schiffer expressed no remorse and made no request for leniency. Nor was he cowed by the judge's citation. Brashly he asked for a hearing before another judge in which he might challenge the court's biased reasoning. Wilson summarily denied this request but allowed Schiffer to stay out of jail on a $2,500 bond while pursuing an appeal. Eventually Hoffa's black knight of the bar served his sentence in full. The judge also issued a letter of reprimand to Frank Ragano for the Mob lawyer's crass attempt to overhear jury discussions as his co-counsel Schiffer shouted in the background.

Hoffa's sentencing was a watershed event for him and for Bob Kennedy, the culmination of the government's seven-year effort to convict the IBT boss of a serious crime. And for the first time in his thirty-two years as a Teamster, Hoffa squarely faced a career-ending term in prison. The nation's most notorious labor leader would remain free as his appeal went forward but his downward slide had begun. His three convicted co-defendants were in similar straits and three of his other associates were under indictment on jury-fixing charges. Most notable among the latter group was Zeno Thomas Osborn, the Nashville lawyer who had thrown his mind, heart and soul into Hoffa's defense in the Test Fleet case. Tommy Osborn was the prime example of his client's corrupting influence, and certainly the most empathetic character to be caught in its web. His pending trial would be a cliffhanger for everyone involved in it.

CHAPTER 8

"The Most Contemptible Piece
of Trickery and Fraud"

The convictions of Hoffa and his three henchmen bolstered Walter Sheridan's claim that the IBT boss had led the "most massive" jury-tampering effort in the history of the federal courts. Less than a month later, convictions of two more Hoffa cronies confirmed that view. Again before Judge Wilson, this time in Nashville, Neal and Hooker sent Lawrence "Red" Medlin to jail for attempting to bribe Test Fleet juror James Tippens with a $10,000 payoff. In early April, 1964, another Nashville jury found Henry "Buster" Bell guilty of offering a black bartender $30,000 to influence the votes of black panelists on the same list of prospective jurors. Teamster flacks argued that insufficient evidence linked these men's deeds directly to Hoffa, but everyone else knew these jury fixings were part and parcel of Hoffa's modus operandi.

In the wake of these successful prosecutions the only unsettled charge of jury rigging by a Teamster associate was against Z. Thomas Osborn, Hoffa's leading defense counsel in the 1962 Test Fleet trial. Osborn's case was unique in two respects. It was the sole instance of a Hoffa lawyer being accused of attempting to influence a jury. It also promised to show, as no other, how Hoffa's corrosive influence could provoke a formerly law-abiding citizen into criminal behavior at the risk of destroying his unblemished reputation, his closely knit family and even his life.

This last episode had begun about two months before the start of Hoffa's Chattanooga trial. On November 7, 1963, Walter Sheridan received a long-distance telephone call at his D.C. office from Robert Vick, a former member of the Nashville police force. Acting as a would-be private eye—with alleged contacts in Nashville's underworld as well as its law enforcement establishment—Vick had phoned Sheridan twice before, claiming knowledge of further jury-fixing efforts by Hoffa-connected individuals. Because of Vick's shady reputation and his lack of supporting evidence, Kennedy's chief investigator had paid him little mind. Sheridan now reluctantly answered Vick's latest call out of a nagging sense of duty, resigned to listen patiently to more of the ex-patrolman's tiresome chatter. Without warning Vick tossed him a live grenade: Tommy Osborn, the Nashville lawyer who had done a superb job of defending Hoffa in the Test Fleet case, had just directed Vick to offer $10,000 to a prospective member of the jury panel in Hoffa's upcoming jury-tampering case.[1] Not wanting to discuss details on the phone Sheridan asked his informant to meet him at 9 a.m. the next morning in the chief investigator's office in the Nashville courthouse. It was already late afternoon in Washington, but having flown so often to Tennessee's capital he had a travel agent's familiarity with flights between the two cities. He headed south on American Airlines' 2:00 a.m. flight that night and met with Vick the next day at the appointed hour.

On hand with Sheridan to hear the former policeman's story were Neal, Hooker and local FBI agents Steele and Sheets. Vick began by saying that Osborn had recently asked him to come to his office and look over the names of panelists to be called for jury duty in Hoffa's forthcoming trial. If he knew any of them, Osborn wanted to talk with him about making contact. One name on the panel immediately stood out: the ex-policeman's cousin Ralph Elliott from Springfield, Tennessee. It was then, Vick continued, that Osborn made his shocking proposal: Vick was to offer Elliott $10,000 for his vote, to be paid in two chunks. Hooker and Neal looked at each other in utter disbelief. The Tommy Osborn they knew would never make such an offer. At age forty-four he was among Nashville's most prominent lawyers and civic activists. Hooker knew him as a long-time fellow barrister and good friend. Neal accorded Osborn the same respect the latter gave to Hooker. But Vick stuck to his story. Asked to put it in a form that would subject him to a charge of perjury if untrue, he did so with a signed and notarized affidavit.

Both lawyers realized the former policeman's word was not enough to convict such a highly respected member of the community. The only way they could hope to prove Vick's charge was to get a recording of Osborn repeating his instructions to his former accomplice, now his accuser. Asked if he would return to the lawyer's office and secretly tape their conversation, the world-weary, seen-it-all ex-lawman shrugged "Why not?" With that settled, the FBI's Steele went to Judge Miller's office seeking a warrant to use a hidden device. Equally stunned by Vick's affidavit, Miller authorized the electronic search as requested.

After one false start Vick met again with Osborn and successfully completed his mission. FBI agents observed their informer on his way to Osborn's office and as he exited an hour later. They kept him in sight until other agents picked him up in an unmarked car, assuring that no one outside of Osborn's office building had tampered with the tape before or after its message was recorded.

After a few preliminaries Vick and Osborn got down to business:

Osborn: Did you talk to … Elliott?

Vick: Yeah, I went down to Springfield. … [H]e got to talking about the last Hoffa case being hung, … and some guy refusing $10,000 to hang it, see, and he said the guy was crazy, he should have took it. And so we talked … discreetly … about … five thousand now and five thousand later. … So he seemed very respective [sic] … to hang the thing for five now and five later. …

Osborn: Then tell him it's a deal.

Vick: Tell him what?

Osborn: That it's a deal … and when he gets on, he's got to be certain that he'll just be talking to you and nobody else.

Vick: All right. You want to know when he's ready … for the five thousand. Is that right?

Osborn: Well, no, when he gets on the jury. … I know that if we go to trial before that jury he'll be on it, but suppose the government challenges him. … Where are we then?

Vick: Oh, I see. I see.…

Osborn: All right, so we'll leave it to you. … Your next contact will be to tell him that if he wants that deal, he's got it. … The only thing it depends upon is him being accepted on the jury. If the government challenges him, there will be no deal.

Vick: All right, if he is seated.

Osborn: If he's seated.

Vick: He can expect five thousand … and then five thousand if it's a hang. Is that right?

Osborn: All the way, now!

Vick: Oh, he's got to stay all the way?

Osborn: All the way…

Vick: I'm going to play it just like you told me previously, to reassure him and keep him from getting panicky … I have reason to believe that he won't be alone, you know.

Osborn: Tell him there will be at least two others with him … We'll keep it secret. The way to keep it safe is that nobody knows about it but you and me. …[2]

The recording of Osborn's voice was devastating. He had undeniably instructed Bob Vick to tell prospective juror Elliott to expect $5,000 if he was "seated" as one of the twelve to try Hoffa for jury tampering, and $5,000 more for a vote of acquittal. When Vick said that Elliott "seemed very 'respective' … to hang the thing for five now and five later," Osborn shot back, "Then tell him it's a deal," and that "there will be at least two others with him."

The prosecution team gave Judge Miller a transcript of the audio tape and together they listened to the recording. Miller was aghast, shaking his head as if to reject Osborn's damning words. He called Judge Gray, who came immediately to listen to a replay of the malodorous tape. The two judges then called Osborn and told him to appear before them the next afternoon in Miller's chambers. They advised him they had received "information of a substantial nature" concerning jury tampering in connection with Hoffa's pending trial, and that Osborn himself was among the suspects.[3] They had some questions for him and he was free to consult with counsel before answering. Realizing that a request for legal representation from a lawyer of his stature might raise doubts about his innocence—and never dreaming the judges' "information" might include a tape of his conversation with Vick—he came to their chamber alone. The judges asked if he knew anything about such jury-tampering efforts; whether he had made any such attempt or talked to anyone else about doing so, and whether he had talked with anyone about influencing a member of the jury panel named Elliott. To all of these questions Osborn answered "No." With that, Judge Miller handed him a previously prepared order directing him to appear at a hearing ten days later to "show cause" why he should not be disbarred from practicing law in the federal district courts of Middle Tennessee.

Osborn scurried back to his office, his heart pounding and his thoughts racing wildly. Frantically, he telephoned Vick's home. Answering his call the ex-policeman's wife told the lawyer she did not know where her husband was or when he might return. Osborn called back every hour until midnight, sounding more desperate with each failed attempt. What Mrs. Vick did not say was that a deputy marshal from Judge Miller's court was in her house for the night, to protect her and the Vick children. Nor did she disclose that her husband had taken a room at a local Holiday Inn accompanied by FBI agents Steele and Sheets.

The next morning Osborn asked Jack Norman, Nashville's preeminent criminal defense lawyer, to go with him to Judge Gray's office. There they learned everything the judge knew about the charge and received from him copies of Vick's affidavit along with the taped conversation between Osborn and the retired policeman. Although shocked at this revelation, the stricken lawyer nevertheless decided to go it alone, hoping to get by with a censure. He sought and received a hearing before Judges Miller and Gray in the latter's chambers in which he admitted that the voice on the tape was his and that it had been correctly transcribed. But the idea to approach prospective juror Elliott, he said, was Vick's and not his; the former policeman, not he, had requested their meeting. Furthermore, he continued, he had doubts about the plan and had not decided whether, in the end, he would allow his hired investigator to carry it out. The judges then brought in FBI agents who described Vick's wiring and their observation of him going to and from the lawyer's office. Osborn asked them no questions and declined the judges' offer to call Vick as a witness. They promised the now-humbled suspect a prompt decision.

Their order, issued the next afternoon, was biting in its criticism. In so many words they called Osborn a liar. He had not been entrapped; he had himself initiated the discussion about buying off Elliott and had led the way throughout. His "brazen attempt to bribe and improperly influence a prospective juror [was]... a callous and shameful disregard of duty, [showing] such a lack of moral fitness and sense of professional ethics" that disbarment from the federal courts was his only appropriate punishment.[4] News of the November 20 disbarment order spread rapidly. The following morning a director of the Nashville Bar Association, the group poised to elect Tommy Osborn its next president, said the city's legal community was in a "profound state of shock."[5]

Certain that a criminal indictment would follow his disbarment, Osborn asked Norman to be his lawyer. As the younger man's longtime friend and mentor, Norman could not resist Osborn's plea and agreed to represent him for no fee. When the indictment came as predicted Hooker and Neal reluctantly accepted Bob Kennedy's mandate that they be the prosecutors at the disgraced lawyer's trial. The stage was now set for high courtroom drama.

****

If Hooker was the David Boies of the Nashville bar, Norman was its Johnnie Cochran. About six feet tall and one year younger than his fellow barrister, Norman was courtly in manner, intimidating in anger, and always in control. His high forehead was topped with curly graying hair; the jowls of his ruddy, rounded face shook in tempo with his animated speech. He had the bulk of an upright bear but was more often described as "leonine," probably because of his commanding voice and magnetic presence that dominated a courtroom. Seigenthaler had seen Norman up close and in action. "No film or portrait can recreate [his] image...before a jury: the jutting jaw ... the compelling voice that would ring like a bell, penetrate leather-lined courtroom doors, echo through corridors or, at his whim, drop to a whisper so that back-bench jurors would lean forward to catch the loop of his logic."[6]

In one respect Norman's involvement in Hoffa's tribulations had come full circle. The Teamster boss had first asked the esteemed defense lawyer to represent him at the Test Fleet trial. Having acted as a special prosecutor in the trials of several Nashville Teamsters, Norman had declined, recommending that Hoffa hire Osborn. Though well aware of

Lawyers Jack Norman (left) and John Hooker awaiting a jury's verdict in an earlier case, 1961. Norman was the defendant's lawyer and Hooker the state's special prosecutor. Courtesy of John Jay Hooker Jr.

the Teamster boss's questionable reputation, Osborn was excited at the thought of representing a nationally known figure. He saw it as "a tremendous professional opportunity, ... the case of a lifetime."[7] At their first meeting Hoffa had stoutly maintained his own innocence. He complained bitterly of Kennedy's arrogant abuse of the attorney general's office to mount a personal vendetta against him. These charges resonated with Osborn's populist sympathies, his empathy for the working man, and his belief that every individual, no matter how powerful, was the underdog in a fight with big government. He had soon heard enough and eagerly agreed to become a member of Hoffa's defense team.

Unlike Saul on the road to Damascus or Bernadette at Lourdes, Osborn had experienced no epiphany. His eventual conversion to Hoffa's cause stemmed from the accumulated experiences of a lifetime. With the instincts of a self-made, church-going Kentucky farm boy, he had gradually come to believe Hoffa was not a criminal but a victim. In Osborn's view, big government and the business establishment had combined to punish a labor leader who was too aggressively outspoken for membership in their club, and whose rise to power threatened their dominance. Hoffa's charisma and Osborn's ambition united in a volatile mix. The people's lawyer and the hard-driving Teamster boss became blood brothers.

As Osborn saw things, evidence in the public record justified his view. Kennedy was using men of his own stripe to carry out his personal feud with Hoffa. Chief investigator Walter Sheridan was Osborn's case in point. Soft-spoken but hard as tempered steel, Sheridan, in Osborn's view, was guilty of using wiretaps and other illegal devices in his pursuit of evidence, and of trampling on the rights of those he questioned. Neal "was the toughest and most ambitious ... lawyer" of the Get Hoffa unit, "a little powerhouse with a big mind, a permanently puffed chest, and a robust self-esteem to match." With Seigenthaler as its new managing editor, "the *Tennessean* ... was clearly in bed with the Kennedys, and its offices were being used to interview prosecution witnesses. ..." The FBI had tapped Osborn's home telephone, or so he assumed, and "as far as he could see, the fix was in all over town."[8]

This mindset and Osborn's expression of it were reminiscent of his famous client. On first learning that Judges Miller and Gray had disbarred Osborn, the Teamster boss's hair-trigger temper sparked a fiery outburst. The judges' decision was a "travesty on justice." They had conspired to "set up and entrap" Osborn, in order "to take away from me a competent lawyer to represent me in this [jury-tampering] case."[9] This was classic Hoffa; he was the sun around whom everyone else revolved.

Aware that Judges Miller, Gray and Wilson would have irreconcilable conflicts if assigned to preside at Osborn's trial, judicial overseers on the US Sixth Circuit Court of Appeals gave the job to Judge Marion Speed Boyd of the federal district court of West Tennessee. The case would be heard in Nashville, Osborn's hometown. Known to lawyers as "Speedy" Boyd—more for the dispatch with which cases moved through his court than his middle name—the Memphis jurist ran a tight ship. His cases started at the appointed hour and went beyond regular closing times when necessary to keep his trial schedule current. Overly argumentative lawyers were brought up short. Rulings on motions and objections came firmly and quickly. Known for fairness and impartiality, Judge Boyd rarely fraternized with his peers, publicly or privately. These traits, as well as his lack of ties to the Nashville establishment, made him an ideal choice to try the case against Osborn in the latter's hometown.

Osborn's trial began in Nashville on May 25, 1964. After Walter Sheridan and FBI agents laid the necessary groundwork, Hooker called for the government's chief witness to take the stand. Robert Vick was the epitome of the vulnerable, disreputable and undependable witness on whom prosecutors often had to rely to prove a criminal defendant's guilt. The kindest thing that could be said about Vick was that he did not inspire trust. He was stooped and slightly built, with a face resembling six miles of hard road. His gaze was shifty, his statements halting. His body language was a panoply of inner conflict. As a retired policeman he lived hand-to-mouth, supplementing a small pension with odd jobs for lawyers and private investigators. But he was also the informer who had secretly recorded Osborn, and the prosecutors could not put the audio tape into evidence without his testimony.

On direct examination by Hooker, Vick was fairly straightforward. He had first gone to Osborn in 1962 in an effort to supplement his earnings as a Nashville policeman. The lawyer had taken him on as a part-time assistant to get background information on prospective jurors in the Test Fleet case. Osborn had hired him to do the same job in connection with Hoffa's jury-tampering case. Vick also confirmed the circumstances in which he had recorded his conversation with Osborn. The tape of their meeting then went into evidence and was played in the courtroom for all to hear.

On cross-examination Norman decimated Vick's character and credibility. Throwing the witness's own past statements back into his face, Osborn's lawyer exposed the ex-policeman as a conniving schemer willing to contradict himself and otherwise change his story as necessary to further his own interests—all with an utter disregard for the truth. The nervous informer squirmed uncomfortably in his seat, acknowledging he had met several times with FBI agents who had turned over written reports of their meetings to Hoffa's defense team. Norman had also acquired audio tapes of several recent conversations among Vick and three Teamster agents, secretly recorded at Osborn's request. Didn't you tell these Teamsters, Norman asked, "that you had a letter in your pocket from Attorney General Kennedy" promising to educate your three children if "you would stay with them in this investigation?" "I don't recall it," said Vick, "but if I did, it wasn't true."[10] "And didn't you remark to one of these men that the FBI had promised to guarantee your local government pension if you went to work for Osborn?" "No," said the witness, "but if I did [say that] I was joking."[11] "Did you ever make anybody a price for your testimony under oath in this court?" "I may have," said Vick lamely. "I don't recall."[12] Knowing he now had the witness on the run, Norman bored deeper. After reminding Vick that he had sought, in writing, the FBI's "protect[ion] from prosecution in return for furnishing information," the defense lawyer scathingly demanded, "Did you tell the government that?" "Yes, sir," said Vick. "Did you mean it?" Norman roared. "Well," said the flustered witness, "I don't know if I meant it or not."[13]

The next morning Osborn took the stand in his own defense. "A tall, grand-looking man with sandy hair [and] an easy manner," he made a good witness.[14] At ease in the courtroom, he often spoke directly to the jury, occasionally removing his glasses and rubbing his brow in concentration, then gesturing as he gave a well-phrased answer. When asked by Norman about his meeting with Vick, Osborn said the ex-policeman mentioned that he had a second cousin on the jury panel, who he could "talk to ... if you want me to." "I told him," the defendant continued, that "he had been in trouble enough and to leave it alone."[15] He said that Vick, undeterred by that earlier brush-off, returned to Osborn's office unbidden, wearing the hidden tape recorder. His visitor's intent, he said, was to entrap him into joining Vick's venal scheme to persuade prospective juror Elliot to vote for Hoffa's acquittal.

The jury listened carefully to the personable witness's forthright responses to his own lawyer's questions. Osborn had clearly impressed them favorably. On Hooker's cross-examination of the younger lawyer he trod softly and asked only a few questions. A personal attack on Osborn would have backfired; the prosecution's case, he knew, now rested on the jury's reaction to the taped recording of Osborn's voice.

After several witnesses testified to Osborn's good character, the defense rested. On the prosecution's rebuttal, Judges Miller and Gray told the jury how Osborn had lied to them, and with that the evidentiary phase of the trial ended. At this point the prosecution's hopes were muted. The taped conversation between Osborn and Vick was incriminating, but it also supported the image of Vick created by Norman's cutting cross-examination: he was a man who would sell his soul to the highest bidder, a petty crook who had enticed an honest if somewhat overeager Osborn to do things the successful lawyer would never have considered on his own. Both sides felt that the closing arguments, set to begin the following day, would decide the trial's final outcome.

Neal made the first of the prosecution's final arguments, accurately summarizing all of the evidence heard by the jury in a light favorable to the government's case. Vick was not on trial, and "your decision" should be based not on the ex-patrolman's testimony, but on Osborn's own words on the hidden tape. "Take [the written version of] it into the jury room with you and read it. This is what convicts Mr. Osborn, sad as it is, and not Vick."[16] He then curtly dismissed Osborn's claim of being led or goaded into misconduct by the former policeman. That's "like saying a jackass led a fox into a trap."[17] And he reminded the jurors that the defendant had admitted sliding into an unholy alliance with his charismatic client. "I [went] gradually from [being a] lawyer for Hoffa," Osborn had testified, "to a point where I had respect for him, and then friendship for him, and then identification with him."[18] That confession, said Neal, was a clear sign of Osborn's guilt.

Norman's turn came next. Putting his heart and soul into this last chance to sway the jury he spoke for almost two hours. To establish a rapport with his listeners he began softly, mixing self-confidence with an air of genuine humility. He told how he had referred Hoffa to Osborn in the first place, and the deep regret he felt for having done so. "But for this act," he said, sadly shaking his leonine head, "none of us would be in court today." Turning his attention to Vick and warming to his subject, Norman exuded disgust, the gray curls of his hair shaking with indignation, his eyes flashing with anger. His forehead and upper lip were beaded with sweat, his face flushed. With a voice ranging from a whisper to a barely suppressed roar, he destroyed Vick's character and artfully planted the idea of Osborn's entrapment by the government as the only reasonable explanation for his client's questionable conduct. When he ended, the issue of reasonable doubt was almost tangible, covering the hushed courtroom like a pall as the old lion walked slowly back to his seat at the counsel table.

All eyes were now on Hooker, his burden made heavier by the power of Norman's appeal. He rose and moved slowly toward the front of the jury box, his head bowed, his eyes fixed on the floor. As was his wont, he rubbed his chin, collecting his thoughts, determined to choose just the right words to break the spell cast by his adversary. Then, lifting his head and assuming his most benign countenance, he slowly swept the jury with his gaze, silently reestablishing the bond he had developed with them during the trial. He spoke sincerely to them of his agonizing pain at having to prosecute his friend and colleague. "Ladies and gentlemen of the jury, this is the saddest, darkest day of my career. But there was a dark, dark day before this, ... the day that Tom Osborn got mixed up with James R. Hoffa ... and his trail of jury fixing. And how poisonous... this thing has been. How many lives has it crushed? Isn't it a tragic thing that the defendant Osborn didn't heed the warning?"[19]

Hooker then became the indignant prosecutor, on the attack and in full voice.

> "I am not surprised that my distinguished friend, one of the greatest trial lawyers the South has ever produced... never mentioned a single, solitary word that Tom Osborn had said on that tape. And I am asking: don't you convict him on the testimony of Vick, [who] might as well have been a mechanical man....I'm asking you to convict the defendant, if you find him guilty beyond a reasonable doubt, *on his own voice.*"[20]

Dropping to one knee in front of the jury he added, "I hope you won't regard me as irreverent when I say... that I have gotten down on my knees at night like this and asked God that justice, and only justice, be done in this case."[21]

Having kept the jurors alert and focused on his theory of the case, Hooker then reviewed the transcript of Osborn's hearing before Judges Miller and Gray when he first appeared before them, in chambers, on suspicion of jury tampering. Quoting at length from the judges' questions and Osborn's answers, he left no doubt that the lawyer's lies were intended to mislead and deceive his official interrogators. He emphasized Osborn's admission that his taped conversation with Vick was "in sum and substance ... correct."[22] Hooker's final point seemed to strike a chord in the jurors' hearts. If Osborn "had just come forward and said, 'Yes, Judges, I was misguided. ... I wanted to win this case so bad, I made a mistake. Please forgive me. ...' [But] I didn't hear him say he was sorry in this trial, really...."[23]

Judge Boyd assigned the case to the jury about 7:30 in the early evening of May 29, the trial's fifth day. For those who had followed the proceedings it was hard to predict where they might come down. The courtroom's prevailing sentiment was that the jury would find the defendant not guilty. "Osborn thought he was about to be acquitted, as did everyone else who had witnessed Norman's devastating assault on Vick and the government's case. Entrapment was the only possible explanation for Tommy Osborn's aberrant behavior."[24] Osborn's friends were upbeat and encouraging. Hooker and Neal were subdued, knowing the jury had listened with apparent sympathy for the attractive defendant. Sheridan glumly awaited the verdict and at one point, reflecting the power of Norman's summation, the normally unflappable investigator said to Seigenthaler: "We've lost this case."[25]

At 10:30 p.m., three hours after giving the case to the jury, Judge Boyd was ready to call it a night. As he moved to leave his chambers a marshal appeared with surprising news: the jury had reached a verdict. No one had anticipated such a quick decision, and at this late hour only the judge and his courtroom officers, along with lawyers for both sides and Osborn's diehard friends, were in court when the jury foreman rose to announce the verdict. On the charge of attempting to influence a jury panelist, he said, "We find the defendant Z.T. Osborn guilty." Gasps of surprise and disbelief arose from the Osborn camp as the defendant and his lawyer listened to the verdict in stoic silence. Norman declined the judge's offer to have the jury members individually polled and Boyd dismissed them with profound thanks. Several weeks later, after denying the defense's motion for a mistrial, he sentenced Osborn to three and a half years in prison.

The shame of a felony conviction had a deeply corrosive effect on this self-made son of an itinerant minister. He put on his best face with friends and former colleagues, most of whom empathized with his claim that Vick had maliciously enticed him to commit a crime he would not otherwise have considered. But he would not be consoled, and on the denial of his appeal in the fall of 1966 he went to prison feeling depressed and alone. Several months later Maclin Davis, Osborn's law partner, learned that Vick, ever the loose cannon, had told a friend that Walter Sheridan had promised him money and a job for entrapping Osborn. Based on that discovery, Davis asked Judge Boyd to vacate the imprisoned lawyer's sentence. Sheridan forcefully denied Vick's charge. When Boyd refused to grant Osborn a new trial, Davis vowed to take the case all the way to the nation's highest court.

As the appeal wound its way forward, Osborn received an early release from prison after serving two and a half years of his sentence. Now permanently disbarred from practicing law in Tennessee he struggled to re-enter society as a real estate salesman. He held a slender hope that the Supreme Court, still considering whether to hear his appeal, would grant him the relief he so desperately wanted. In January of 1970 came the black news that it would not, a shattering blow to Osborn's already frail emotional state. On the afternoon of February 2, 1970, his wife came home, noting her husband's car in the driveway and expecting him to be there. Finding the house empty and fearing the worst for her increasingly despondent husband, she reported his absence to the police and called Mac Davis. "Davis arrived just in time to see a young ashen-faced policeman step out of the garage. Tommy Osborn had put a .38-caliber police revolver beneath his chin and fired. He was fifty years old."[26]

Shock waves from Osborn's suicide raced across Nashville. No one felt worse about his death than John Hooker, Osborn's co-prosecutor, who immediately sought consolation and companionship with his son John Jay, and with Hal Hardin, a young lawyer friend. Late that evening, as Hardin and Hooker shared a diminishing bottle of Jack Daniel's sour-mash in the elder lawyer's study, the phone rang and Hooker answered it.

"Well, I hope you're satisfied now, you sonofabitch," said the caller, and hung up.[27] Hooker's sadness lessened over time but stayed with him until he died in his sleep ten months later.

****

The guilty verdict in the Osborn case was the fourth time a jury had found the Teamster boss and one or more of his associates guilty of attempting to influence the votes of prospective or seated jurors. In light of these consistent findings in multiple cases, most lingering skeptics were persuaded that Hoffa was guilty as charged and that Bob Kennedy's campaign to put him in prison was a fight for justice, not retribution. Over the next weeks and months, however, as Hoffa and his convicted associates pursued their appeals, the Teamsters' public relations team pressed hard to refurbish their leader's tarnished image. Their efforts were surprisingly successful: the media kept Hoffa's name in the public eye, and a dozen or so US senators and congressmen, sensitive to the labor icon's resilient political power, continued to speak out on his behalf. And as always, Hoffa continued to be his own best advocate.

CHAPTER 9

"Like Jesus Christ on the Cross"

Outwardly unfettered after posting bail in Chattanooga, Hoffa was actually on the government's invisible leash. Unless his lawyers could find a legal flaw in the conduct of his jury-tampering trial he was headed for prison. Their job was to pursue his appeal all the way to the US Supreme Court and he could do little to help them. Rather, he would devote his time and energy to Teamster business, focusing on his reelection as the IBT's president at its next general convention two years away. If he could avoid incarceration until then—meanwhile negotiating contracts and otherwise promoting the rank and file's interests—opponents would be hard pressed to unseat him. He also made plans for avoiding a worst-case scenario. He would choose a trusted associate to join him on the convention ticket as his anointed successor, someone who would keep the presidential seat warm if and when he went to jail. Upon his release, the regent caretaker would return the scepter to him and he would again take the throne. Or so he saw the future.

Seven years of the Teamster presidency had addicted Hoffa to the power of his office. It was he who had stimulated and shepherded the Teamsters' exponential growth. It was he who had put money in the Teamsters' pockets and pride in their hearts. He alone had earned and retained the membership's overwhelming support. Now, amid swirling troubles and darkening skies, he stayed hopeful as he developed a strategy for staying in office. As a self-reliant pragmatist he felt no need for spiritual guidance, and it was just as well. Had he prayed for heaven's help, God would have laughed.

Well aware that he was his own best advocate, Hoffa also knew that only a professional public relations campaign could refurbish his tarnished image. To lead this effort he turned to the IBT's Vice-President Harold J. Gibbons, his executive assistant. Gibbons's point man would be Sidney Zagri, the international union's chief lobbyist and top tactician. For the foreseeable future, "Saving Jimmy" would be their full-time job.

The three men got together at the IBT's spacious offices on the boss's first day back in Washington. Out of their meeting came a clear strategy. Hoffa would concentrate on shoring up support for himself and his administration among local union leaders and their members. Gibbons would intensify his speaking schedule before gatherings of high-level officials from government, business and the media. Supplementing his public appearances would be private sessions with small groups and one-on-one meetings with key individuals— all arranged by Zagri. The PR chief himself would aggressively lobby Capitol Hill with personal contacts, letters and telephone calls. He would stimulate grass-root letter-writing campaigns to national and state office holders, and urge local union groups to come to Washington and make their case personally to their senators and representatives.

The Gibbons-Zagri public relations campaign featured two closely coordinated tactics. Defensively, it would portray the IBT boss as an innocent victim. It would also promote the steady growth of union members' earnings under Hoffa's leadership, and his lifelong concern for their welfare. Offensively it would attack the principal source of Hoffa's troubles: the unceasing efforts of Attorney General Robert Kennedy and his DOJ minions to railroad an innocent man into prison. The campaign's additional targets were the mass media, most of which were subservient supporters, in Hoffa's eyes, of Kennedy's vendetta. The IBT message's bottom line: this abuse of power by government and the media—the country's two most formidable institutions—not only wronged Hoffa, it threatened the individual rights of every American citizen.

****

Harold Gibbons, still the Teamster boss's number two man, was the linchpin of the International Brotherhood's administrative office. Like Hoffa, Gibbons was a child of limited formal education but blessed with innate leadership skills and energy to spare. Like many other labor activists who came of age in the depths of the Great Depression, he was a Socialist. Though his views mellowed in later years, his commitment to workers' welfare was deep and permanent. His first job was in adult education, teaching English to Chicago's burgeoning immigrant population. Seeking higher wages for himself and his colleagues he formed a union of fellow instructors. With a head for business and a capacity to inspire his peers, Gibbons gradually gained recognition as a rising star within the labor movement during the depressed economy of the 1930s. In 1941 he accepted a call to become the director of a group of CIO unions in Saint Louis. Six years later he led those unions into an independent organization which in 1949 he merged into Teamster Local 688. Within three years he became Local 688's president and ultimately the recognized leader of the combined Teamster unions in the greater Saint Louis area. He retained those positions throughout his time at the IBT with Hoffa.

In his early years in Saint Louis Gibbons fostered numerous strikes, often joining picketers in their marches and sit-down protests. On these occasions encounters with the police were commonplace, and usually ended with a rough ride to jail in a paddy wagon. I went on "more than a hundred trips from the picket lines to the shithouse," he told one interviewer years later.[1] He also fought against attempted inroads by organized crime. In 1953 a group of Saint Louis racketeers known as the Workman Gang threatened a takeover of Local 688. Aware of Hoffa's reputed underworld connections and his success in heading off similar challenges, Gibbons sought the help of his powerful Detroit counterpart. Alert to opportunities for gaining the allegiance of Teamster leaders in other cities, Hoffa came willingly to the aid of his brother unionist. Arguing against compromise he warned Gibbons—ironically and prophetically—that if he put gangsters on his payroll, organized crime bosses would soon take over. His advice, in classic Hoffa-ese, was "to get yourself a pistol, and the first son of a bitch who walks in the door, you shoot him in the head."[2] Hoffa also furnished his Saint Louis colleague with personal bodyguards and joined him in meetings to rally the support of union members. These tactics succeeded and Gibbons retained his power. Over the years, however, the social-minded unionist hired Barney Baker and other thugs as union "organizers," clear evidence that Gibbons's reign had its dark side.

Under his leadership the combined Teamster operation in Saint Louis became a model of labor reform, providing benefits to its members on an unprecedented scale. Workers received health care under a comprehensive plan paid for by employers and bought food at cost from a union-operated grocery store. They spent leisure hours at a recreation complex featuring indoor and outdoor swimming pools, tennis courts, a gymnasium and a golf course, all built with union funds. In the early 1950s, before *Brown v. Board of Education*, Gibbons led his members in a campaign to desegregate Saint Louis's public schools. Well before the civil rights movement went nationwide his Teamsters picketed whites-only theaters and joined with blacks at restaurant sit-ins. All the while his union grew and prospered along with the power and reputation of its progressive leader.

Later in the 1950s Gibbons was elected a vice-president of the Central States Conference, an IBT organization headed by his future boss. Soon after Hoffa assumed the IBT presidency in 1957 he brought Gibbons to Washington as his right-hand man. The two men worked well together despite their differences in philosophy and style. Hoffa was Mr. Outside, more at home in the field, mingling with his troops and negotiating with employers. Gibbons was the IBT's inside man, heading a large managerial staff of his own choosing and comfortable in his dealings with Washington's hierarchy of politicians, bureaucrats and national media representatives.

In their personal lives the two men were polar opposites. Hoffa dressed simply in bus driver gray suits and white socks, at least until Josephine, irritated by media critics of her husband's drab outfits, forced him to spruce up his wardrobe. Severely self-disciplined in his habits he scorned rich food, tobacco, alcohol and extra-marital sex. He lifted weights in his office building's new gymnasium, worked late and went to bed early. Despite his socialist orientations, Gibbons, on the other hand, was an overt hedonist. Suave and articulate, he led a sybaritic life of fine wine, gourmet food and sexual liaisons with a variety of women. He was a heavy smoker and a fashionable dresser. On the road he traveled first class and stayed in first-class hotels. In Washington he favored the haunts of power-lunchers. Dinners were at the city's best restaurants, often with a female companion. His expense accounts for these perks were notoriously large but also fully disclosed, and no one ever accused Gibbons of stealing a dollar or accepting a payoff.

Despite their differences—though it took the straight-laced Hoffa a while to accept his lieutenant's philandering—the members of this odd couple were inseparable. Having wives who chose to stay at home with children in Detroit and Saint Louis, respectively, they shared a luxurious two-bedroom suite at Washington's upscale Woodner Hotel. Each valued the other's skills and their different contributions to the IBT's success. An effective administrator, Gibbons built a talented staff dedicated to the labor movement and to the Teamsters as its most dynamic segment. He approached problems as a result-oriented pragmatist. He spoke the language of everyone he dealt with, from rank and file workers to business leaders and government officials. As one newspaper reporter wrote, Gibbons "uses four-letter words to convey four-syllable ideas."[3] He also excelled at improving the Teamsters' image in the minds of influential outsiders, from the lecture halls of Ivy-League universities to the private dining rooms of Washington's Metropolitan Club, then the city's most exclusive male bastion.

Gibbons and Hoffa shared mutual respect as self-made men of humble origins. Each esteemed the other's courage and grit. In their early years in Saint Louis after one difficult bargaining session with employers Hoffa said admiringly, "Gibbons, there are some men in Detroit who dislike me—but those fellows back there actually hate you."[4] Each gave something of immense value to the other. The stoical Teamster boss offered the class-conscious Gibbons a unique opportunity to live the high life he craved. Through Gibbons, Hoffa escaped the daily grind of managing what was rapidly becoming the nation's largest labor union. Theirs was a truly symbiotic relationship.

Sid Zagri, Hoffa's chief publicist, was a Gibbons protégé. As a young man Zagri spent two years at Harvard Law until the Depression forced him into the workplace to earn enough money to complete his education. Within two years he reentered school at the University of Wisconsin where he earned a law degree in the late 1930s. Attracted to the labor movement, he went to work for Gibbons in Saint Louis and accompanied his boss to Washington in 1958 when the latter answered Hoffa's call. Euphemistically named vice-president for community relations, Zagri became the IBT's chief lobbyist and public relations specialist. Like his leader, the legally trained promoter thought big. Soon after joining the IBT staff Zagri came up with the idea for a political action program named DRIVE, an acronym for Democratic, Republican, Independent Voter Education. Through this vehicle, Zagri suggested, each of the Teamsters' 1.5 million members should be asked to make voluntary contributions of fifty cents per month, a potential of $9 million annually. Though Hoffa thought of him as one of Gibbons's eggheads, the industrious lawyer soon gained the Teamster boss's confidence. A husky six-footer weighing two hundred twenty pounds, Zagri mirrored Hoffa's swagger and pugnacious personality.

In 1959, as the US Congress debated a new labor reform bill, Zagri led the IBT's offensive against it. He prepared a set of extensive changes to the legislation—"fifty-nine pages of bill-gutting amendments," according to *Time* magazine.[5] At the same time he persuaded Gibbons to host a series of breakfasts at Washington's Congressional Hotel for all 435 members of the US House of Representatives, twenty to twenty-five at a time. Others to be invited at the IBT's expense included union leaders from the home districts of each Congressional attendee. It would be a costly and time-consuming project, a scheduling nightmare. But Zagri pulled it off as more than 250 legislators enjoyed a free breakfast over the course of several months. Most of these invitees were unmoved but a significant number promised support for the proposals put forward by Gibbons and his energetic lobbyist.

Overall, Zagri's in-your-face style got mixed reviews and results. To get the support of Teamster and other local union leaders he yelled at them "like a crusader on a trailer-truck parking lot."[6] "Get a delegation down here tomorrow morning," he ordered a New Jersey Steelworker, "and tear [your Congressman's] door down." Such urgings brought union activists to Washington in impressive numbers but Zagri's aggressiveness alienated many others. House Speaker Sam Rayburn, responding to the claim that he supported the lobbyist's proposed amendments, said it's a "damn lie." Reacting to similar pressure by the Teamster flack, Representative Edith Green of Oregon fumed, "He can go to hell."[7] Those were harsh words, rarely uttered publicly by politicians in that more mannered era, and in the end Zagri's contentious style reminded many legislators of the tactics often attributed to Hoffa. Some of these legislators, previously on the fence but now repelled by the Teamsters' point man, found the courage to vote "aye" on the labor reform bill.

Congressman Frank Thompson Jr. of New Jersey, a friend of labor but not of the Teamster boss, was among those blistered—in his case, literally—by Zagri. Inspired by the PR chief's condemnation of Thompson as labor's enemy, some overzealous unionists made so many threatening calls to the New Jersey politician he reported them to the FBI. One or two of these callers, perhaps remembering the Victor Riesel incident, decided to teach the New Jersey representative a lesson. Driving to his office on a hot August morning Thompson stopped at a traffic light with his front windows open. Almost immediately a Ford pickup truck pulled up beside him on his left. A man in the truck's passenger seat leaned out the window and with a large syringe squirted a stream of liquid at the startled congressman. "Only bad aim saved Frank Thompson from serious injury. The liquid was sulfuric acid, and the little that did hit Thompson burned a hole through his shirt and raised a blister on his arm."[7]

The legislation Zagri so vehemently opposed was passed by the Congress and signed into law by President Eisenhower. Known as the Landrum-Griffin Act, it had real teeth. For the first time unions were required to adopt and publish written constitutions and bylaws. Detailed financial reports had to be filed annually and made available for public inspection. Employers had to disclose payments to their employees for union-related activities. Union elections were henceforth to be held by secret ballot. Secondary boycotts were severely restricted and willful violations of the law were made criminal.

Given labor's power at the ballot box, Bob Kennedy believed the McClellan Committee's exposure of widespread corruption and Mob influence within the Teamsters and other unions might not have been enough, alone, to force the passage of this tough new labor law. In his view it was Hoffa's continued hold on the IBT presidency that pushed the legislators over the top. Jimmy Hoffa "was the symbol in the minds of the members of Congress of what needed to be corrected," said Kennedy.[8]

By the late summer and fall of 1962, Kennedy's Department of Justice had tightened the circle of investigations and pending cases surrounding the Teamster boss. These included the Test Fleet trial in Nashville and the pending Sun Valley trust-fund case in Orlando. By then, Zagri had developed a clique of senators and representatives he could count on for support. At his bidding they went into action. In an August speech on the Senate floor Homer Capehart, an Indiana Republican, called for a formal investigation of alleged collusion between the DOJ and federal judges in Florida to postpone Hoffa's trial on the Sun Valley charges. In September of 1962 eleven members of the House of Representatives delivered anti-Kennedy orations based on the same grounds. Days later Republicans Hiram Fong, a senator from Hawaii, and Congressman Glenn Cunningham of Nebraska, joined the pro-Hoffa chorus. The prepared remarks of these fourteen legislators had a common base, many of them including phrases, sentences and even an occasional paragraph copied from material supplied by Zagri. As noted by labor columnist John Herling, Zagri stood in the wings as "the ghostly master of ceremonies" at these pro-Hoffa performances on the floors of the House and Senate.[9]

These concerted congressional calls for an in-depth investigation of the DOJ were based on a relatively minor charge: that government lawyers were dragging their feet in the prosecution of the Teamster boss's criminal trial in Orlando. Zagri claimed this was prejudicial "forum shopping," an effort to try Hoffa first in Nashville, a more Kennedy-friendly venue. Whatever the merits of this complaint, it hardly justified a congressional uproar. It was like a call for war against Nicaragua for its failure to give the US ambassador a timely welcome in Managua. Zagri's only purpose was to demonstrate the Teamsters' political clout at high levels, giving a foretaste of the lobbying campaign that would grow more intense as Hoffa's troubles worsened.

****

Grady Partin's incriminating testimony during Hoffa's 1964 jury-tampering trial alerted Teamster stalwarts to the depth of their difficulties. While his lawyers hurled objections at Judge Wilson and cried foul to the media, William Bufalino put in an emergency call to Sid Zagri from IBT's Chattanooga headquarters in the Patten Hotel. To paraphrase his basic message: they're killing us down here. Bob Kennedy's lawyers sent a traitorous Louisiana liar into our midst as their secret agent. The FBI is tapping our phones, bugging our hotel rooms, following our every move with hidden cameras and electronic listening devices. So put out the word to our Washington supporters. Demand their help in stopping Kennedy's malicious persecution of their best friend in the labor movement.

Zagri told Bufalino he was already on the move. The first evidence of his renewed zeal, sparked during the first days of Hoffa's jury-tampering trial, was a series of letters first disclosed to the press by Chuckie O'Brien several days after the conclusion of Partin's testimony. Letters, O'Brien said, had been sent to Senator James Eastland of Mississippi and Representative Emanuel Celler of New York, chairmen of the Judiciary Committees in their respective houses of a Democrat-controlled Congress. The letters charged illegal surveillance of Hoffa and his Teamster associates on a massive scale by Kennedy's FBI. Proof came soon of Zagri's effectiveness. Senators Everett Dirksen of Illinois, Ernest Gruening of Alaska, Olin Johnson of South Carolina, Herman Talmadge of Georgia, and Hugh Scott of Pennsylvania—three Democrats and two Republicans—all expressed outrage at these allegations of clandestine snooping. Chairman Celler received similar complaints from Representatives Arch Moore of West Virginia, a Republican, and Claude Pepper of Florida, a Democrat. These congressional complaints were perfect examples of un-researched, shoot-from-the-hip outbursts—irresponsible but in many ways typical.

This latest demonstration of Zagri's muscle produced immediate results. In mid-April, six weeks after Hoffa's conviction, Chairman Celler's office announced that a special subcommittee of the House

Judiciary Committee would hold hearings on Zagri's charges of illegal wiretapping and electronic surveillance of Hoffa and his colleagues by the FBI during the Chattanooga trial. This political posturing resonated strongly with Fred J. Cook of *The Nation*, a nationally circulated and self-styled "progressive journal of opinion" published weekly since 1865. Studs Terkel called Cook "the finest investigative reporter in the land."[10] Ralph Nader also chimed in: I am "doubtful there has ever been a better, more dauntless and more unsung investigative reporter."[11] Cook's article, entitled "The First Full Account of a Fateful Trial" appeared in the April 27, 1964 issue of *The Nation*. Covering twenty-four pages it contained almost 25,000 words.

Cook had listened to Zagri's version of the Hoffa story and swallowed it whole: in its willful persecution of the Teamster boss, the government had employed "espionage and [illegal] surveillance" in a sinister "vendetta" to Get Hoffa.[12] Claiming the Hoffa camp had recently acquired and used similar resources to conduct "counter-espionage and surveillance," Cook said the world could now see, for the first time, that Kennedy's DOJ had conducted a form of "jungle warfare violating basic principles of justice."[13] His view echoed the Teamsters' party line that the Hoffa camp was merely fighting fire with fire. Ignored were the FBI's categorical denials of wiretapping or electronically surveilling Hoffa or his lawyers, having tracked only the movements of King, Campbell and others suspected of jury tampering. Leaving unchallenged the fact that the Chattanooga trial had produced nothing to rebut the FBI's disclaimer, Cook fecklessly concluded that only Judge Wilson's consistently "favorable" rulings for the prosecution had kept evidence of such abuses out of the record. But Cook could point to no data, factual or legal, to back up his charge. He simply printed the Hoffa camp's unsupported allegations as fact.

Cook enlarged upon his vendetta theme with the argument that the government was energetically manipulating the media in order to influence the courts. Citing only a *Life* magazine article praising Partin for his courage in testifying against his powerful boss, the biased reporter wrote, "The entire weight of the FBI and the Justice Department seems to have been thrown, not into trials, but into [media] campaigns to insure that the [government's] confidence of guilt would be upheld by the courts."[14] Nothing else in the article supported this sweeping claim of the DOJ's attempted manipulation of the media. Cook then devoted several pages to the proposition that Partin's testimony was inconsistent and, in his layman's view, "inadmissible." "The government's case," he asserted, was "born in the impropriety of planting an informant in Hoffa's suite, [and] founded on the quibble that this impropriety did not taint the charge it produced."[15] Never mind that Hoffa had invited Partin into his inner sanctum, and that the jurors had been free to reject Partin's testimony if, for any reason, they disbelieved it.

Cook was an articulate spokesman for a rich vein of contemporary hostility to big government. His reputation as a skilled investigative reporter lent credence to his words. In 1964 many still feared the United States was moving toward George Orwell's vision of *1984*. To them—and to others who bought into the image of Robert Kennedy as Big Brother using the FBI to punish his political enemies—government wiretapping and electronic "espionage" of any kind were anathema. "Stings" and other secret police operations had not yet come into vogue. Covert surveillance was reluctantly accepted by most people if, as in Hoffa's Chattanooga trial, judges had given their prior approval. But Cook simply overlooked this "technicality" as he might have called it while invoking the ire of the fearful. To him, the FBI's watchfulness and the clandestine use of an agent provocateur, a term he applied to Partin, was "a performance that vitiated basic guarantees of the American system of justice."[16]

Zagri made sure that Cook's lengthy article in *The Nation* got attention. One week later Roland Libonati, a Democratic congressman from Chicago and member of the House Judiciary Committee, went to the House floor to demand a full inquiry into the DOJ's conduct of the Hoffa trial. Exhibit 1 to his remarks was Cook's long article which he put into the *Congressional Record*. Voicing their support of Libonati's call were Representatives Bill Brock of Tennessee and Clarence Brown of Ohio, both Republicans. The *Chattanooga Times*, whose reporters attended every day of the jury-tampering trial, saw things differently. Its editorial page called Cook's piece "the most wildly distorted magazine article we have seen this year, ... the definitive propaganda treatment of the Hoffa side, all the way."[17] Referring to Congressman Libonati's floor speech, the paper also noted that the son-in-law of Chicago Mafia boss Sam Giancana was on Libonati's staff. The relevance of that disclosure required no elaboration.

Zagri saw to it that Cook's contentious article was mailed to every federal judge in the United States. He also sent thousands of copies to the Teamsters' local unions in Chicago for distribution to passers-by at the city's street corners and subway stations. He chose the Windy City because the trial of Hoffa and seven co-defendants for defrauding the Teamsters Pension Fund began there on the same day that the Cook story appeared in *The Nation*. This was the Sun Valley case, originally set for trial in Orlando but later moved to Chicago, the site of the Teamster Pension Fund's home office. Hoffa had been indicted in this case for taking a concealed interest in a Florida land development company, known as Sun Valley, and putting Teamster monies in escrow as collateral for an initial bank loan to the new company. He was also charged with using additional Teamster funds in secret payoffs to get himself out of the deal when his ownership became suspect. The other six defendants were alleged to have participated, one way or another, in this scheme.

Bill Bittman, an assistant US Attorney in the DOJ's Chicago office, was called to take over the government's case only two weeks into the Sun Valley trial when Abe Poretz, the prosecution's chief lawyer, became ill. The facts in this case were voluminous, requiring intense study by the new counsel. Bittman rose to the occasion and the trial went on for another two and a half months. At the end, attorneys for both sides prepared a series of detailed charts to support their final arguments to the jury. Foolishly hoping that their number and complexity would hide his tactic, defense lawyer Charles Bellows decided to doctor his presentation, thus matching his client's fraud with his own. Bittman alertly sensed that the evidence actually presented during the trial did not support the data on his opponent's charts, or the conclusions Bellows drew from them. The DOJ lawyer went through the trial record that night and found it contained none of the exhibits cited by the defense.

Confronted with this fact the next day in open court Bellows stated that the missing documentation was being flown to Chicago that morning. His lame excuse infuriated Judge Richard Austin, who instructed the jury to disregard the tainted charts and the arguments made from them. Though not decisive, the defense lawyer's attempted deceit no doubt helped the jury find Hoffa guilty on four counts and the six other defendants on two to nine counts each. In mid-August Judge Austin sentenced Hoffa to five years in prison, to be added to his existing eight-year term for jury tampering.

Although these convictions did not make Zagri's whitewashing job any easier, some die-hard Republicans and anti-Kennedy Democrats, like programmed robots, cited Zagri's claims of government abuse as a basis for renewing their charges of misconduct by RFK's Justice Department. A faction of the House Judiciary Committee, led by Democrat Libonati and Republican William C. McCulloch of Ohio, voted twenty to thirteen to hold a hearing on whether the DOJ "had infringed upon the constitutional rights of any individual."[18] The Committee's announcement of this decision did not mention the Teamster boss's name but it was covered with Zagri's fingerprints. Chairman Celler, who voted not to hold a hearing, made that clear. "This all grows out of the Hoffa agitation," he said. "The resolution does not mention names, but this undoubtedly will be called the Hoffa resolution." In Celler's view the bipartisan vote to investigate the DOJ was the unjustified act of an "unholy coalition."[19]

That evening, NBC's *Huntley-Brinkley Report*, television's most popular news program, commented on the House Committee's action. David Brinkley, rarely if ever afraid to risk political brickbats, spoke softly but with withering effect in his trademarked sardonic style:

> Today, surprisingly, the House Judiciary Committee voted to do what the Teamster lobbyist asked them to do—investigate the Justice Department. Chairman Celler ... opposed it but was outvoted, mainly by Republicans and southern Democrats, some of whom have old scores they would like to settle with the Justice Department.... One member, Mathias of Maryland, asked [that] they not investigate any case now before the courts.... But the Republican and Democratic zeal for Hoffa's civil rights was so great they voted him down.
>
> Now there will be a lot of pious mouthing about civil rights, but the spectacle here is that a committee of congress is dancing to Jimmy Hoffa's tune, investigating criminal cases now in the courts—a kind of political help that convicted criminals are usually not able to command."[20]

Like the Energizer Bunny, Zagri went far and wide to advance his missionary cause. In August of 1964 he kept the Hoffa story alive at both the Democratic and Republican National Conventions. Responding to his plea, the Republican Platform Committee approved a plank calling for an investigation of the Justice Department. About the same time Zagri struck pay dirt in the halls of academia. Law professors Daniel M. Berman of American University and Philip Kurland of the University of Chicago wrote letters to Chairman Celler supporting Hoffa's cause. Both were highly respected in their fields, particularly Kurland, whose 1996 obituary referred to him as "the pre-eminent constitutional scholar of his generation." These letters were a prime example of academic outrage replacing scholarly investigation.

In late August Bob Kennedy announced he was leaving the office of attorney general to seek election as the Democratic nominee in the upcoming race for the US senate seat held by Republican Kenneth Keating of New York. Heading the Democratic ticket in the November election would be Lyndon Johnson for president and his running mate Hubert Humphrey for vice-president. Seeing a new market for his venomous propaganda Zagri created a bogus political committee called "Democrats for Keating-Johnson-Humphrey." Under cover of that non-existent group he sent half a million pamphlets into New York State. Distributed by Teamster locals, these flimsy sheets painted Kennedy as anti-labor, anti-Semitic and even anti-Italian. An equal number of Committee fliers went to Harlem only, attacking RFK's civil rights record though in fact he and Burke Marshall, the DOJ's assistant attorney general for civil rights, had done more than any other federal government officials up to that time to promote the civil rights of blacks and to protect the lives of freedom fighters and their supporters.

Zagri's efforts on behalf of Senator Keating were ineffectual. New York voters—especially its metropolitan Democrats—are flattered to have nationally known figures ask for their votes, even those like Bob Kennedy, who established state residency less than three months before election day. Not surprisingly the Democrats chose the Massachusetts newcomer as their Senatorial candidate who then went on to win a substantial victory in November. From Hoffa's point of view, however, Kennedy's return to Washington in late 1964 was the least of the Teamster boss's problems. The weight of two felony convictions bore heavily on his shoulders. There was growing unrest among the fourteen members of the IBT's executive board over their leader's precarious position. One of them, though only one, was willing to say publicly what was on the minds of many. John B. Backhus of Philadelphia, a long-standing Hoffa opponent, complained that the Teamster boss had "done too much damage to the union's reputation" and should be replaced.[21] The "damage" Backhus had in mind included the courtroom convictions of IBT members during Kennedy's three and a half years as attorney general. During that period, Hoffa and 125 of his Teamster officials and associates had been found guilty of federal crimes.[22]

As his own appeal dragged through the courts Hoffa grew increasingly frustrated. Adding to his discomfort, Edward Williams, the Teamsters' longstanding general counsel, ruled that the IBT boss could no longer use union funds to pay his personal lawyers. In late October, 1965, with one eye on that problem and the other on the next year's general convention, Zagri staged a gala event in New York City to honor his boss and fatten Hoffa's depleted pocketbook. Held at the City's newest "world-class hotel and convention complex," the Americana Hotel on Seventh Avenue, it was a blowout. Sixteen hundred paid guests enjoyed a sumptuous dinner featuring slabs of roast beef, salmon filets, and baked Alaska for dessert. Speakers were listed in a program whose cover proclaimed the honoree's name in gold letters. A thirteen-piece orchestra provided musical interludes. At Hoffa's entrance, with the band playing "Hey, Look Me Over," the crowd rose and cheered wildly. Smiling and waiving his way to the head table, the guest of honor acknowledged their acclaim. Momentarily at least he could forget his mounting troubles.

The October salute to Hoffa raised $150,000, something over $1 million in current dollars. Throughout the evening Hoffa basked in photographers' flashbulbs and the beaming smiles of enthusiastic well-wishers. Waves of goodwill flooded toward him from a boisterous crowd obviously getting their money's worth. The evening's speakers knew their audience and how to bring them to their feet. Reflecting the Teamster boss's oft-repeated complaint, dinner chairman Thomas E. Flynn passionately denounced Hoffa's prosecutors as persecutors. "He's been crucified. His troubles are nothing but a vendetta from top to bottom." Cecil B. Moore, president of Philadelphia's NAACP chapter, painted the picture even more graphically in what had to be the evening's topper. "He's just about like Jesus Christ who died on the cross. Bobby Kennedy was on one side [and] some ... Teamster ... informers on the other." John J. O'Rourke, the event's New York host, presented Hoffa with a check representing the ticket proceeds. The honoree could use the money as he wished, said O'Rourke, "perhaps as a gift to some charitable institution."[23] But Hoffa knew where charity began. Accepting the crowd's praise with gratitude he took the money with relief.

Delighted with the dinner's success Zagri made plans for similar occasions in several other cities. These events would strengthen Hoffa's support among union members and help to pay the team of lawyers now pursuing his appeals. But such efforts could not completely contain the fallout from his two criminal convictions. Employers fought Teamster attempts to organize their companies by reminding their employees that the IBT boss had been sentenced to thirteen years in jail. "Do you want to put your faith in people like this?" they asked.[24] And a few brave Teamster officials let it be known they might seek the union's presidency if Hoffa became "unavailable." One of those who went public was Einar Mohn, an IBT vice-president and perennial favorite son among his Teamster brethren on the West Coast. Harold Gibbons, whose rank as the IBT's first vice-president made him its "acting president" if the office became vacant, did not try to dissuade supporters who talked up his possible candidacy.

While Hoffa publicly took the high road in his effort to stay out of prison he plotted secretly with his supporters in the shadows. Their target was Robert Vick, their goal a recantation of the ex-policeman's harmful testimony in the trial of Tommy Osborn. Teamster lawyers had filed a second motion for a new trial in Hoffa's jury-tampering case on the ground that Vick was a paid government agent while working for Osborn during the latter's preparations for the Chattanooga trial and had disclosed the defense team's strategy to the prosecution. Osborn's conviction, they argued, deprived Hoffa of his constitutional right to the services of the lawyer of his choice.

Don Vestal, a Nashville Teamster who had hired Vick to work with him in organizing a plant's workforce, went to Hoffa in 1965 seeking financial support for his attempt to increase Local 327's membership.

The IBT boss responded that money was available if "the little guy in Nashville," a/k/a Vick, would help Hoffa get a new trial. For such assistance Vestal could promise "the little fellow" $20,000.[25] When his money-raising effort failed, Vestal turned to George Broda, the Nashville business agent who had partnered with Ewing King in an attempt to influence a juror in the Test Fleet case. Broda, after talking with "Detroit," told Vestal that if he could persuade Vick to change his testimony, "You can write your own ticket."[26]

Teamster agents kept up the pressure. In addition to the $20,000 bonus, Hoffa's Executive Assistant James Harding, through an intermediary, offered to find a job for Vick outside the United States with an income of $18,000 per year. Still, the elusive ex-policeman was non-committal. About a month after Hoffa's testimonial dinner in New York, Red Vaughn, a former business agent for the Nashville's Local 327, asked Vick just how much money it would take for him to assist in the boss's effort to stay out of jail. When Vick told him to get lost, Vaughn's face darkened into a threatening scowl. "Some cold night," he said, "they [may] drag your body out of the river."[27]

In early 1966, as murmurs of internal Teamster dissent grew louder, a decision of the United States Supreme Court reinvigorated Hoffa's faltering campaign. On January 31 of that year, to the surprise of lawyers on both sides, the Justices announced they would review his jury-tampering conviction, now almost two years old. Taking an unusual tack they agreed to address only one issue: whether Grady Partin's testimony should have been stricken for having been obtained through a violation of the defendant's constitutional rights. For Hoffa the ordering of a new trial on that basis would be a decisive victory. Without Partin's eyewitness statements that the Teamster boss had knowingly controlled and encouraged his underlings' attempts to influence Test Fleet jurors, the government's charges against him would crumble.

The Supreme Court's timing was also in Hoffa's favor. He would remain a free man until the high court ruled, which would not happen until the court's fall term, well after the IBT convention scheduled to begin in Miami on July 4. For the next five months the PR team led by Gibbons and Zagri went forward in high gear, as did Hoffa himself. His real strength came from the union's rank and file. While some IBT directors were ambivalent—particularly those two or three who might succeed him—the union's members had never wavered in their loyalty and were solidly behind him. Knowing how to get their blood up the Teamster boss spoke defiantly to worker gatherings at every available opportunity. To rousing cheers of "Go get 'em, Jimmy!" and "We're with you all the way!" he vowed to fight to the end, to "continue the struggle … no matter how bad it becomes."[28] He sailed into the Miami convention that summer on the crest of their support.

Echoing Hoffa's testimonial dinner orators, podium speakers at the IBT's 1966 convention alternated between bombast and locker room exhortation. The Teamster boss was the most important American since George Washington, said one. John English, the IBT's feisty secretary-treasurer, then brought the delegates roaring to their feet. Jimmy "says he's not guilty … I say he's not guilty, and the executive board says he's not guilty. Come what may, we don't care! The hell with everybody!"[29] Joining the throng of well-wishers were two Democratic US senators, Zagri's way of bringing a touch of class to the circus-like atmosphere. In his waggish but persuasive style Eugene McCarthy of Minnesota pointedly criticized one of Hoffa's pet bugbears, the media. The press, said McCarthy, must "give as much protection as it can to those who are accused," clearly implying their failure to do so in Hoffa's case. Edward Long of Missouri, one of the Teamster boss's most reliable political supporters, got up-close and personal. While looking directly at a beaming Hoffa, Long said, "You delight your friends and amaze your enemies. Keep on fighting them, Jimmy!"[30]

Thus energized, convention delegates raised Hoffa's annual salary by 33 percent to $100,000. They increased members' dues by 20 percent to six dollars per month. Ignoring their general counsel's warning they authorized the use of IBT funds to pay Hoffa's personal lawyers in criminal cases, including past-due fees of more than $1.2 million. They also gave Hoffa unprecedented power to establish procedures for negotiating nationwide and area-wide contracts, and to submit employers' offers to local unions when their own officials chose not to do so. And as the cherry on top of Hoffa's rich chocolate sundae, they confirmed his choice of Frank E. Fitzsimmons for the newly created office of general vice-president. Fitzsimmons was the longtime vice-president of

Detroit Local 299 and a member of the IBT board since 1961. Under the new bylaw he would automatically become the union's president should the office become vacant. A true Hoffa sycophant, at least up to that time, Fitzsimmons was widely viewed as a dim bulb, his boss's handyman and gofer. Had he run for the presidency in an open race against Gibbons or Mohn he would have lost. But what Hoffa wanted Hoffa got—in this case, someone he believed would merely dust the furniture in the displaced president's office and follow the instructions of his former boss, even if they came from a prison cell. Perhaps it was this assumption that would have amused God most.

In early October of 1966 the United States Court of Appeals for the Sixth Circuit upheld the convictions of Hoffa and the other defendants for trust-fund fraud in the Sun Valley case. But this was a distant cloud compared to the imminent Supreme Court hearing on the IBT boss's appeal from his guilty verdict in Chattanooga. Two justices had recused themselves from the case: Byron "Whizzer" White because he had been JFK's legal counsel and Bob Kennedy's deputy attorney general, and Abe Fortas, who in private practice had represented dissident Teamster members in a suit against the IBT. Joseph A. Fanelli, the Teamster Bar Association lawyer chosen to represent Hoffa, appeared before the remaining seven members of the high court. Though his argument offered no new legal theory it had a powerful emotional appeal. Particularly intriguing was the government's failure to act on the kidnapping and other criminal charges brought against Partin four years earlier. This failure to prosecute, said Fanelli, was clearly a quid pro quo for the testimony of the alleged spy sent secretly by the DOJ into Hoffa's camp during the Test Fleet trial. This made Partin's entry into Hoffa's headquarters an unreasonable search of his client's private space in violation of the Constitution's Fourth Amendment. Further, disclosure of Hoffa's self-incriminatory statements, along with Partin's access to confidential discussions between the Teamster boss and his lawyers, violated the due process requirements of the Fifth Amendment. These infringements, Fanelli protested, made a mockery of justice itself. The American Civil Liberties Union filed an *amicus* brief taking Hoffa's side against Big Brother government. Partin's presence was an illegal "search" of Hoffa's premises, argued the ACLU, in part because the informer had "conceal[ed]…his role as a government spy and… pass[ed] himself off as a loyal friend."[31]

Presenting the government's case were Fred M. Vinson, the recently appointed assistant attorney general of the DOJ's Criminal Division, and "instant law" Nathan Lewin, Hoffa's gadfly in his Tennessee trials. They reemphasized the reasons why the judgments of the lower courts should be affirmed. In sum they argued that Partin may have decided to come to Nashville on his own, but Hoffa had invited him into his inner sanctum. Sheridan and FBI agents had told Partin to report any evidence of jury tampering and nothing else, orders which he had strictly obeyed. Whatever may have motivated Partin to play this role, the government had made no plea bargains with him, and no promises of monetary compensation. Judge Wilson had properly let the jury decide what weight, if any, to give to Partin's testimony. Vinson's points made a good case both legally and factually. But this was the Warren Court, known for assiduously protecting individual rights from arbitrary infringements by big government. Evaluating their chances, Vinson and Lewin were not yet ready to break out the champagne and cigars.

There was considerable speculation among informed lawyers that the Supreme Court would overturn Hoffa's conviction. As a Washington pundit had once observed, the justices also read the newspapers. They were well aware of the charges in the media and in Congress of electronic snooping by Bob Kennedy's Get Hoffa Squad. In this they shared, to one degree or another, the public's concern with the growing power of "big brother" government and its use of newfangled gadgets to secretly invade private sanctuaries. Moreover, in two recent cases, the court had ruled that the government's use of an informer violated a suspect's right to speak with counsel in confidence. Citing these cases, a former federal prosecutor and criminal procedure expert wrote in the *Atlantic Monthly*, "With the Supreme Court passing on the means used to catch Hoffa, the identity of the enemy within is less clear. … When the appeal is discussed in legal circles, the usual question is not whether Hoffa will win, but how he will win."[32] If these lawyers were correct, the court would effectively be saying that the more powerful "enemy within" was the government itself.

The court surprised these speculators. On December 12, only two months after hearing arguments, the justices issued a 6–1 decision upholding Hoffa's jury-tampering conviction and jail sentence. Joined by Justices Hugo L. Black, William J. Brennan and John M. Harlan II, Justice Potter Stewart wrote the court's opinion. One by one, Stewart struck down lawyer Fanelli's arguments. "Partin ... was not a surreptitious eavesdropper.[33] He was [with Hoffa] by invitation. ... The Fourth Amendment [has never been held to] protect a wrongdoer's misplaced belief that a person to whom he voluntarily confides his wrongdoing will not reveal it."[34] Regarding the Fifth Amendment's protection against self-incrimination the court said that Hoffa's "incriminating statements were [not] the product of any sort of coercion, legal or factual." Made in Partin's presence, they "were wholly voluntary."[35] Nor was Partin's mere presence in the Teamsters' camp a violation of Hoffa's Sixth Amendment right to consult confidentially with his counsel. Even if the informer had overheard lawyer-client conversations about the defense's strategy in the Test Fleet case, he could still testify to Hoffa's statements about the entirely different matter of attempting to fix the jury. And none of the IBT boss's incriminating words were uttered "in the presence [or] ... the hearing of [Hoffa's] counsel."[36]

Justice Tom C. Clark, joined by William O. Douglas, reached the same conclusion by a different route. They relied on the court's long-standing rule that it should not review findings of fact by two courts below in the absence of a very obvious and exceptional showing of error. Both Judge Wilson and the federal appellate court found that Hoffa had "knowingly and voluntarily" brought Partin into the Teamster's inner sanctum and there was no reason to question these findings.

Hoffa's lawyer, Fanelli, had also made a final overarching claim. The "totality" of the government's conduct, he argued, "offend[ed] ... [the] canons of decency and fairness" that form the basis of American justice. Accordingly, that conduct had violated Hoffa's right to the Fifth Amendment's requirement that the government afford him "due process of law." Not so, said Stewart. In his words, this claim boiled down to "a general attack upon the use of a government informer as 'a shabby thing in any case.'" As such, that claim was "without historical foundation. ... Courts have countenanced the use of informers from time immemorial. ... [It] is usually necessary to rely upon them ... because the criminals will almost certainly proceed covertly ... Partin ... may have had motives to lie. But it does not follow that his testimony was untrue, nor ... that [it] was constitutionally inadmissible. The established safeguards of [our] legal system leave the veracity of a witness to be tested by cross-examination, and [his] credibility to be determined by a properly instructed jury.... The Constitution does not require us to upset the jury's verdict" in this case.[37]

Chief Justice Earl Warren was alone in accepting Fanelli's point as the basis of a dissent. Warren's opinion, at least by today's standards, sounded more like legal advocacy than thoughtful constitutional analysis. As "a jailbird languishing in a Louisiana jail under indictments for ... embezzlement, kidnapping, and manslaughter," Partin was strongly motivated "to work his way out of ... his various legal entanglements."[38] He "surreptitiously ... tape record[ed]" his telephone conversations with Hoffa about meeting in Nashville. Then, "worming his way into Hoffa's hotel suite ... Partin became the equivalent of a bugging device which moved with Hoffa wherever he went."[39] For the services of their informer, Warren continued, the government made "devious and secret support payments to his wife, [along with] ... inferred ... promises not to pursue the indictments" against him. In light of this background, the court did not need to decide whether the government had violated Hoffa's rights. "[T]he nature of the official practices evidenced here is offensive to the fair administration of justice." The court's duty to supervise the conduct of federal court trials required it to "see that the waters of justice are not polluted ... by the testimony of [such] an unsavory informer."[40]

To buttress his opinion Chief Justice Warren then argued hypothetically: "If a criminal defendant insinuated his informer into the prosecution's camp in this manner he would be guilty of obstructing justice."[41] This flawed analogy reflected the angst of a strongly result-oriented reformer. The government's use of an informer to discover crime is markedly different from a criminal's use of an agent to thwart justice by secretly listening to the prosecution's plans, some of which might never be used. Without the use of paid government informers acting under false pretenses there would be no sting operations. No detectives disguised as "ragmen" could silently case neighborhoods with high crime rates or arrest burglars they then caught in the act. And, as Justice Stewart noted, although the statements of a paid government agent may be sullied by the informer's criminal record and contemptible lifestyle—or by a plea bargain made with the prosecution—the duty to evaluate a witness's testimony falls to the jury, not to the courts.

This decision was a heavy blow to Hoffa's cause. Adding to its impact was another opinion, issued by the Supreme Court on the same day, upholding Tommy Osborn's conviction for jury tampering. The justices easily found that the government had acted lawfully in sending an informer into the Nashville lawyer's office with a hidden tape recorder. It was justified, the court said, by the need to test and verify the statements in Vick's earlier affidavit. As a result of this ruling the Teamster boss could no longer claim that by prosecuting Osborn the government had deprived Hoffa of his counsel of choice in the Chattanooga trial. His lawyers filed petitions for reconsideration in both cases but Hoffa came to believe it was no longer a question of whether but when he would go to prison.

William Bufalino, the Teamster boss's loyal counselor, was undaunted. Through a newly created "Friends Of Hoffa Committee" he offered $100,000 to anyone who could show that the government had illegally wiretapped or electronically eavesdropped on Hoffa or his agents. William Loeb, the *Manchester Union-Leader*'s publisher, added to that offer, dollar-for-dollar. This $200,000 pool of new money soon roiled with hungry fish. Benjamin "Bud" Nichols, a self-styled electronics expert from Knoxville, Tennessee, swore that Walter Sheridan had paid him to bug the telephones in the Read House Hotel rooms of the trial's sequestered jurors—an obvious lie as the jurors' rooms had no telephones. Other bottom feeders included Messrs. Frazier, Paden and Cole, Nicholas Tweel's friends from West Virginia, who claimed Sheridan had let them listen to tapes of government wiretaps of Hoffa's telephone conversations. Hazel Fulton, the secretary who had testified against her employer Tweel, swore that Sheridan had played audio tapes, in her presence, of discussions among Hoffa and his lawyers. Of course, neither set of these alleged recordings was produced. A Detroit policeman stated he had tapped lawyer Bufalino's phone on the order of an IRS intelligence agent, a charge the agent denied under oath. A Washington, D.C. promoter and friend of Hoffa alleged that John Hooker once told him that unspecified government lawyers had tapped the Teamster boss's telephone.

Hoffa's lawyers put these charges into twenty-one affidavits which they filed with the Supreme Court as attachments to a Motion for Relief. Their hope was that these claims would bring other justices to Warren's view that the government had strayed beyond the bounds of due process. In response, the US Solicitor General—a position then held by Thurgood Marshall, whom President Johnson would appoint to the court later that year—reported that a thorough search by the Department of Justice had found no evidence of illegal wiretapping or electronic surveillance in connection with the Hoffa jury-tampering case. His report added, incidentally, that Bud Nichols, one of the more vociferous affiants, was the proud owner of a new Cadillac convertible.

Hoffa's public relations campaign picked up speed in February of 1967. Early that month four US senators—Bob Bartlett and Ernest Gruening of Alaska, along with Mark Hatfield and Wayne Morse of Oregon—called for an "in-depth investigation into bugging and wiretapping by the government."[42] Senator Edward Long of Missouri, Hoffa's most ardent senatorial supporter, praised the Teamster boss's leadership to a cheering crowd in Detroit. These protestations were again the handiwork of PR maven Sid Zagri who, with Bufalino, was still on the job. Days later came surprising news that Zagri had died in a penthouse restaurant fire in Montgomery, Alabama. William Loeb, ham-fisted as ever, immediately sent a telegram to Lurleen Wallace, the recent successor to her husband George Wallace as the governor of Alabama. "... [I]t seems incredible to me that a fire should have soared so quickly without artificial stimulation. ... I suggest very careful consideration of this aspect of the tragedy." In a follow-up press release Loeb reemphasized his sick theme. "Only about two weeks ago Zagri cautioned me against revealing the names of certain individuals who were attempting to help Hoffa. ... Don't forget, our opponents will stop at nothing, including murder."[43]

On February 20 another Fred Cook polemic appeared in *The Nation,* entitled *Taps, Bugs, and Spies—Anything to Get Hoffa.* The outraged reporter first praised Chief Justice Warren's "vigorous dissent." Ignoring Walter Sheridan's sworn statement to the contrary, Cook then stated as fact the claim of Bud Nichols, the wiretapping "expert" from Knoxville, that Nichols and Sheridan had bugged "all the phones" in the jurors' hotel rooms during Hoffa's Chattanooga trial, phones which later proved to be nonexistent. On that faulty premise Cook concluded that "Hoffa's telephone lines and hotel suite must [also] have been thoroughly tapped and bugged."[44] He conceded that Nichols's accusations might be suspect in light of the reward offered for such assertions. He also acknowledged the Knoxville wire-tapper's unsavory record of having served jail time for forgery, and of having been sentenced to six months of hard labor during his first army hitch and charged with desertion during his second. But Nichols was worthy of belief, said Cook, because his statements were corroborated by *"four public officers"* (Cook's emphasis).[45] Three of these "officers" were none other than Frazier, Paden and Cole, the surveillance specialists from Huntington, West Virginia, whom Nicholas Tweel had brought to Nashville during the Test Fleet case. Cook did not clearly identify the fourth "officer," and saw no irony in accepting the claim that the West Virginia threesome were Tweel's "business associates" who had come to Nashville only to discuss matters of insurance.

The Nation's biased reporter also naively assumed that Allen Dorfman, the Mob-affiliated insurance executive from Chicago, had holed up with Hoffa in Nashville for several days during the Test Fleet trial solely for legitimate business reasons. The circumstances of the Chicagoan's death years later perhaps gave Cook second thoughts. In 1982 Dorfman was convicted and sentenced to prison for attempting to bribe US Senator Howard Cannon of Nevada. In January of 1983, days before his scheduled incarceration, Dorfman was murdered in a gangland shooting in the parking lot of a suburban Chicago restaurant. Word on the street was that mobsters feared that their victim, in order to gain early release from jail, would reveal new details of the Mob's ownership interests in Las Vegas casinos. Taking no chances, their hit-men ended Dorfman's career with extreme prejudice.

In his February article Cook tried to avoid criticizing the iconic Thurgood Marshall for the latter's report exonerating Kennedy's Justice Department from Hoffa's charges of illegal surveillance. The writer's adroit tap-dancing on this point could not hide his condescension. "It is not necessary to interpret the evidence detailed above as casting doubt on Mr. Marshall's word," he wrote. "More likely, he is one of many Americans who have not yet grasped the extreme sophistication with which certain government agencies cut the corners of veracity."[46] For Walter Sheridan, vilified in Cook's article as a perjurer and felonious wiretapper, this slap in the face stung too sharply to be ignored. Ordinarily soft-spoken and unflappable, RFK's chief investigator reciprocated in kind. "In fact," he wrote, "it was Mr. Cook who was again participating in the ... truly sophisticated prostitution of veracity in which Hoffa's agents and apologists had been engaged for some time. The filing of blatantly false affidavits in courts—now even in the Supreme Court of the United States—and the peddling of lies in the Congress and in the press to influence the courts, was almost incredible in its arrogance. That was the real sophistication."[47]

On February 27 the Supreme Court denied Hoffa's motion for relief, saying it was properly a motion for a new trial for Judge Wilson to consider. The only open question now was the date the union leader would enter prison, a matter also in the hands of the Nashville trial judge.

As the Supreme Court was writing "finis" to Hoffa's appeal, Frank Chavez, the IBT's Puerto Rican chieftain, left San Juan for Washington in order to pay his boss a final visit. Chavez was by anyone's definition a thug. He was also one of Hoffa's strongest Teamster supporters, a loyalty he displayed in many ways. He had come to Nashville in 1962 during the Test Fleet case as evidence of his support. In early 1964—perhaps stimulated by the start of the Chattanooga trial, which he also attended—he wrote a heartless letter to Robert Kennedy, who was still in deep mourning for his assassinated brother. "Sir," Chavez began, " ... The undersigned is going to solicit from the membership of our union that each one donate whatever they can afford to maintain, clean, beautify and supply with flowers the grave of Lee Harvey Oswald. You can rest assured contributions will be unanimous."[48] Consistently in and out of trouble, Chavez was tried in Puerto Rico in 1965 for obstruction of justice. In that case his attorneys were Mob lawyer Frank Ragano and the ubiquitous Jacques Schiffer. True to form, Schiffer so alienated the presiding federal court judge that he was evicted from the courtroom. "If I ever see you on this island again," the judge warned mockingly but to the point, "I'll have you arrested for practicing law without a license."[49]

In early 1967 the realization that Hoffa was headed to prison pushed the vengeful Chavez to the brink of derangement. He came to Washington intent on killing Bob Kennedy, now a US senator and in Chavez's view the sole author of the Teamster boss's destruction. Carrying a pistol and accompanied by two armed bodyguards he went to the IBT's offices to meet with his leader. On hearing the Puerto Rican's plan Hoffa reacted with the same spontaneous energy and physical courage that had carried him through many similar situations. "Give me that goddamn gun," he demanded. "The last thing we need is another investigation."[50]

In the face of this forceful reaction the would-be terminator backed down and reluctantly returned to his island home. Not long thereafter, in the heat of an argument, one of Chavez's bodyguards shot and killed him. Hearing the news while in prison, Hoffa reacted in character. As he had cursed Gibbons for lowering the flag after JFK's assassination, he now empathized with the man who revered the former president's murderer. Through messengers, he ordered his successor at IBT head-quarters to send "a key aide to ... Puerto Rico [to] take care of the Chavez family."[51]

In Nashville on March 6, 1967, Judge Wilson denied Hoffa's motion to delay the date of his imprisonment. He ordered the Teamster president—the office Hoffa still occupied—to report to the US Marshals' office in Washington at 9:00 a.m. the next day for transportation to the federal penitentiary in Lewisburg, Pennsylvania. Having no further issue with which to challenge the judge's deadline, the Teamster Bar Association was finally silent.

CHAPTER 10

"Booked, Fingerprinted, Showered and Deloused"

March 6, 1967, the Teamster boss's last day of freedom, started peacefully enough. Son Jim Hoffa and daughter Barbara Crancer had flown to Washington the preceding afternoon to spend the night with their parents in Dad's hotel suite. The next morning, as the ailing Josephine lay sleeping, Hoffa and his children shared an early breakfast with Barbara acting as their short-order cook. The IBT president then went off to work as if it were just another day. Hoping to wind up his affairs in time, he planned to join them all for dinner. When he called that afternoon to say he would have to work late they were disappointed but not surprised.

Hoffa found the IBT headquarters in turmoil. Staff members sought last-minute instructions for tying up loose ends. Well-wishers hoping for a final handshake mingled in the building's anterooms and hallways. Lawyers and their secretaries worked on a series of legal documents requiring the boss's approval. Telephones jangled with calls from supporters, some of whom wanted to block the roads leading to his prison site, wherever it might be. Days earlier he had spoken to an angry group of Detroit Teamsters planning a city-wide strike to protest his jail sentence. Don't do it, he had told them. "Stay on the job. That's the best way you can help me."[1] To the calls now coming into his office, he repeated himself more forcefully. "No strike! No strike!" he yelled. "Don't fuck up my chances of getting out soon!"[2]

Last-minute wrangles continued into the evening with sandwiches and soft drinks brought in for dinner. Lawyer Morris Shenker and five associates were still working on papers for filing in one or another of Hoffa's ongoing legal battles. Their boss insisted on reading drafts of every page, challenging the wording, rearranging the arguments and discarding some points altogether. At 2:00 a.m., finally satisfied, Hoffa was astounded to learn that the exhausted secretaries had been sent home. With no one to type his corrections, and some of the documents requiring his signature, their filing would be delayed indefinitely by his imminent incarceration. He stormed around the room, cursing his hapless lawyers and finally hurling a heavy chair across the conference room table into the opposite wall with a resounding crash. When he finally got back to his apartment his family had not waited up.

Minutes before 9:00 a.m. the next morning, Chuckie O'Brien's car pulled up in front of the federal courthouse at 333 Constitution Avenue N.W., the official home of US Marshals in the District of Columbia. Beside the driver sat Hoffa. He had wisely chosen to say good-bye to his family in the privacy of his apartment before Chuckie picked him up. A horde of reporters awaited them, tipped off to the time and place of the Teamster boss's surrender by someone from the marshals' office or perhaps from the union's PR team. This would be his final public appearance before entering prison, his last chance to make headlines. As he emerged from O'Brien's car, bare-headed but wearing a raincoat against a drizzling rain, a wave of media representatives surged toward him, microphones aloft, cameras clicking away. Ignoring their shouted questions a grim-faced Hoffa pushed his way to the courthouse entrance and then turned to confront his interrogators.

His demeanor that morning was the calm after the preceding day's storm. Containing himself in the face of imminent confinement the convicted labor leader transformed what might have been a verbal brawl into a farewell address. True to form he castigated the political establishment and the national media for bringing him to the lowest point of his long career. "This is a very unhappy day in my life. . . . The government has wire-tapped, room-bugged, surveilled and done everything unconstitutional it could do."[3] Then, looking upward and addressing union members directly, he continued, "None of the courts, none of the legislators, understand your problems … only you, who work for a living … understand that. It's not just Hoffa they are doing this to. If they can do this to Hoffa they can do this to any citizen. I urge everyone to beware of the constitutional rights they are losing. That is all I have to say, gentlemen."[4] With that, he turned and entered the building.

Morris Shenker and an associate lawyer awaited their client inside the courthouse that morning. When Hoffa came in they escorted him to the office of Chief Marshal Luke Moore. Shenker got permission to put in a call to Chattanooga's Judge Wilson, who was considering the defense team's last ditch request, filed days earlier, to postpone their client's imprisonment on the ground that urgent Teamster negotiations needed his personal participation. When the lawyer had difficulty making a connection, Hoffa impatiently yanked the handset away from him. As he did so the phone's bottom piece dropped downward, dangling from its connecting wires. "You must have been bugged lately," he said to Marshal Moore, "because it looks like somebody forgot and left a screw loose."[5] But no one laughed at Hoffa's attempt to lighten the atmosphere and the call was postponed.

The prisoner's black mood returned when marshals led him in handcuffs to the midnight blue car that would take him to jail. Inside they put a chain around his waist and clamped his legs into metal rings firmly anchored in the vehicle's floor. "As if, for Christ's sake, I was John Dillinger or somebody … I don't know where the hell they thought I was gonna run to."[6] As the marshals' car got under way their new prisoner used his raincoat to hide the shame of his shackles.

A few lingering reporters stood watching as Hoffa's auto pulled out of the federal building's garage. Among them was Clark Mollenhoff, bureau chief of the *Des Moines Register's* D.C. office, the first investigative reporter to spark the interest of Bob Kennedy and the McClellan Committee in wholesale Teamster corruption. More than any other member of the fourth estate Mollenhoff symbolized to Hoffa the media's biased hostility and the role it had played in his downfall. A large man with a penetrating glare and the perpetual smirk of a born skeptic, Mollenhoff could have doubled for Raymond

Burr in the role of Perry Mason. As their eyes met, the sight of his old adversary waving farewell was too much for Hoffa. Already chagrined and now infuriated, he reacted instinctively in the only way his chains would permit. Tightly constrained between two marshals the prisoner spat contemptuously at the object of his hate. The marshal on his right could only wipe the spittle off the vehicle's closed side window as Mollenhoff's startled image faded in the distance.[7]

Three more carloads of marshals joined Hoffa's entourage. In mid-afternoon the caravan arrived at the gates of the federal prison in Lewisburg, Pennsylvania, where the convicted felon was to begin serving his eight-year sentence for jury tampering. To avoid the ignominy of being handcuffed and hustled into a government vehicle under armed guard, Hoffa could have bypassed the marshals and gone directly to Lewisburg. But he chose not to, probably in the forlorn hope that Judge Wilson would grant a last-minute extension of his reporting deadline.

Upon his arrival, like all new inmates, he was "booked, fingerprinted, stripped [and] run through a delousing shower."[8] The only concession to Hoffa's celebrity status was that he was processed alone. In prison garb he spent his first twenty-four hours of incarceration in an isolated cell. The next day he was moved to permanent quarters, a 7½- by 10-foot single cell furnished with a chair, narrow bed, toilet and small locker. Metal bars separated the cell from a prison corridor leading to a courtyard, whose windows provided the new inmate's only sense of the outside world. The difference between the Teamster boss's luxurious apartment and his Taj Mahal office space in Washington and this austere, depressingly small confinement area could not have been greater.

Lewisburg was a medium security prison whose inmates ate at small tables and had access to televison, weekend movies, library books, schoolroom classes, craft shops, baseball, volleyball and other means of exercise. Cells were wired to receive radio broadcasts via furnished headsets. Each prisoner worked at an assigned task—such as re-stuffing mattresses, the job given to Hoffa—for about two dollars per day. Prison guards were unarmed. Supervised small groups of inmates with good records were allowed into town to work on projects of civic worth. The visitors lounge was a brightly decorated area where prisoners could meet with family members at open tables. The price paid for this privilege was a thorough search of each prisoner after his visit, including all body cavities, to prevent the smuggling of incoming drugs.

Like most prisons Lewisburg was a forbidding monolith of cold gray stone. It was a place where "your guts were tested," where "it takes three months to get over the feeling that the world has ended. It was overcrowded with "lifers, ... gunmen, forgers, burglars and safecrackers."[9] Inmates with money could buy heroin, marijuana, amphetamines and barbiturates on the prison's black market. In those early days of anti-anxiety drugs, guards were authorized to hand out tranquilizers like popcorn. Rapes were commonplace but there was nothing fellow inmates could do about it. "So you just sit there or lay on your bunk," said Hoffa, and "pretty soon the screams are over." And "you'd sure as hell better have a knife to protect yourself, [particularly] if you're between twenty-one and thirty. Everybody has a knife because where there's metal there's a weapon. You have a metal bunk, you have a knife."[10]

Of lesser consequence, but grinding in its daily annoyance, was the prison's repulsive and sometimes inedible food. Perfectly good meat and produce arrived at Lewisburg's loading area but much of it mysteriously disappeared. What remained was fouled by ex-guards turned cooks who could barely slice bread. Hoffa claimed to have single-handedly improved the dining room menu as a result of the respectful relationship he had established with Noah Aldrich, the institution's warden. One day—after several of his complaints to Aldrich's office had gone unanswered—he refused to eat the grayish slop ladled into his bowl. It was bubbling, he would write, not from heat but from swarming maggots. Arms folded, he told the guard to send for the warden, saying that he and the men in line would eat nothing unless their calls for improved service were answered. His ploy worked. The warden came and told the cooks to serve something else that day, also promising to pay more attention to the quality of the prisoners' meals in the future. The one thing he refused to do, however, was to sample the food himself.

Despite the food's poor quality, the boredom of idle hours and the prison's oppressive atmosphere, Hoffa's physical and psychological health improved greatly in his new surroundings. He had come to Lewisburg with stomach ulcers and a serious but controllable form of diabetes.

Both conditions were due in part to excess weight, inadequate regular exercise and the stress of workaholic hours. On the day of his incarceration prison officials confiscated his diabetes pills and ulcer medications, never to be returned. Medical consultation was not available; prisoners got to see a real doctor only when the guards decided they needed emergency treatment. The prison's daily regimen, however, took over and did wonders for Hoffa. Distasteful food resulted in a much lower caloric intake. Having plenty of spare time he exercised daily. And with growing confidence that his imprisonment did not threaten imminent physical harm, the constant pressure he had so long endured now subsided. He was buoyed by the thought that good behavior would get him paroled well before completion of his full sentence, particularly if his Sun Valley conviction got overturned on appeal. After two months of incarceration he was back in fighting trim.

A natural leader and proven survivor, Hoffa gained other inmates' acceptance by treating them like fellow workers in a local union. He cemented relationships with many fellow inmates, upon their release from prison, by finding jobs for them within the widespread network of Teamster unions and other labor groups whose members remained his steadfast friends. After several months inside the walls he organized an informal committee to assess prisoner complaints and make whatever recommendations they thought proper. In keeping with jailhouse politics his four-man group included a black, a Puerto Rican and a white former army major. Hoffa also gained rapport with the prison's guards, once jokingly offering to organize them after overhearing several complain about their working conditions. Solidifying his successful integration into the Lewisburg way of life was his ability to convince the prison's gang leaders he was no threat to their influence. Trusted by them, he became their spokesman with the warden.

Under Lewisburg's rules inmates were not allowed to make telephone calls. Prisoners could write letters but only to seven people named by them and put on a list. Visitors were limited to lawyers and close family members, with the latter held to three hours per month. Attorney-client conversations were virtually unrestricted as long as they stuck to legal issues—a restriction difficult to monitor and subject to being overlooked by favor-hungry guards. Indeed, by twisting these rules, Hoffa beat the system to a pulp. He added son Jim to his list of attorneys, and had Chuckie O'Brien legally declared his "foster son." Always a reliable gofer, O'Brien also acted as Josephine's chauffeur on her regular monthly visits. Between the two of them, plus one or two trusted counselors, Hoffa could wheel and deal on Teamster matters with assurance that his orders from prison would be confidentially relayed to their intended recipients.

Frank Fitzsimmons, chosen by Hoffa as his temporary replacement, initially played the lap-dog role expected of him. As the IBT's general vice-president and senior manager, Fitz faithfully carried out his ex-boss's instructions. In the autumn of 1967 he led the union's team in negotiations with trucking company executives on a national wage and hour contract, with Hoffa calling the tactical shots from his cell. The loyal surrogate also took orders from Lewisburg on the "awarding of Central States Pension Fund Loans and other major matters."[11] And in the cavernous D.C. office of the Teamster president—a title Hoffa had not relinquished—the name plate on the former occupant's desk along with his collection of family photographs and mementos was left undisturbed. Also left in place was Hoffa's prized plaque inscribed with the maxim *illegitimi non carborundum* whose words now rang a bit hollow. The bastards might not have ground him down, but they had put him out to pasture.

On the morning of June 5, 1968, word reached Lewisburg that Bob Kennedy was clinging to life in a Los Angeles hospital after being shot in the head the previous evening. Twenty-four hours later came news that Kennedy had lost his fight for survival. Hoffa no doubt expressed himself privately on the death of his arch-enemy, but first revealed his feelings in an authorized biography published posthumously. "I can't honestly say that I felt bad about it. Our vendetta had been too long and too strong. Over the years I'd come to hate him and yet when he got it I felt nothing. But … a hell of a lot of people felt the same way I did about him." He also quoted from a story in Knight Newspapers particularly critical of Kennedy as "the object of … widespread, passionate loathing."[12] Hoffa also cited the words of a highly partisan letter written by an aging Dwight Eisenhower in March, 1968, at the beginning of the presidential primary season, before RFK's assassination. Robert Kennedy was "shallow, vain and untrustworthy," wrote the former president, a "man …

without "a single qualification … for the presidency." With his brashness undiminished by age, Hoffa then concluded: "If you think I pass those [views] along with satisfaction, you're right."[13]

At the time of his nemesis's death, Hoffa had been in prison for a year and three months. During that period Fitzsimmons had assured his IBT colleagues that he was doing everything possible to shorten the time their former leader would spend in prison. Teamster lawyers, he said, were pressing an appeal in the Sun Valley case and still burrowing for evidence that would force Judge Wilson to reconsider Hoffa's jury-tampering conviction. Though he could not publicly elaborate on the latter effort, it involved continuing pressure on Partin to disavow his testimony. Combining threats of serious physical harm with virtually unlimited offers of money, Teamster agents were pursuing Partin as relentlessly as Hoffa claimed Kennedy had gone after him.

In the fall of 1968 Fitzsimmons took a strong stand in favor of Richard Nixon for president. His support produced huge contributions of money to Nixon's campaign and hundreds of thousands of Teamster votes in the Republican candidate's successful election. Soon thereafter Fitz let it be known that John Mitchell, former Wall Street lawyer and Nixon's new attorney general, was an ally in his effort to free Hoffa. "Don't rock the boat," he told IBT officials, "I'm taking care of it with Mitchell."[14] He also said repeatedly that he would not seek the IBT presidency if his mentor were released from prison before the convening of the Teamsters' next national convention in mid–1971, more than two years away.

Hoffa was reelected president of Detroit's Local 299 in December of 1968 while in prison. By early November, 1969, he had served one-third of his eight-year sentence for jury tampering. This made him eligible for parole because his five-year sentence from the Sun Valley case was still on appeal. When his lawyers petitioned the US parole board for his release it was denied without explanation. Though his behavior had been spotless, the board was reluctant to release him until the courts made a final ruling on his pension fraud conviction. With the understanding that he could reapply for parole in March, 1971, the model prisoner's only option was to tough it out until then.

As the ensuing months of Hoffa's imprisonment fell from the calendar, the power and perks available to the Teamsters' top dog gradually took hold of Fitzsimmons. He had a $100,000 annual salary, a private plane, and, like Gibbons, a bottomless expense account. Although his fellow Teamsters never showed him the genuine respect they had given Hoffa, he got their self-serving deference. As a result he began to feel stronger in the performance of a job he had gained primarily as a result of his perceived weakness. Thereby self-deluded, Fitz gradually eased some of Hoffa's friends out of their jobs at the Teamsters' D.C. headquarters, opening the former president's office to a few of his own loyalists. He also gave increased responsibilities to the regional union officials he trusted. As things turned out these steps would lead eventually to internal discord. Local and regional Teamster officials, seeing the general vice-president for the weak leader he was, began to show increasing independence. Either because Fitzsimmons saw the trend toward less top-heavy management as inevitable or genuinely believed that a dispersion of power would strengthen the union in the long run, he made no effort to stop it. This gave Teamster officials outside of Washington further incentive to assert their growing influence. Many of these newly energized underlings were the Mob-connected ruffians Hoffa had brought into the union but kept under control. It was a simmering stew that would eventually come to a full boil.

Until recently, Anthony Provenzano had been the highest-ranking gangster in the Teamster organization. A mafioso from Union City, New Jersey, "Tony Pro" was a captain in the Genovese family. He was actively involved in the management of several family-owned businesses whose employees were Teamster organized. He had joined the union in the mid-fifties, become a staunch Hoffa supporter, and then elected president of Teamster Local 560 and of New Jersey's Joint Council 73. Based on information developed by the McClellan Committee, Eisenhower's DOJ indicted Provenzano in 1959 on charges of extortion. Awaiting trial in 1961, he was elected an IBT vice-president with Hoffa's blessing and the charges against him were dropped. No other union official was more grateful to, or supportive of, the Teamster boss. In recognition of the two men's relationship, Zagri chose Tony Pro as one of the speakers at the plush New York fund-raising dinner honoring Hoffa in 1965. Indicted again for extortion shortly thereafter, and then tried and found guilty, Provenzano received a sentence of seven years. The convicted New Jersey gangster entered the Lewisburg penitentiary ten months ahead of his friend Hoffa.

A shrewd survivor in a dangerous world, Provenzano came to Lewisburg with a reputation as one of the best-connected members among the New York-New Jersey Mafia families. Fleshy but physically powerful, with a gangster's heavy-lidded countenance and a gaze that became coldly cruel at the slightest challenge, Tony Pro radiated a commanding aura. These attributes gained him immediate acceptance into the prison's underground hierarchy, removing him from threats of physical harm and harassment that greeted most new arrivals. He also knew how to work the system to acquire special privileges. He lived in a room with a real bed in an area formerly occupied by prison staff members. Though he ate with other prisoners in Lewisburg's dining area, he wangled a note from the prison's doctor citing his chronic stomach troubles and ordering him to be fed from the staff's menu. Avoiding the swill eaten by other inmates was probably Provenzano's most welcome perk and certainly the clearest evidence of his power to flaunt his special status without fear of retribution by his prison peers.

On Hoffa's arrival at Lewisburg Tony Pro welcomed his friend and mentor with an inmate's equivalence of open arms and a warm embrace. He got the newcomer a seat at his mealtime table, introduced him favorably to the leaders of prison cliques and used his influence to provide Hoffa with protection against peer abuse. When the irrepressible Teamster boss occasionally risked retaliation by calling a black prisoner "a nigger son of a bitch" or yelling "spic bastard" at a Puerto Rican inmate, Provenzano managed to still the waters.[15] In doing so he may literally have saved Hoffa's life.

Hoffa returned the favor some months later when a stomach constriction seriously threatened Provenzano's health. Even as the mobster's weight fell dramatically, prison guards adamantly refused his request for a hospital examination in the town of Lewisburg. Realizing the gravity of his friend's condition, Hoffa blew a gasket. He told the warden that if Tony Pro were not immediately sent for an outside diagnosis he would take the case to the media and order his lawyers to sue the warden and the federal government for inexcusable prisoner abuse. "Within hours Provenzano was transported to a local medical center where he underwent surgery."[16] The operation was a success and the recovering patient knew exactly who had saved him from almost certain death.

Back in good health and quickly reverting to type, the Mafia *caporegime* went to Hoffa for additional help. His problem was that the Landrum-Griffin Act of 1959 prohibited persons found guilty of certain crimes, including extortion, from holding union office for a period of thirteen years from their conviction dates. That provision would keep him out of Teamster officialdom for several years from the date of his release and he would therefore be unable, during those years, to receive pension credits at the level of a union officeholder. What he wanted was for Jimmy to push for an amendment to the IBT bylaws that would enable Provenzano—and other ex-cons who might be similarly affected—to receive pension credits at an officer's level when they returned as non-officer Teamster employees. Hoffa knew what such an effort could cost him in several areas, whether or not successful. In the short run such obvious intervention in Teamster affairs would be frowned on by members of the US parole board when he came before them. Over the longer term, Congress and the Justice Department might well take action to prevent such a transparent effort to evade the law's restrictions.

Tony Pro's request put the jailed Teamster boss between a rock-pile and a granite prison wall. Though anxious to keep the good-will of his long term supporter he could not risk the consequences of granting the mobster's request. Provenzano, with a word to his Mafia soldiers, could make an enemy wish he had never been born. But Hoffa was still the enraged bull who hated a red flag, whoever might be waving it. After a fleeting moment of internal debate he turned Provenzano down flat. Unable to resist a chance to gore the man he still viewed as a Teamster subordinate, he snarled, "It's because of people like you that I got into trouble in the first place."[17] Some bystanders reported that this remark led to an exchange of pushes, prods and words of intense ill will, ending with an ominous warning from Tony Pro: "Old man, yours is coming. You're going to belong to me!"[18] This confrontation provided a rare look behind the veil of Hoffa's repeated insistence that the presence of mobster-affiliated Teamster officials was a necessary and controllable part of his union's growth. It also solidified an enmity between the two men that would grow stronger with each passing year.

During Hoffa's jail term his supporters went to considerable lengths to keep his name in the public arena, along with his claim of victimization by a corrupt government. "Free Jimmy Hoffa" groups surfaced periodically in various cities and towns. Occasionally they came to Washington's Capitol Hill, protesting the union leader's "political" incarceration and urging renewed investigations by their congressional representatives. On February 14 of each year since Hoffa's imprisonment a banner-towing airplane had flown over Lewisburg's courtyard with the message "Birthday Greetings Jimmy Hoffa."[19] In the spring of 1970, three years after the Teamster boss's incarceration, the White House received a petition containing over 250,000 signatures urging a presidential pardon and a commutation of Hoffa's sentence. The media covered many of these events, a sure sign the imprisoned labor leader remained in the public eye.

In January of 1971 the US Supreme Court upheld the Teamster boss's conviction in the Sun Valley pension fraud case. The justices found no reversible error in Judge Austin's trial rulings, and affirmed his decision to add the IBT boss's five-year sentence to his time for jury tampering rather than consecutively as Hoffa's legal team had requested. Two months later, however, the lawyers filed a second application for his early release from prison on parole. By then he had served almost one-third of his combined sentence of thirteen years and hoped the finalization of his Sun Valley sentence would not influence the parole board's judgment. He had been a model prisoner from day one, and Josephine's worsening health could also help his cause. For the past several months she had been in and out of the hospital due to a heart attack and a series of small strokes. But her husband's hopes for early release were short-lived. The board denied Hoffa's latest request, advising him he could reapply for parole again next year. Using their broad discretion under the law to avoid arguable explanations, they gave no reason for their decision.

As if to lessen the impact of the board's refusal, Hoffa was given a five-day "emergency furlough" to visit his ailing wife, who was now in a heart specialist's care at a California hospital. He would need to return to Lewisburg with proof of his travel but no marshals would accompany him. His only restraint was that he must devote his time exclusively to family meetings and Josephine's health issues. As his jailers probably anticipated, he completely ignored this limitation. He spent time each day with his wife, daughter, son, and grandchildren, but also welcomed Fitzsimmons, Gibbons and a stream of other Teamster visitors to his suite at the San Francisco Hilton for talks about more than the weather. Outwardly Hoffa appeared to be his old self but his four years of incarceration had dampened his spirits and his cocky demeanor. At a minimum he faced another fifteen months of imprisonment with no assurance that a third application for parole would then be granted. Adding to his discomfort was the need to decide, well before the Teamsters' fast-approaching annual convention, whether to seek reelection as the IBT's president. This cloud of uncertainty followed him back to his waiting prison cell where it materialized into a dilemma.

On the one hand, Hoffa feared what might happen if he resigned the Teamster presidency. Fitzsimmons, the union's general vice-president and acting CEO, would become its new president later in that year of 1971, consolidating his power. The longer Hoffa remained in jail with no official Teamster connection, the more difficult it would be for him eventually to regain his old office. Also strengthening his temptation to seek reelection at the upcoming June convention was the conviction that he was still the rank and file's favorite. His friends and advisors confirmed this view. The solid New England supporters who had protested on his behalf in the nation's capital were now circulating a petition to keep him in office "wherever he may hang his hat."[20] His reelection to the union presidency while at Lewisburg would keep Fitzsimmons off balance, at least until Hoffa's next opportunity for parole in mid-1972. If then released, he could walk back into his opulent office, his head held high and his power fully restored.

On the other hand, parole board members might see his retention of Teamster office, along with his continuing receipts of per diem payments, as a lack of remorse on his part and evidence of his union's disrespect for the administration of justice. If so, then his reelection to the Teamster presidency while in prison might solidify the board's reluctance to set him free at his next hearing. His lawyers also felt that a formal resignation from the IBT and Local 299 presidencies, along with his leadership roles in various Teamster councils and conferences, would constitute "significant new information" entitling him to an expedited rehearing well before the mandatory fifteen-month hiatus he otherwise faced.

Abandonment of his union connections thus might be the key to unlock Lewisburg's gates very soon, though probably not in time for a last-minute addition of his name to the ballot at the Teamsters' upcoming convention in July. Without these connections he would be in limbo until the IBT's next convention in 1976, but he would be out of his prison hell-hole and anything could happen in the intervening five years. Besides, even the faintest hope of attending the Miami Beach convocation as a free man stirred a compelling vision. Like Julius Caesar returning to Rome from a successful siege, Hoffa would enter the Florida convention hall to wild acclaim, a triumphant conqueror of the forces out to destroy him, the rank and file's once and future king.

But that was a daydream. The IBT's executive board told Hoffa they needed to know forthwith whether he would seek reelection as their president. On June 3rd, after a final painful analysis, he sent two messages to the directors via son Jim: he would not seek reelection to the office he had held for fourteen years, and he supported Fitzsimmons as his successor. His official resignation from all of his Teamster offices came some two weeks later in the form of a hand-written note mailed to the board at the unions' D.C. headquarters. It said simply, "I agree not to be in organized labor as a officer [sic]."[21] Though sounding somewhat offhand, this one sentence artfully took him out of office but set no time parameters on his absence or his potential return. Whether or not his resignations at this moment were well advised, they set in motion a series of events that would lead to his ultimate downfall.

Immediately upon receipt of Hoffa's resignation the board held a special meeting in Miami Beach and dutifully nominated Fitzsimmons to continue as the IBT's chief executive. At its convention three weeks later, having received Hoffa's endorsement, Fitzsimmons easily won reelection. The executive board's vice-presidents, whose individual powers had grown steadily under Fitz's loose reins, wanted to keep him in place. Tony Provenzano, William Bufalino, Allen Dorfman and other mob-related Teamster officials had thrived under Fitz's weak leadership. Not only had he allowed these racketeers to decide who got Teamster loans and who received kickbacks from them, he did not demand, as

Hoffa had, a piece of the action for himself. With all of this support Fitzsimmons had no trouble banning pictures of Hoffa in the convention hall. In his acceptance speech the union's new president made only one passing mention of his former boss.

President Nixon had been on vacation at his winter White House in Key Biscayne at the time of the IBT executive board's June meeting. In an extraordinary and unprecedented move for a sitting president, Nixon stopped in at the board's gathering to sit briefly with them and to congratulate Fitzsimmons on his new role. This was a clear sign of the close relationship between the two men, and of the power accorded the union's new boss as a result of the president's quest for Teamster support in his 1972 reelection campaign. Surely, thought Hoffa's family, friends and well-wishers, Fitz would use his new power to press harder for presidential clemency for the victim of Robert Kennedy's vendetta, now in his fifth year of incarceration. Fitzsimmons did exert such additional pressure but, as later investigations would show, his work for the imprisoned Teamster included equal efforts to protect his own place in the sun.

The prisoner and his advisers decided that Hoffa's son Jim, now a licensed attorney, should play a leading role in the effort to free his father. Citing the elder Hoffa's resignation of his Teamster offices, the young lawyer wrote to the parole board asking for reconsideration of their earlier decision in light of his father's new move. Jim also advised them that his mother had recently suffered a relapse causing her health to deteriorate. He stressed that the elder Hoffa intended to teach and lecture, live on his pension and care for his ailing wife. The board granted his request and set August 20 as the date for a new hearing.

Thus encouraged, Hoffa's son entered the parole board's hearing room at the Department of Justice expecting a receptive atmosphere. He had met earlier with Will Wilson, chief of the DOJ's Criminal Division, who had reacted positively to the news of Hoffa's resignation from Teamster offices and the cancellation of income from them. The young Hoffa had interpreted Wilson's cordial attitude and sympathetic words as an encouraging sign that the board, under Wilson's oversight, would also realize the merits of the elder Hoffa's case. Thus its negative posture on the morning of August 20 came as a total surprise. The board expressed concern with the union's agreement to pay Hoffa $1.7 million even though this was a lump-sum settlement of the retirement benefits due him under the Teamsters' pension plan. Board members seemed upset by its size, and probably by unexpressed doubts of how long Hoffa would stay retired. They noted the union had agreed to hire James P. Hoffa as the IBT's counsel on an annual retainer of $30,000, and to continue Josephine's income of $40,000 per year as the head of the Teamsters' political action committee. The board also put probing questions to Jim about his father's alleged ties to organized crime.

The gloom cast by these questions caught the Hoffa team by surprise which turned to stormy outrage before the day ended. That afternoon the board unanimously denied the prisoner's application for parole, advising him he could try again in June of the next year. "Double-cross" and worse were the epithets thrown at the board, the Department of Justice, and the Nixon administration. One of the Teamster lawyers said bitterly, "At least when Bob Kennedy gave his word, he kept it."[22] This reaction reflected the ingrained cynicism of Hoffa's world—the belief that everyone in a seat of power had his or her price, and that all were motivated solely by selfishness and greed. This was also the code of the underworld, misplaced here but nevertheless followed: if you agreed to be fixed, you had better stay fixed. And in the custom of gangsters now more prominent than ever in Teamster officialdom, a positive word and a knowing smile was taken as a commitment. Breach the deal and you are a rat, more than likely a dead rat. Will Wilson, for example, after saying he would "try to help," became a filthy double-crosser who failed to deliver. In this corrosive environment everyone who could have helped but did not—the attorney general, the president, and the president's aides—were traitorous co-conspirators because that was the way the government did business. They all worked together and posed as your friends but failed you in the end. Hoffa's team, like their boss, would have scoffed had anyone suggested that the parole board's eight members, appointed by the president and approved by the Senate, might simply have acted with a measure of independence and responsibility.

To Hoffa's supporters, the parole board's members were tight-ass, turf-protecting bureaucrats obstinately blocking the release of a model prisoner. Incensed by the board's decision, these allies redoubled their efforts to persuade the Nixon administration to use the power of the presidency to grant the Teamster boss the freedom he now deserved. Five days after the board's action, William Loeb sent a telegram to the president, urging him to free Hoffa "with a stroke of your pen."[23] Two days later Fitzsimmons met with Attorney General Mitchell to express his displeasure and to urge executive clemency. Fitz also met with Charles Colson, a top assistant to John Ehrlichman, Nixon's chief adviser on domestic affairs. As the White House's point man on the Hoffa matter, Colson had been heavily courted by Fitzsimmons ever since Hoffa's imprisonment. As their relationship grew closer Chuck Colson became the new Teamster boss's most trusted contact within the Nixon administration.

During the fall of 1971, Maurice Stans, Herb Kalmbach, Murray Chotiner and the president's other political operatives were already eyeing next year's reelection campaign, more interested at that stage in hard cash than in promises of future votes. In those pre-Watergate days, politicians were not subject to the intense oversight of today's high-tech media and their virtually unlimited sources and outlets. Thus when the stakes were large enough, some campaigns took money from questionable sources with full knowledge it was tainted. Jack Anderson, who had taken over Drew Pearson's nationally syndicated newspaper column the "Washington Merry-Go-Round," reported that "a source close to the Teamsters claimed the union had raised more that $750,000 for Nixon's 1972 reelection campaign. Another source said that 'much of the money came from Las Vegas gambling lords whose casinos. were financed by the Teamsters' pension fund.' A third source, 'close to the president, [said] the amount was smaller. But all ... agreed that a huge cash collection was turned over to ... [the Nixon campaign] on behalf of the Teamsters by crime-connected Allen Dorfman.' "[24] A later report put the amount of the Mob's contribution to the Nixon war chest at $1 million, half of it raised by Dorfman, the other half by Tony Provenzano, and delivered to Colson in a Las Vegas casino.[25]

Though all such gifts went unreported there can be little doubt that the IBT's combined contributions to Nixon's reelection campaign were the largest amounts credited to a single source. Collected in part as the skim from casinos, prostitution rings and some legitimate businesses owned or controlled by Teamster-affiliated mobsters, they helped give Fitzsimmons the power to make almost any reasonable request of the president with the expectation it would be granted. At that point the Teamsters' contributions served two purposes: they confirmed the union's commitment to Nixon's reelection and guaranteed its leaders open access to administration officials sympathetic to the IBT's goals, one of which was Hoffa's immediate release.

In his Labor Day speech in September, 1971, Fitzsimmons called upon Nixon to pardon Jimmy Hoffa. He continued meeting with Colson, with whom he was now extremely close, and by the end of October the pieces seemed to be falling into place. Wanting the public to see Hoffa's release in the most favorable light, Colson began to spin the president's plan to the press. On November 4 he met in the White House with Clark Mollenhoff, the anti-Hoffa newspaper reporter who had spent a year on Nixon's staff as the president's "ombudsman" before resigning his position in mid–1970. Colson told Mollenhoff that in his most recent meeting with Fitzsimmons the subject of Hoffa's release never came up—most likely a flat-out lie. Then, after getting the newsman's agreement to hold off printing what he was about to hear, he got to the point: the president was considering a grant of executive clemency for the jailed Teamster "as an act of compassion" during the upcoming holiday season. "It is inevitable," he continued, "that Hoffa will be free [on parole] next summer."[26] But if it came at that later time, Colson explained—just as the president's reelection campaign went into full swing—Hoffa's parole would be criticized as purely political, an election year move by Nixon to get the labor vote. It would not bring the excitement and gratitude of Hoffa's supporters that an earlier release, this December, would surely generate. Colson then gave a transparently false excuse for bringing the reporter to his office: the president, he said, wanted the former ombudsman's advice.

How Mollenhoff responded is anyone's guess, but he delayed writing a story on Colson's disclosure though it ran completely contrary to his investigative nature. On December 19, at a party given by William O. Bittman, Hoffa's prosecutor in the Sun Valley trial, a "reliable source" told Mollenhoff the announcement of Hoffa's release was scheduled for the following week. That additional source freed the journalist from his commitment to Colson, and his bylined story appeared the next day, scooping all other papers. Four days later, untroubled by the story, Colson called Mollenhof with an invitation to meet in the White House that afternoon with John Dean, a junior White House aide, for a background briefing. Dean, a "pleasant and naive young man," told Mollenhoff that just that morning President Nixon had signed an order commuting Hoffa's sentence, and that the former Teamster boss was on his way out of prison as they spoke.[27] He then added with feigned offhandedness: Hoffa's release papers prohibited him from engaging "in the direct or indirect management of any labor organization prior to March 6, 1980," the date on which his thirteen-year prison term would have been served in full. Any violation of this condition would automatically render the commutation order "null and void in its entirety." This critical provision would keep Hoffa out of Teamster affairs for almost nine more years.

The final push for presidential forgiveness of Hoffa's sentence had begun only three weeks earlier. On a word from Colson that the time was ripe, Fitzsimmons told Morris Shenker that the Department of Justice would now look favorably on a petition seeking executive clemency for Hoffa. A few days later Shenker's petition was on the attorney general's desk. Mitchell's response

Jimmy Hoffa leaving federal prison on December 23, 1971 as a result of President Nixon's commutation of Hoffa's 13-year sentence to 4 ½ years, the time served.

showed clearly that his office's machinery had been thoroughly greased. Customarily, the DOJ's pardons attorney would first seek the written views of the Criminal Division's lawyers and of the judges and prosecutors who had handled the prisoner's trials. White House lawyers would also have a chance to comment. None of that happened here. Within two weeks, after discussing the matter only with pardons attorney Lawrence Traylor, Mitchell recommended to Nixon that he commute Hoffa's sentence. The president did so, signing the commutation order on December 22. Christmas came this year on a Monday, and they wanted Hoffa free by then. They barely made it. Hoffa walked out of prison in the late afternoon of Saturday, December 23.

Barbara's husband Robert Crancer was the family's designated driver to bring Hoffa home. Informed in a call to his motel room that the prisoner was ready, Crancer drove to the prison and met his father-in-law in the warden's office. Looking a bit haggard in one of his old gray suits but in a buoyant mood, Hoffa was reading his "Conditions of Release," the standard form all parolees had to sign before leaving. Its boiler-plate restrictions did not seem particularly onerous: no drugs, no excessive use of alcohol and no guns of any kind. He would have to report regularly to his Detroit parole officer, and for the next two years seek advance clearance to travel outside his home area. Any future law violation would also violate his parole status and jeopardize his freedom. Hoffa felt comfortable that he could live with these restrictions. He had a standing agreement with Dave Johnson, Local 299's new president, that on his release from prison he would be Johnson's assistant. In this position he would have access to his former Teamster associates and a springboard for his eventual return to the IBT's helm. Seeing nothing in the papers before him to threaten these plans or seriously hamper his expected lifestyle, he signed the release document without reservation. Cheered by a watching group of inmates he then walked with Crancer through Lewisburg's front gates to freedom.

The two men drove to a small airport near Williamsport, Pennsylvania, where a Teamster jet sent by Harold Gibbons awaited them. Their plane took them first to Detroit where they picked up son Jim and then flew on to Saint Louis, now the Crancer family's hometown. There they would join Jo, Barbara, and granddaughter Barbara Jo for the holidays. Alerted to Hoffa's arrival, reporters from the Saint Louis media greeted him as he walked into the private plane terminal. The newsmen's first shouted question sought his reaction to the conditions placed on his parole. "Which one do you mean?" he asked. "The one that says you can't hold union office," they told him. Surprised, he begged off, saying he wanted to join the family members anxiously awaiting his arrival. Son Jim immediately got on the telephone to confirm the bad news, a bitter blow that ruined what would have been a joyous reunion. "Hell," his father said later, "if I'd known of those conditions I never would have accepted the commutation. I'd have been free without any conditions in 1974"—because by then he would have been eligible for parole on the basis of good behavior.[28] And as Colson had suggested, Hoffa might well have convinced the parole board to release him as early as 1972 at his next scheduled parole hearing just a few months away. He was sick at the thought of what might have been.

Hoffa's surprise and disappointment were genuine, but not because he had hoped to seek Teamster office anytime soon. His plan was to regain the Teamster union's presidency in 1976. What shocked him was that the restriction on his holding union office had been put in writing with an expiration date in the spring of 1980. During his furlough from prison to visit Jo's San Francisco hospital room in early 1971 he had told Fitzsimmons simply that he would relinquish his Teamster offices without specifying the length of his absence. As reported by an associate with him at the time, Hoffa had spoken in his typical shorthand. "It was the kind of thing he just said 'yeah, yeah' to when someone mentioned it."[29]

What seems most likely is that as Fitzsimmons's hold on the IBT presidency strengthened, he had discussed with close confidants the possibility of getting Hoffa's release conditioned on his honoring what they considered his "promise" to stay out of organized labor. In meetings and conversations with Colson, Fitzsimmons doubtless urged that this restriction be quantified and put in writing. With John Dean's help, and a clearance from Haldeman, Ehrlichman or both, Colson formulated the time frame: Hoffa could not hold union office until March 6, 1980. From their political perspective this date had beautiful symmetry. It was the day on which Hoffa's thirteen-year sentence would have been served in full, and until then it protected Fitzsimmons against challenge by his main adversary.

Upon Hoffa's release from prison his 59th birthday was six weeks away. He had spent forty tumultuous years as a labor activist, ten of them as the Teamsters' president. Under his leadership the IBT had become the nation's fastest-growing union and eventually its largest. A pension settlement near $2 million promised him and Josephine a lifetime of financial comfort. He had earning power to spare. On the lecture circuit his fees would match those of a former US president. Profitable affiliations awaited him at trucking companies and at labor-oriented non-profits. He had paid society its due and had the unshakeable admiration of millions of his fellow citizens. But in Hoffa's soul burned a flame quenchable only by the recapture of his former position. He left Lewisburg as strongly addicted as ever to the smell of truck fumes and the roar of idolatrous Teamster crowds. He missed the challenge of employer bargaining sessions and the deep satisfaction of a successful negotiation. He felt diminished without a steady stream of callers wanting help or advice and by his consequent inability to take care of "his people."

Two high barriers made the road back to the Teamster presidency seem virtually impassable: the lengthy term of the commutation order's restriction, and the fact that Fitzsimmons, the "caretaker" president, now had a solid hold on the IBT leadership. On the first count, Hoffa felt there might be some legal basis for challenging the government's limitation on the way he could earn a living. With regard to unseating his successor, he told himself that his own popularity within the union, and his ability to handle Teamster malcontents—even those affiliated with organized crime—would facilitate his return to office. He knew that the union's mobsters had become more firmly entrenched under Fitzsimmons but believed he could regain the loyalty of those whom he had originally brought into the union. While these thoughts helped to rationalize his decision, it was an unabated lust for power and its fruits that again drove him to press his luck, to choose the path of conflict and predictable danger. This time, however, it would lead to a dead end.

CHAPTER 11

"Some Day, Somehow, I Will Return"

Following the family's year-end holiday in Saint Louis, the senior Hoffas went off to their Miami condominium for three weeks in Florida's abundant winter sunshine. They returned to Detroit in late January to begin Hoffa's life as an ex-convict on two years of supervised parole. Though barred from union officialdom, he was free to meet with former Teamster associates and attend their social functions. He could also accept speaking engagements throughout the country, donating to charity his fees from business groups and refusing honoraria from non-profits. To working stiffs everywhere he was a heroic veteran of their cause; to others he was a celebrity whose appearance guaranteed a good crowd. Wherever he went—to restaurants, parking lots, hotel lobbies and on city streets—friends and strangers greeted him with a "Hiya, Jimmy," some even going out of their way to shake his hand and wish him good luck. A model of equanimity in his early months of freedom, he disclaimed any hard feelings toward President Nixon for delaying his return to union office. When asked about his relationship with Fitzsimmons he professed no quarrel with the new Teamster boss.

Later that year he met Edward "Big Ed" Lawrenson, a fellow ex-con who had recently founded the National Association for Justice.

Intrigued by Lawrenson's mission to improve jailhouse conditions and help freed criminals reestablish their lives, Hoffa made the NAJ his primary activity and in time became the director of its Crisis Center. In this position he traveled extensively, praised the Association in numerous forums, and gave liberally of his funds to its cause.

Hoffa's behavior in these first months of freedom was admirable but not altogether altruistic. With his parole conditions in effect until March of 1973, he knew better than to test their limits and risk returning to prison. In his words, Lewisburg had been a "hell on earth, only hell couldn't be this bad."[1] His bedrock objective—his obsession—was to regain the IBT presidency at the international union's next convention in 1976, four years hence. It was not beyond hope, he told himself, that his civic service and charitable acts could earn him a full presidential pardon by then, ending the longer restriction on his holding union office. But that was a long shot, and for more direct help he turned to lawyers who had served him well in the past. Eager to counsel such a potentially valuable client, they suggested he consider challenging the legal basis of Nixon's restrictive order. Was this restriction a lawful exercise of the US president's broad power to pardon, or was it an after-the-fact form of additional punishment and therefore unconstitutional? Over the next several months he hired three law firms to research those questions in depth.

Another phase of Hoffa's legal attack, led by Teamster lawyers now in his personal employ, was already under way. Their never-say-die goal was to overturn his 1964 jury-tampering conviction by having the courts throw out Grady Partin's testimony. For seven long years, Hoffa's hope of destroying Partin's credibility had clung to life like a comatose patient on a respirator. Success in this mission would amount to a full acquittal because without Partin the feds had no case. Elimination of the jury-tampering charge would leave intact only his conviction for loan fraud in the Sun Valley matter. His prison time of four years, nine and a half months, plus a credit for good behavior, would amount to full service of Sun Valley's five-year sentence. That would mean he should have been released from Lewisburg without restrictions of any kind. With their removal he could seek reelection to the IBT presidency in 1976, a contest he felt confident of winning.

Ammunition for this continuing court battle could come only from Grady Partin. Ever since Partin's surprise appearance at the Chattanooga trial, Hoffa loyalists had pressured the Louisiana Teamster to renounce his claim that the IBT boss had masterminded the efforts to fix the Test Fleet jury. William Loeb and other sycophants had lambasted the DOJ for its failure to press the long-pending criminal charges against Partin. Hoffa's musclemen had threatened to send the turncoat Teamster to the hospital or worse. Other shady characters had approached him with huge payoffs for a recantation of his testimony. Heading this latter effort was Carlos "The Little Man" Marcello, the Mafia boss of New Orleans, who had collected markers totaling $2 million from a coalition of Teamster-aligned mobsters for a "spring Hoffa" fund.[2] For Partin's cooperation Marcello's minions had also promised to help resolve his antitrust and other legal problems which they, ironically, had helped to instigate. They also offered him enough cash—$1 million, Partin had once said to some Louisiana friends—for a lifetime of financial independence.

These overtures made Partin's life miserable but in the end were unsuccessful. During one discussion with Marcello's henchmen he said that Sheridan had planted him in Nashville to get information on the Teamster boss's defense strategy during the Test Fleet trial. He also implied that "the government had pressured him into testifying against Hoffa and ... told him what to say."[3] But he did not specifically retract his claim that Hoffa had led the jury-tampering effort, and he refused to put into an affidavit the rambling and often conflicting words attributed to him in this interview. Hoffa's lawyers examined the unsigned document prepared by Marcello's interrogators but never offered it as evidence of a recantation. Instead, in a final attempt to discredit the Louisiana Teamster, they filed a third retrial motion with Judge Wilson. In it they charged Partin with perjury for falsely denying that he had recorded a conversation with Ewing King concerning the latter's effort to fix a Test Fleet juror. The government easily disproved the charge and Judge Wilson summarily dismissed the motion. When, in 1973, the Sixth Circuit Court of Appeals upheld Wilson's decision, Hoffa's lawyers again petitioned the Supreme Court to hear the case. The odds that the justices would review the matter and rule for their client were about those of winning a national lottery, but the potential reward was a chance for him to regain the Teamster presidency, worth more to Hoffa than any lottery's pot of gold. As expected, the high court refused to reopen the case, finally bringing closure to his jury-tampering conviction after a decade of challenges.

This post-prison attempt to overturn the verdict of the Chatta-nooga jury was only one sign of Hoffa's submission to his demons. His successor's increasingly independent ways had been gnawing at him since his days at Lewisburg. While in jail Hoffa had tried unsuc-cessfully to appoint a successor to John English, the IBT's retir-ing secretary. "Name Gibbons," he had ordered from his prison cell. "I can't," Fitzsimmons had replied.[4] His reason, it would later emerge, was that "Red" Dorfman, a member of Chicago gang formerly headed by Al Capone, had reminded the IBT's caretaker president of their "deal" that the secretarial job would go to "Tom Flynn, a Teamster official from Chicago."[5] Hoffa's frustration at being unable to control his pliable successor continued into his post-prison days, heightened by the galling realization that Fitz's pliability had made him the tool of the mobsters now opposed to having Hoffa back in charge.

Fitzsimmons could easily have been mistaken for an over-indulgent Irish bartender, out of place in his palatial D.C. office and rumpled pinstripe suit. Seemingly affable but plagued with a chronic stomach ulcer, Hoffa's anointed successor was deferential in his dealings with other men of power. Teamster insiders who had worked with Fitz as the IBT's general vice-president and now as its general president saw him as insecure and fearful. As one of them put it, "Everybody knew he had no balls."[6]

Hoffa's former lackey had quickly grown accustomed to his perk-laden presidency. A generous paycheck, a virtually unlimited expense account, club memberships and a private jet airplane soon seemed indispensable. Golf was his favorite form of recreation, with two or three rounds his weekly average. He found particular solace on the green fairways of California's La Costa Resort and Spa, a favorite watering hole of Las Vegas casino owners amid the golden hills of California just north of San Diego which he visited regularly. If his plane left Detroit early enough he could get in eighteen holes that same afternoon. Once, when he left his clubs at home, his pilot famously flew back to fetch them for the next day's round. Also contributing to

Fitz's luxurious life atop the Teamster summit was his growing political clout. President Nixon, seeking reelection, paid increased court to the leader of the only major labor union endorsing his 1972 candidacy. The doors of the White House and the Department of Labor were always open to the new IBT boss. Fitz occasionally got a ride to La Costa on Air Force One when Nixon flew to his summer White House in San Clemente.

Hoffa's long hard fight to win the Teamster presidency had strengthened his ability to keep the office once he gained it. Fitzsimmons had become the union's chief executive simply by serving as his boss's faithful gofer, and his malleability contrasted sharply with the dictatorial style of his mentor. During Hoffa's imprisonment Fitz had steadily increased the autonomy of IBT's vice-presidents, gradually shifting the allegiance of these regional leaders from their former boss to their new president. He had enlarged their power by diminishing his own, but their increased authority assured him of their support. Thus the weakness that had initially attracted Hoffa to him was, ironically, the primary trait solidifying Fitzsimmons's grip on the union's highest office.

The Teamster officials gaining most from Fitzsimmons's benevolent passivity were those connected to organized crime. Hoffa had brought the mobsters into the union and allowed them to gain control of some of its largest locals and regional councils. In return for the benefits bestowed, he had demanded a share of their action through payoffs and loan kickbacks, always in cash and under the table. More in fear than in generosity, Fitz had given them greater power just for the asking, with no price tag attached. Vincent Piersante, for many years head of the Michigan attorney general's criminal division, summed up the difference. "The Detroit Mob had a high regard for Fitz because he was easy to get along with," said Piersante. "He'd do whatever they wanted him to. ... [W]ith Hoffa it was always a tough negotiation."[7]

Leading the pack of profiteers was Allen Dorfman, installed years earlier by Hoffa as the manager of the Central States pension fund as a concession to Paul "Red" Dorfman, a Chicago mobster and Allen's stepfather. Multi-million dollar loans to Mafia-connected syndicates during Hoffa's presidency helped to build many of the original Las Vegas casinos, including the Dunes, the Stardust and the Desert Inn. Through the fund, Teamster dues financed dog tracks in Florida and a jai alai fronton in Connecticut. The largest of these early loans, $94 million, went to the construction of the La Costa Spa. Before going to prison Hoffa had thrown the younger Dorfman a bouquet worth a fortune. He told Fitzsimmons: "Allen speaks for me on all pension fund questions. He's the guy in charge while I am gone."[8]

When Hoffa entered Lewisburg the Central States fund had assets of $400 million, with Teamster dues surging ahead at the rate of $14 million per month. With the authority bestowed upon him by his departing mentor, Allen Dorfman came into his own. Fitzsimmons dutifully had the fund's board of directors name the Chicago strongman its "Special Consultant." A handsome former physical-education instructor who kept himself fit, Red Dorfman's stepson was, on the outside, "suave, charming, clever and witty."[9] He looked and acted the part of a no-nonsense young executive, supremely comfortable as the newly empowered manager of the Teamsters' largest pension fund. When he recommended an applicant the loan was made with few questions asked. Often the borrower was a straw man whose only qualifying assets were a clean record and the silent backing of a gangland partner. In times of stress, however, the younger Dorfman's cruelty surfaced to show that while he and "Red" Dorfman did not share the same blood, he was his stepfather's star pupil. One critic, after being threatened with "a concrete overcoat," called him "the most vicious, crooked, scary guy you'll ever meet."[10] It was no wonder, then, the press reported that "Frank Fitzsimmons hardly makes a move relating to financial matters without consulting Dorfman."[11]

Hefty segments of Teamster fund loans were burdened by Mob-demanded kickbacks or discounts, each resulting in some portion of workers' dues going into mobsters' pockets. But as measured by the marketplace, Dorfman's operation was a success. Despite these rake-offs, the fund's value had doubled by the time of Hoffa's release on parole, making its manager one of the nation's most powerful bankers. His tacit understanding with Fitzsimmons was that each gang-connected Teamster official would get his fair share of pension fund loans. Supposedly representing the Teamsters' rank and file, Dorfman was in truth working for the Mafia.

Also flourishing under Fitzsimmons's reign was Hoffa's prison buddy and Genovese capo Anthony Provenzano. Of all the Teamster-associated officials, Tony Pro had probably profited most from his close relationship with Hoffa. With handsome salaries from several Teamster positions, he had been described in 1963 by *Newsday* columnist Murray Kempton as "the highest-paid labor boss in America."[12] Out of prison now, Provenzano looked and acted like a character from a Hollywood gangster movie of the day. Tall and handsomely swarthy, his muscular frame smoothed but not hidden by the flab of high living, he was usually seen in a sharkskin suit with a diamond ring on his pinkie. In any guise he was an ominous and intimidating physical presence. The Landrum-Griffin Act forbade him, as a convicted extortionist, from holding union office for five years following his release from prison but not from hobnobbing with union leaders. He became Fitzsimmons's active but unpaid consultant and his frequent companion on and off the La Costa golf course.

Through renewed contacts with Mob-connected owners of Las Vegas casinos, Provenzano was one of the largest money raisers for

Portrait of Anthony Provenzano meeting with newsmen outside his posh island home on Florida's Intracoastal Waterway. August 6, 1975.

Nixon's reelection campaign of 1972. Through his control of a New Jersey bank he also made loans to members of other crime families, including those allied with Pennsylvania mobster boss Russell Bufalino. With Bufalino and others he formed "labor-leasing companies" to hire truck drivers at less than union wages. These companies contracted with trucking corporations to supply drivers at below-market rates, thereby displacing higher paid Teamster employees while Fitzsimmons and his IBT cronies looked the other way. These sweetheart deals were taking millions of dollars from Teamsters' pockets in the mid-Atlantic region and threatening to spread westward. By the early '70s Tony Pro had become a force to be reckoned with on many fronts. If Hoffa feared any man, it was the mafioso from New Jersey.

The bitter disagreement between Provenzano and Hoffa, begun at Lewisburg, had turned their symbiotic friendship into implacable hostility. Their relationship worsened when the New Jersey mobster grew more powerful under Fitzsimmons. On one occasion, when both were out of prison, the two men met face-to-face in Miami. A day or so later, describing their encounter to a fellow Teamster, Hoffa fumed that Tony Pro "threatened to pull my guts out [and] kidnap my children if I continue to attempt to return to the Teamster presidency."[13] He was also convinced that Provenzano had encouraged Fitzsimmons's efforts to block the former Teamster boss's return to power, and was continuing to do so. "They must pay," he confided angrily to Frank Sheeran, a Delaware Teamster official Hoffa had brought into the union several years earlier who now doubled as Russell Bufalino's hit man. "Something has to be done about Tony Pro." Accustomed to such talk, Sheeran took his friend's words seriously. "You get the go-ahead" and I'll take care of him. "I got a good man who can drive me." "I'll be the driver,"[14] Hoffa responded, a sign to Sheeran that the former Teamster boss was only letting off steam. But Hoffa's words left no doubt the anger behind them was white hot.

As time went on, despite warnings that he was heading for trouble, Hoffa told friends that nothing could stop his quest for the IBT presidency. In the spring and fall of 1973, three events gathered like stars in propitious conjunction to lead him along this dangerous path.

The first of these was the expiration of his parole term and the behavioral restrictions that went with it. Next was his decision to begin a federal court proceeding to nullify Nixon's ban on Hoffa's holding union office. Finally came former Attorney General John Mitchell's disclosure, in a deposition taken by Hoffa's lawyers in preparation for his planned lawsuit, that Fitzsimmons had first spoken to Mitchell about granting early release to the Teamster boss in June of 1971. This flatly contradicted Fitz's claims, begun in 1968 and regularly repeated, that he was in close contact with Mitchell on this matter. Hoffa, who saw Fitzsimmons's fabrications as a sign of long-standing disloyalty, was furious. Unable to contain his anger and frustration he began openly to call Fitzsimmons a liar, and to accuse him of having pressured Colson and other Nixon aides to add the restrictive language to the president's commutation order.

Fitzsimmons responded in kind, taking the wraps off his behind-the-scenes effort to block the challenge of his former mentor. During Hoffa's time in jail, the caretaker president had put Hoffa's son and wife on the Teamster payroll. He now fired them both. Other potential troublemakers got similar treatment, most notably Harold Gibbons, the IBT's vice president who would have become its president if the prison-bound Hoffa had put the union's interests ahead of his own. Fitzsimmons revoked all of Gibbons's titles and perks except the elective office of the IBT's first vice-presidency, leaving Hoffa's former top aide with a minimal salary, a meager expense account and no power. Having inherited the autocratic powers of his predecessor, Fitz summarily fired several more Hoffa loyalists, including Nick Morrissey, Boston's longtime Teamster boss and ardent Hoffa supporter. When asked by Morrissey, " 'Why are you destroying me?' Fitzsimmons replied: 'If you're loyal to Hoffa you're disloyal to me. ... [He] is not coming back, and ... I'm the boss.' "15

In the case of Chuckie O'Brien, Fitz took a different tack. O'Brien had faithfully promoted Hoffa's cause among the Teamsters' rank and file while the man he called "dad" or "the old man" languished in jail. Soon after the prisoner's release Fitzsimmons exiled Chuckie to a union outpost in Alaska, cut his salary and sharply reduced his expense account. But as Hoffa's outspoken criticisms increased, his successor decided to lure O'Brien into the Fitzsimmons camp. Like Saint

Peter reprieving a hell-bound sinner, Fitz offered to reassign Hoffa's spoiled protégé from the Alaskan wasteland to the sunny clime of Hallandale, Florida. There, with his salary raised and his credit cards reactivated, Chuckie would supervise twenty or more Teamster Locals in the southern region. Showing his true colors O'Brien took the bait and became a Fitzsimmons convert. Then, after several months in the cushioned luxury of his

Portrait of Charles O'Brien leaving courthouse after testifying "uncooperatively" at a federal grand jury's inquiry into Hoffa's disappearance 37 days earlier. September 4, 1975.

new job, he likewise went public—prominently pinning on the lapel of his jacket a large button announcing "I'm for Fitz."

Fitzsimmons's counter-intuitive decision to rescue O'Brien raised several questions. Why would he dismiss other Hoffa loyalists and lavishly reward someone so close to the ex-IBT boss? And why would Chuckie, whom Hoffa had protected and promoted like a second son, turn traitorous in the hour of his benefactor's greatest need? Answers to these questions lay in the two men's characters and in O'Brien's relationship with Anthony Giacalone, a member of the Detroit Mob and former Hoffa ally.

Sylvia Pagano, Chuckie O'Brien's mother, had been a close friend of Josephine Poszywak since their youthful days as laundry workers in Detroit. While visiting Kansas City, Pagano met and married Sam Scaradino, alias Frank "Bing" O'Brien, a driver for local mobsters. Not long after Chuckie's birth his father committed suicide by hanging. Sylvia then moved back to Detroit where she found a new husband, but was again married only a short while. Following her second husband's death in 1940 she and Chuckie, then six years old, moved in with the Hoffa family for a while. Since then, Hoffa's fatherly instincts had shown clearly in his dealings with Chuckie. Perhaps he saw in Sylvia's child much of himself. The young O'Brien was short and stocky, fast talking and quick to take offense. Their close relationship made some think the teenager must be the Teamster boss's illegitimate son.

Over the years Hoffa's coddling of the wayward O'Brien lent support but no proof to that speculation. When Chuckie dropped out of high school at age seventeen, Hoffa appointed him a business agent for Local 299. When he cashed $600 in worthless checks at a drugstore, his surrogate father made them good. When he spent $1,000 hosting a dinner for the Detroit hockey team, charged it to Local 299 and had it rejected, Hoffa paid the bill. When O'Brien went to jail for falling behind in alimony payments to his divorced first wife, his forgiving guardian brought them up to date. Before leaving for prison in Lewisburg, Hoffa appointed his protégé an "international organizer" for the IBT at a higher salary with unspecified duties and an open-ended expense account. He also put O'Brien's name on the list of Teamster officials Fitzsimmons was told "not to touch" while the convicted labor leader was "away." Chuckie drove Jo to Lewisburg on visitation days, doubling as the prisoner's occasional messenger boy.

The Hoffa family treated the young O'Brien as a brother to son Jim. This arrangement lasted until Sylvia, an attractive woman then in her mid-thirties, caught the eye of Anthony "Tony Jack" Giacalone, a local gangster of about the same age. Not long after their meeting she moved to an apartment with Chuckie in tow, courtesy of her married lover. Their relationship grew apace with Tony Jack's wealth. Sylvia's son and Joey Giacalone, the mobster's son, became close friends even as the bond between O'Brien and young Jim Hoffa gradually weakened. For the rest of his life, Chuckie would refer to the elder Giacalone as "Uncle Tony."

Anthony Giacalone began his working life as an apprentice to the Zerillis, a prominent family in Detroit's mafiosi with interests in local gambling, loan sharking, prostitution and "protection" rackets. As the family's "enforcer," Tony Jack pressured delinquent debtors, pimps and business owners to pay up or suffer the painful consequences of not doing so. For this he became known as the "King of the Streets."[16] His proficiency in that role earned him managerial positions in the family's legitimate businesses, including distribution companies with Teamster-organized employees. In this way Giacalone and Hoffa fed each other in a classic symbiotic relationship. Tony Jack's employees added to Local 299's size and wealth while the Zerilli family got easy access to Teamster loans from which both men took individual cuts. Giacalone also prospered as a silent partner in a business to sell overpriced health insurance to Teamster members. His sole contribution in return for 20 percent of the company's revenue was providing introductions of its management team to Teamster officials.

By the time Hoffa went to prison in the

Anthony Giacalone walking to courthouse. "I don't have anything to say," Anthony "Tony Jack" Giacalone (right) told newsmen before entering a federal grand jury room during the investigation of Hoffa's disappearance. September 8, 1975.

spring of 1967, Giacalone had become the Zerilli family's top lieutenant. He was also recognized by the FBI as an important figure in the nation's network of organized crime. Already well off, his power and wealth grew steadily in the Fitzsimmons years. Symbols of his sybaritic lifestyle—in addition to his mistress—included a three-story residence in Grosse Point, Detroit's most fashionable suburb, Tennessee walking horses in a nearby stable, and a penthouse condominium in Hallandale, Florida. His only extraordinary outlay for maintaining these luxuries was the support of his free-spending wife, whom he kept happy in part because she was Tony Provenzano's cousin.[17]

This was the set of relationships in which Fitzsimmons decided to reward Sylvia O'Brien's son even as he punished Josephine and young Jim Hoffa. By the time the elder Hoffa left prison, Giacalone was solidly in Fitz's camp. With the former Teamster boss barred from union office for more than eight years, Tony Jack's defection was irreversible. It was apparent that Chuckie would go down the drain unless he, too, changed sides, and so it was arranged.

O'Brien's decision to abandon his lifelong benefactor was consistent with the demands of his environment. Living in the shadowed fringes of organized crime had heightened his instinct for self-preservation and his fear of making a wrong move. The only life he knew was that of a Teamster agent, which paid far more than he could earn as a bartender or nightclub bouncer, the other jobs for which he might be qualified. The pressure on him to join Fitzsimmons was thus intense. But his blatant disloyalty to Hoffa, the only caring father-figure of his misspent youth, revealed O'Brien's true character. Sylvia O'Brien's son was a highly self-centered ingrate.

Fitz's retaliation against his opponent's family members and other supporters thickened the storm clouds over his former boss's comeback trail. Hoffa saw their dark masses but was undeterred. Though he no longer served the IBT's rank and file, he was still their favorite. They wrote him letters of support. "Bring Back Jimmy Hoffa" stickers appeared on their trucks. Many went out of their way to drive by his Lake Orion cottage just to honk their horns or to make a quick stop to say hello. A poll conducted by *Overdrive,* truckers' most-read trade magazine, confirmed his ongoing popularity. Published in early 1974, the votes showed 83 percent of the surveyed respondents favoring Hoffa as the next international union president. Elated by this overwhelming vote of confidence, he resolved to fight even harder to regain his former position.

To qualify as a presidential candidate at the IBT's 1976 convention Hoffa had to hold some lesser Teamster office, from shop steward on up. David E. Johnson, his successor as the president of Detroit's Local 299, had been his friend and staunch supporter since 1935. A veteran labor leader now his sixties, Johnson had announced that he would retire from union office in 1974. But that was before Hoffa needed him, and at the latter's urging Johnson agreed to run once more for the Local's top job. To establish his old friend's credentials for the IBT election, he agreed to name Hoffa as one of 299's business agents if and when the ban on his holding office was removed, with a token salary of $15,000 per year.

This news sent Fitzsimmons into personal overdrive. He had cleared the way for his son Richard—who had succeeded his father as Local 299's vice-president—to become the union's president upon Johnson's departure. Now, both Dick Fitzsimmons and Dave Johnson were opposing candidates for its leadership. With Johnson supporting Hoffa's planned return to power, the Fitzsimmons team wanted to stop him by any means necessary. Young Fitz's vice-presidential running mate was the Detroit Teamsters' most forbidding muscleman, the six-foot, 245-pound Rolland McMaster. McMaster had earned his reputation as Hoffa's chief enforcer in the mean streets of the labor movement's earlier years. Years later, after losing his left eye, he could get his way with people simply by glaring at them with his good eye as his glass implant stared blankly into space. Now in the Fitzsimmons camp, McMaster had the necessary financial resources and he knew how to use them. Recruiting a Fitzsimmons helper by long distance telephone, he rasped, "Are you working? You want to come to Detroit? ... I got a project going. We got unlimited money to upset Dave Johnson and disrupt the whole goddamn operation.... Unlimited expenses, and I'll take care of your wages. There's no ceiling on it, but we gotta succeed."[18]

No stranger to labor turmoil, Dave Johnson knew his opponents would play rough. As a Hoffa supporter during the years of his friend's incarceration, he had been the target of periodic violence. In 1970, hired thugs had beaten him viciously. Under cover of night they had shattered his office windows with gunfire. In separate events, shotgun pellets had taken one eye of a local union official, fire had destroyed another's barn, and a bomb damaged the home of still another. In his current race for reelection, Johnson received an ominous signal. At 3:20 a.m. on the morning of July 7, 1974, an explosion rocked his Elco cabin cruiser at its mooring in the lake behind his elegant suburban home. With no one on board, the prized forty-five-foot boat, shattered and smoking, sank where it lay. Authorities found no evidence of a mechanical or electrical malfunction, and while McMaster and his heavyweights were suspected, none was ever charged. In the end, Johnson and the young Fitzsimmons reached an uneasy peace. They would run as a team, each seeking to retain his respective office in the Local election to be held in December of that year. This compromise was a victory for Hoffa. If he could somehow remove the shackles of Nixon's restrictive order, Johnson's continuation as Local 299's president might be the former Teamster boss's stepping stone to the IBT presidency.

In the months preceding these maneuvers several legal consultants had advised Hoffa to challenge the constitutionality of the provision in Nixon's commutation order banning him from union office for almost nine years following his release from prison. He finally followed this advice and in March of 1974 hired Leonard B. Boudin, a respected New York City civil rights attorney, to bring a lawsuit asking the courts to declare this restriction null and void. Well-known for his representation of Paul Robeson, Fidel Castro and others with leftist or Marxist views, Boudin also defended Daniel Ellsberg for releasing the Pentagon Papers and Dr. Benjamin Spock for protesting the Vietnam War. Though Hoffa's brand of self-reliant conservatism did not fit this mold, the politically liberal lawyer admired the Teamster boss's accomplishments and "liked [him] personally."[19] He also found the case intriguing. "This is the first time a president of the United States has imposed a condition on the commutation of a sentence with respect to a man's livelihood. ... A president shouldn't be running the labor movement."[20]

Hoffa's case went to trial in a D.C. federal court before Judge John H. Pratt without a jury on June 5, 1974. Boudin made a strong argument that in limiting Hoffa's right to hold union office Nixon had exceeded the Constitution's limitations on the pardoning power of the chief executive. This restriction, Boudin urged, amounted to an additional penalty for his client's crimes which the president had no authority to impose. As such, it violated Hoffa's Fifth Amendment right of protection against double jeopardy. It also illegally infringed on his right of free association under the First Amendment, and his right to earn a livelihood under the "liberty" clause of the Fifth. Though couched in these legalisms, Boudin's basic argument was that the eight and a half-year prohibition on holding union office was, to Hoffa, a greater penalty than the additional time he would otherwise have had to serve in prison.

Unimpressed, Judge Pratt upheld Nixon's order in a comprehensive if not thoroughly persuasive opinion issued on July 19. The president's broad constitutional pardoning power, he noted, included the right of commutation, the forgiving of an original sentence in exchange for time served. The only limitation on the power to commute was that any restrictions coming with it—which in Hoffa's case included typical parole conditions and the restriction on holding union office—must be "reasonable and lawful." The eight and a half-year restriction was reasonable, in the judge's view, because it was intended to curb further abuses of the kind that had led to the Teamster boss's conviction, a proper government goal of great public interest. It was not additional punishment for a past crime. It limited Hoffa's conduct, not his freedom of speech, and did not unduly restrict his freedom of association. And for good measure, Judge Pratt reminded the plaintiff that he had vowed, in his commutation request, to "enter the educational field on a limited basis as a teacher, lecturer or educator," using his substantial Teamster pension to support himself and his family.[21] Hence his claim to having been deprived of a means of earning a living was also without merit.

Naively anticipating a ruling in his favor, Hoffa had called a press conference in his Detroit office. The reporters would assemble at a time coinciding with a promised telephone call from Boudin relaying Judge Pratt's ruling. To supplement his expected victory, Hoffa planned to confirm, then and there, his candidacy for the IBT presidency. It was a disastrous decision, certainly one that Boudin, like any prudent lawyer, would have advised against had he received wind of it. The call detonated an explosion of criticism and blame, with Hoffa flailing his lawyer in such harsh and abusive terms that even the reporters, accustomed to his outbursts, were taken aback. Moments later, with the news media still present, he took a call from his wife complaining of noise being made by repairmen at their Lake Orion home. His anger spent, her husband soothingly told her not to worry, the workmen would be done soon and he would be home in a couple of hours.

Hoffa followed this classic performance by reconciling with his lawyer the next day. He and Boudin agreed that the judge's opinion upholding Nixon's restrictive order was wrong and should be appealed forthwith. Boudin felt strongly that the issue was not whether the almost nine-year ban on Hoffa's holding union office would serve a useful social purpose, as Judge Pratt had ruled. Plainly and simply, to keep a man from re-engaging for several years in the only work he had ever known was an additional penalty, beyond the power of the president to impose.

Boudin's colleagues thought he had an even chance of convincing the US Court of Appeals to overrule Judge Pratt and eliminate Hoffa's onerous restriction. Those odds would have skyrocketed in Hoffa's favor if the views of President Nixon and his aides on this subject had been made public. Only years later, when the government lifted the veil on portions of the infamous Oval Office tapes, did the president's intent to penalize the former Teamster boss solely for political purposes become abundantly clear.

On December 8, 1971, a few days after the filing of Hoffa's petition for clemency with Attorney General John Mitchell, Nixon discussed the matter in his office with aide Charles W. ("Chuck") Colson. He had already decided to commute Hoffa's sentence to time served.

> RMN: I've had a long talk with Mitchell. It cannot be done through the parole board. It has to be done through—it's commutation of sentence rather than pardon, which, of course, means that he still does not have his civil rights. Which is good. Mitchell will handle it all himself…I told him to discuss the situation directly with Fitz.
>
> CWC: Good.
>
> RMN: Tell him what we had, and that—I didn't let on that we had any other channels at all.
>
> CWC: No. No.
>
> RMN: Also, and he, Mitchell, will do the Loeb bit.
>
> CWC: Excellent.
>
> RMN: Loeb has been in contact with him, anyway. He says it's a terribly dangerous thing. But Mitchell has his own ways. He's pretty clever this way.

CWC: Oh, yeah.

RMN: But we've decided to go on it, and that's that. And I said, "Well, John, it's in your hands. I don't want to hear anything more about it and I'll just be surprised when it's on the list."

CWC: That's fine. Now Fitz was supposed to call me by the end of today, 'cause he—

RMN: You just tell him that the president—you raised it with him—the president has had a talk with Mitchell. He'll hear directly from Mitchell. And that Mitchell will work out whatever is satisfactory.... All the messages have been conveyed and Mitchell is completely on [garbled].... So Fitz will know you've talked to me, I talked to Mitchell, we're all agreed, but that Mitchell is going to handle it now, Fitz, and gee, Fitz, let us play our game now, boy.

CWC: [Laughs] Well, yeah, no worry with that—

RMN: Tell him that the president's concern was to be sure—he wants this done, and done the right way. And.... when he talks to Mitchell...he should not convey to Mitchell he's talked to you, of course.

CWC: No, no. He knows that.

RMN: But he's to say to him that—but tell Mitchell everything he wants, and that Mitchell will do it. How's that sound?

CWC: Oh, that's perfect I mean, that's all I need. I mean, he just needs that signal. And I think that'll pay enormous dividends.

RMN: All right. Well, that's the way it goes.

CWC: We'll take a little heat, but—

RMN: Oh, the hell with heat.

CWC: It's not gonna—

RMN: We'll take heat on a lot of other things, too.[22]

Nixon's determination to please Fitzsimmons, the labor leader to whom the president was most indebted, shone through this conversation. Fitz was "to tell Mitchell everything he wants... and Mitchell will do it," a commitment Colson and his boss agreed would pay "enormous dividends."

The next Oval Office discussion of Hoffa's release took place in the early afternoon of December 22, 1971, the day before Hoffa's release from Lewisburg. H.R. Haldeman, Nixon's chief of staff, brought the commutation order to the president's desk for signing. Their conversation revealed that Fitzsimmons's fondest hopes had come true.

HRH: Here's the annual clemency [inaudible; background noises include the scribbling sounds from Nixon's pen as he signs the documents].

RMN: You'll want to put that out. . . . Great. Please all the hard hats.

HRH: [inaudible]—in that you give him clemency with the understanding that he cannot hold office or be a member of any labor union, or even be involved in the affairs of them. Any labor union.

RMN: Oh, good. It's great.

HRH: [reading text] "That upon the condition that the said James R. Hoffa will not engage in direct or indirect management of any labor organization prior to March 6, 1980"—which is when his sentence would normally—

RMN: Expire.

HRH: "And if the aforesaid condition is not fulfilled, this commutation will be null and void in its entirety and" [inaudible].

RMN: [not fully audible—stops? fucks?] him.

HRH: Now that [not fully audible—stops? fucks?] him really, because [crosstalk] actually, we handled—he suffered, because if we did nothing he gets a mandatory release in 1975 and he'd be out and he could go back into the union and do anything he wants. So we put five more years' restriction on him than he would have had under the law. And his wife is still very ill; so we played the personal thing, that it serves no useful purpose to society to keep him locked up any more.

RMN: His wife is ill?

HRH: Yeah, see, she was so ill that at the jail, in Lewisburg, the prison warden was letting him out for two weeks, to go home to be with his wife, because she's been dying.

RMN: I see.

HRH: Uh, earlier this year, and then she didn't. But she's still very ill. So they're going to put it on the illness, and the five year, and the condition. And I think we came out pretty well on it. [inaudible] Teddy Kennedy will jump all over us, saying [inaudible]—

RMN: [inaudible][23]

Contrary to Judge Pratt's finding, these Oval Office conversations showed that the decision to block Hoffa's return to office was purely political, unrelated to protecting the public interest. Nixon and Haldeman clearly recognized that if Hoffa had simply served the rest of his term and been released later for good behavior he would have been free to pursue the Teamster presidency. But the commutation order, they also noted, would bar Hoffa from union office for "five more years," thereby keeping him from "doing what he wants." Nixon's conversation with Colson made clear that the president's sole intent was to satisfy Fitzsimmons and "please all the [labor union] hard hats". Had these discussions among the president and his aides been known at the time, Judge Pratt would almost certainly have found that Nixon lacked authority to impose his politically inspired restriction, thereby freeing Hoffa to challenge Fitz for the IBT presidency at the international union's next general convention. With that freedom, he would have had no reason to pick a fight with anyone but his successor. IBT Board members who had prospered under Fitz's rule and might fear a loss of their perks and privileges, but Hoffa could simply have promised a continuation of their favored status. Still a hero to the union's rank and file, he would have received their full support.

But the taped conversations lay hidden in the White House vaults and the court's negative decision became a watershed event in Hoffa's life. From this point on, the ostracized labor leader began to spin slowly out of control. He had counted on the lawsuit to provide an escape hatch from his sinking ship, and his agonized reaction to the judge's decision reflected the depth of his disappointment. Ever wishful, however, Hoffa let himself dream that the Watergate scandal might lead to Nixon's impeachment, bringing into the Oval Office his good friend and fellow Michigan resident, Gerald Ford. Ford might then grant him a full pardon, freeing him to hold union office.

Further emboldened by President Nixon's subsequent resignation, Hoffa developed a new plan some knew, even then, was delusional. To implement this new scheme he sought and gained the cooperation of his ever faithful friend, Local 299's President Dave Johnson. Together they would find a Teamster who would nominate Hoffa as a second presidential candidate, along with Johnson, in the Local's upcoming election in December. This would undermine Johnson's earlier agreement with the younger Fitzsimmons to form a coalition ticket, but so be it. The new candidate would not speak or campaign in any other way for the office. All electioneering would be carried out by subordinates who would operate, in Hoffa's fantasy, with a completely free hand. He would win the election and then immediately withdraw and appoint Johnson as the local union's acting president. As its elected but inactive chief executive he would be eligible to run for the IBT's top office in 1976 without technically violating, he insisted, the commutation order's restriction. And then, if elected, he would dare anyone, including the federal government, to try to unseat him. This contrivance was a measure of Hoffa's desperation, and of the pressures clouding his once clear-headed judgment.

Rumors of the Hoffa-Johnson plan spread along the grapevine, creating astonishment and foreboding among the members of Local 299. News of the fanciful plot shook Fitzsimmons's IBT office like one of McMaster's planted bombs. Hardly believing the reports he was getting, Fitz knew enough about their source and subject matter to take them seriously. He immediately sent word to Local 299 that he would use all available means to quash this rebellion, including, if necessary, an order putting the Detroit union in the hands of hand-picked trustees. Trusteeship, as Hoffa himself had often proved, was the IBT boss's ultimate weapon, challengeable only by prolonged and rarely successful litigation. No one, including the bizarre plan's proponents, doubted Fitzsimmons's power to take this step, or his determination to implement it. Adding to Hoffa's discomfort were newspaper reports that DOJ lawyers had learned of his scheme and were planning a lawsuit seeking his return to prison for violating the terms of his commutation order.

Anti-Hoffa sentiment at the local level grew stronger. Opposition to his latest power-play brought the Dave Johnson-Dick Fitzsimmons coalition to the brink of collapse. It also threatened Local 299's rank and file with a detested trusteeship. In this pressure cooker, Hoffa finally came to his senses and abandoned the harebrained plan to become the Local union's president in name only. He kept after Fitzsimmons, however, taking a swipe at his former sycophant in a year-end interview on a Detroit TV station. "They took Fitzsimmons up to the mountains and showed him the valley and he bought the valley. ... [H]e forgot his friends ... forgot who took him off a truck forty years ago and put him into an executive position."[24] Fitzsimmons responded in kind, calling Hoffa "nuts" and "a liar." He also predicted that his former boss "would never run again for IBT general president." Asked to comment on his opponent's prediction, Hoffa could only insist grimly he would return "some day, somehow."[25] The time left for him to make his move was fast running out.

CHAPTER 12

"My Friend Didn't Suffer"

The crumbling of his plan to sidestep Nixon's restrictive order left Hoffa with only one hope: that the US Circuit Court of Appeals for the District of Columbia would reverse Judge Pratt's decision, freeing him to challenge Fitzsimmons for the IBT presidency. As the autumn of 1974 moved into winter, the appellate court's ruling was months away. In the meantime he would stay on the offensive, touting his own strengths and chastising his opponent at every opportunity.

To reach a wider audience Hoffa turned to the national media. He began with *Esquire*, then in its heyday as the nation's most popular upscale magazine for men. Its March 1975 issue offered articles by Tom Wicker of the *New York Times*, Hollywood's Nora Ephron and British pundit Malcolm Muggeridge. That month's *Esquire* also featured a wide-ranging interview of Hoffa by novelist Christopher Davis. Vocal and volatile as ever, the former Teamster boss played himself up as a self-made, unpretentious homebody. "I don't go out. I do the dishes. I vacuum the floor. I do ... the Laundromat." As for modern society, "It's sick. I read about it; [but] ... goddamned if I can understand it."[1] In times past, he complained, people generously gave of their time and money with no expectation of a return.

Now, however, "You give a bum a buck every day, and the day you miss he'll say, 'Why that son-of-a-bitch, where's my buck?' "[2] He also unloaded on Frank Fitzsimmons, his successor. Fitz was an ungrateful "liar, ... a double-crosser who "failed in every promise he made" He was also an incompetent manager who "didn't know his ass from first base about operations."[3] Fitz's weaknesses reminded Hoffa of a friend's aphorism "You can't get tallow out of a gnat." "Yeah, that's right," he responded grimly, "but you can smash the gnat."[4] *Esquire's* interviewer concluded that "Hoffa thinks that he will now tell everything, as he puts it, and that as a consequence Fitzsimmons could go to prison."[5]

The frustrated ex-Teamster boss was also talking to Jerry Stanecki, an investigative reporter from Detroit radio station WXYZ. Stanecki was one of the few media personalities Hoffa felt he could trust. Staffers at *Playboy*—the successor to *Esquire* as the country's leading T & A magazine respectable enough to gain a USPS mailing discount—got wind of Stanecki's inside track and asked him to do a lengthy piece on Hoffa for their publication. The stiff-necked unionist at first refused to be in a "magazine with tits on the back of my picture" but later relented.[6] A series of wide-ranging interviews by Stanecki, the last of which took place in June, 1975, revealed a high-strung Hoffa on the brink of emotional collapse.

To the reporter's initial questions the former IBT boss replied calmly and frankly. On the subject of his personality: "You've been described as a man with a very big ego. Is that accurate?" "Certainly I got an ego. A man don't have an ego, he don't have any money and he don't have any ambition. ...Actually, an ego is just imagination. And if you don't have imagination you'll be working for somebody for the rest of your life."[7]

On his wealth:

Esquire: "Are you a millionaire?"

JRH: "I would say."

Esq: "We heard that once in a discussion with Jimmy, Jr. you asked 'How many men can come up with $2 million cash immediately?' "

JRH "I would say, exactly right."[8]

And on the use of extreme violence:

> Esq: "Did you ever threaten to kill Bobby Kennedy?"
>
> JRH: "Nope. Another lie."
>
> Esq: "What about killing people?"
>
> JRH: "Self-preservation's a big word. ...."
>
> Esq: "You've never killed anybody?"
>
> JRH: "Never, ... but I'm certainly not going to let someone kill *me*."[9]

When Stanecki moved on to Hoffa's friendships with known mobsters his interviewee began to lose control. After conceding he knew gangsters Moe Dalitz and Meyer Lansky, he said they were "victim[s] of harassment." "Then you don't think [either is] a member of organized crime?" "I don't believe there is any organized crime, period."[10] "But [it's] said that you knew more dangerous criminals than Dave Beck?" "Ah-ha! That's a different question....I know people ... in the big cities. I'm no different than the banks, ... the insurance companies, ... and the politicians. You're a damned fool not to be informed what makes a city run when you're tryin' to do business in the city."[11]

> Esq: "What about Johnny Dio?"
>
> JRH: "Friend of mine. No question about that."
>
> Esq: [Was he] a member of organized crime?"
>
> JRH: "Like you are."
>
> Esq: "Member of the Mafia?"
>
> JRH: "Like you are."[12]
>
> Esq "What about Frank Costello?"
>
> JRH: "The McClellan Committee said just that he was part of a family associated with organized crime."
>
> Esq: "Okay. The Mob, the family, the Mafia. Doesn't it amount to the same thing?"
>
> JRH: Bullshit! Take me. I pick up the phone and call anywhere in the United States. I don't give a fuck what union it is. ... I say listen, I want a favor. No questions asked. ... [The guy] says if

[he] can do it [he'll] call me back. He gets busy, maybe calls six other guys. Now, is that an organized crime? Is that an organized Mafia or some fuckin' thing?.... Some magazine said I control the Mafia. Now, I never heard a more goddamned ridiculous statement in the whole world than that goddamned magazine. They said my good friend Carlos Marcello called the Mob together and put up a million dollars to get Hoffa out of jail. What kind of bullshit is this? ... Yet the newspapers print it, the goddamned books write it. And it's a joke! *Mad* magazine, that cocksucker! They came out with a thing in there about Hoffa. Bullshit![13]

Hoffa's anger cloaked a deep-seated fear of loss: of his career, his reputation, his family's safety and perhaps his life. He turned a deaf ear, however, to suggestions that he hire a bodyguard, revealing a striking blindness to his own profile. "The only guy who needs a bodyguard is a liar, a cheat, a guy who betrays friendship ... I don't cheat nobody. I don't lie about nobody. I don't frame nobody. If I talk bad about people, I tell 'em. So what the hell's people gonna try to kill me for?" To which Stanecki replied, "To get you out of the way. If you win your fight against the 1980 restriction, don't you think somebody will try to have you killed?" "Hell no. Hell no. Ask ... any ten people in the United States whether or not I should have the right to get back in the union, and whether or not Fitzsimmons double-crossed me. You'll get your answer."[14] Hoffa knew that rectitude did not assure victory, nor victimization guarantee reward. But he would not admit, even to himself, that he was playing bet-the-farm poker with cutthroats. He might have a royal flush, but with three aces and a straight razor his gangland opponents held the higher hand.

During this same period Hoffa had a series of talks with Oscar Fraley, an author best known for writing *The Untouchables* with Eliot Ness. In his interviews with Fraley, Hoffa finally got real about organized crime and its influence within the IBT under Fitzsimmons's leadership. He began by admitting to what he called his "two disastrous mistakes." The first was "coming to grips with Robert F. Kennedy in a ... blood feud," thereby getting "railroaded" into a prison term that ended his career.[15] The other was naming Fitzsimmons to succeed him when he should have chosen his next in command, Harold Gibbons. Gibbons, Hoffa believed, would never have sought the president's restrictive order against him, the blame for which he put entirely on his inept successor.

In Fraley's book, published a few months after Hoffa's death, the latter's condemnation of Fitzsimmons mimicked Emile Zola's fiery castigation of the prosecutors of Alfred Dreyfus. "I charge Fitzsimmons with selling out to mobsters and ... racketeers. I charge him with making vast loans from the Teamster pension fund to known mobsters. I charge him with awarding a $1.3 million Teamster public relations program ... to two men with criminal records."[16] No longer in denial, Hoffa forsook generalizations for hard facts: "[I]n a severance-fringe benefit scheme, Fitzsimmons's son Don [and] underworld figure Louis Ostrer ... milked more than $1.185 million out of the pockets of Teamster members in the New York-New Jersey area alone. ... Ostrer and 'Johnny Dio' Dioguardi were [both] linked to the New York Mafia."[17] He identified "Tony Jack" Giacalone as "a reputed Detroit Mafia leader,"[18] and made no bones about what steps he would take to clean the IBT's house if he again became its leader. "Ever since Fitzsimmons took over, the underworld [has held] the balance of power in the Teamsters. ... Well, mobsters be damned ... When I get back, ... heads will roll."[19] Given the historic symbiosis between Hoffa and the Mafia, his apparent willingness to go public with these charges is shocking.

The formation of Hoffa's extensive network of Mafia relationships began in the mid–1930s. At that time he was Local 299's point man in its battles with employers' brass-knuckled henchmen and the club-wielding goons of competitive unions. Needing extra muscle he asked ex-girlfriend Sylvia Pagano for an introduction to Frank Coppola, her lover of the moment and the leader of Detroit's East Side Gang. Coppola put him in touch with Motor City mobsters Santo Perrone and Angelo Meli. Through the latter Hoffa hooked up with his longtime lawyer, William Bufalino, who was married to Meli's niece. He also met and began working with Anthony Giacalone, chief enforcer for the Zerilli family of Detroit.

These Detroit contacts led Hoffa into the underworld of Chicago. Through Perrone, he met the Windy City's Paul "Red" Dorfman, an underling to Salvatore "Sam" Giancana, the ranking member of Al Capone's old gang. Dorfman, in turn, brought Hoffa together with

Joey Glimco, another former Capone associate, and with Dorfman's stepson, Allen. These Detroit and Chicago mobsters took pains to avoid infringing on each other's territories. Any outside crime family looking to do "business" in either place prudently cleared their plans in advance with the dominant families of both cities.

Hoffa used William Bufalino, the future mainstay of the Teamsters Bar Association, to establish a relationship with Russell Bufalino, William's older cousin from Scranton, Pennsylvania, and with Russell's top troubleshooter, Frank Sheeran. The elder Bufalino, underboss and later head of the Joseph Barbara family of Northern Pennsylvania, was known as "the Quiet Don" for his soft-spoken manner. He was also a trustee of the powerful Vito Genovese family of New York City. As the Geneveses' upstate representative, Russell worked closely with his big city counterpart, Anthony "Fat Tony" Salerno. Through this connection the Quiet Don became a partner in highly profitable extortion and labor rackets with Tony Provenzano, the Genovese family's *caporegime* in Northern New Jersey who in earlier years had rapidly become one of Hoffa's chief Teamster lieutenants.

In later years Hoffa met and began working with Carlos Marcello of New Orleans and Santos Trafficante of Miami. These men were suave, firmly entrenched dons, each heading the most powerful Mafia family in their respective states. Both had operated in pre-Castro Cuba, and both were heavily into illegal gambling and drug trafficking in the US. By the early 1970s both had formed alliances with Joe Bonanno, the leader of what had been one of New York City's most prominent Mafia families. Following a bitter feud among these NYC crime bosses ten years earlier—the so-called "Banana Wars"—Bonanno fled the Eastern seaboard and took up residence in Arizona. These three— Marcello, Trafficante and Bonanno—became known as the principal Mafia bosses in the southern United States.

Rounding out the circle of Hoffa's closest criminal associates was Carmine "Lillo" Galante, underboss of the Bonanno family. When Hoffa entered Lewisburg in 1967 Galante was already there, serving a twenty-year sentence for trading in narcotics. A cold-blooded "stone killer," Lillo was known as the "*Capo di tutti Capi*" of the prison's infamous cellblock G, home to 150 long-term inmates.[20] Labeled "Mafia Row" for its high percentage of hardened criminals, this area's population included Tony Provenzano and a score of his mafiosi brethren.[21] Through the unfathomable workings of prison politics but undoubtedly influenced by Hoffa's Mafia connections, Lewisburg's warden assigned the new arrival to Galente's fiefdom. In short order the entire prison population knew that Lillo, the lord of cellblock G, had a new protégé. It was the one time in Hoffa's life he willingly submitted to another's rule.

Lillo Galante was a sinewy fifty-seven-year-old whose daily workouts kept him in fighting trim. Only five feet three inches tall but mean as a snake—with a criminal career dating back to his childhood—he was reputed to have murdered some eighty Mob enemies. Fellow drug-traffickers also credited Galente as the inventor of the "black man" test, a pathologically cruel method of determining the quality of heroin prior to its purchase. In it, an African American male would be injected with a "double bag" of the drug. If the victim became comatose within a specified time, the proffered dope would be deemed "pure."[22] A man of iron will and few words, Lillo made and enforced the rules for the residents of cellblock G. To make sure other inmates showed him proper respect, he went out of his way to get it. On entering Lewisburg's dining hall, he would go directly to the head of the line of those waiting to be served. If hardened black criminals stood at the front, the diminutive Bonanno underboss would snarl, "Get the fuck out the way, niggers."[23] And they did.

In his post-prison days Hoffa's connections with organized crime did nothing to impair his legendary stature among ordinary Teamsters. They believed that if the ex-IBT boss regained power he could control his gangland friends as he had done throughout his career. The rank and file's continuing support was the main source of his belief he could successfully challenge both Fitzsimmons and the mobsters now in Fitz's camp. He saw his popularity within the country's largest and most politically powerful labor union as a monument to his unique leadership talents. He was a well-known if controversial figure in the eyes of the general public. State and national office holders had for years paid him respect based on fear, perhaps the most reliable form of political support. All of these considerations led Hoffa to believe he could safely threaten to "out" Fitzsimmons's ties to organized crime. He was too popular, too powerful, too dangerous a target for Mob retribution.

At the top of Hoffa's list of perceived mobster pals in 1975 were Allen Dorfman and Tony Giacalone, both of whom were leading beneficiaries of his past generosity. He also counted on the friendship of Russell Bufalino, a major recipient of Teamster largess and someone with whom he had never exchanged a quarrelsome word. The Quiet Don's most reliable hitman, Frank ("the Irishman") Sheeran, was the only professional killer Hoffa dared to consider a trusted friend. Years earlier, stimulated by Marlon Brando's portrayal of a union dissident in *On the Waterfront*, Sheeran had decided he could succeed as a business agent in the Teamsters union. To help him move in this direction he sought Bufalino's help. At the Irishman's request, when the two men met in a South Philadelphia bar, his boss made a telephone call to Hoffa and, after explaining why he was calling, put Sheeran on the line. The Teamster boss's alleged first words to his caller were "I heard you paint houses," a gangland code for splattering a shooting victim's blood on nearby walls.[23] "I do carpentry work, too," replied the Mafioso gunman, referring to the construction of coffins and the disposal of bodies. That call, according to Sheeran, got him a job at a local Teamster union in Wilmington, Delaware, where he eventually became the Local's president. It also led to the development of a personal relationship between the two men, and to Hoffa's increasing trust of Sheeran as a friend and supporter. Now, as the former IBT boss desperately sought a return to power, he considered the Irishman one of his most reliable protectors.

In fact, Hoffa was alone in thinking he could openly criticize Fitzsimmons for his alliance with organized crime and simultaneously expect the Mob's support. By early 1975 the Mob bosses' allegiance to Hoffa's successor had solidified. Included within the latter's group of supporters were the three southern dons, along with the principal crime families of New York, New Jersey and Pennsylvania. With Fitz's unquestioning and undemanding approval, Allen Dorfman was spreading Teamster pension fund loans among criminal families like manna from Yahweh. Included within the loan czar's benevolence were his own Giancana family in Chicago and the Zerilli family in Detroit. Russell Bufalino worked hand-in-glove with William Bufalino, his Detroit lawyer cousin, and with Teamster-associated mobsters in New Jersey and Pennsylvania. These criminal barons were now united in their opposition to Hoffa's return. None was about to risk the growing value of his place at the Teamster feeding trough by endorsing a rash insurgent, though it be Hoffa himself.

The ex-IBT boss also misjudged the support he expected to receive from Carmine Galante, his Lewisburg guardian. Hoffa believed his friendship with the ferocious Lillo remained undiminished now that both were free men. Galante, Hoffa felt, was the one mobster whom Provenzano and his allies would not dare to cross. The origin of this error, and the way it played out in the labyrinthine structure of organized crime, is a story of gangland intrigue worthy of Machiavelli at his very best.

****

Galante left Lewisburg prison on parole in 1974. A ranking member of the Bonanno family, his evolving mindset had been strongly influenced by conflicts with other mafiosi, including Carlo Gambino, a member of the infamous Anastasia family of New York. Among the heads of New York City's five Mafia families, no one was more powerful than Gambino. Born in Sicily in 1902, he found his way to New York where he joined the criminal gang led by Alberto Anastasia. Bright, ruthless and ambitious, he rose through the ranks to become the family's underboss. In 1957, at the urging of Vito Genovese, who hoped to expand his power by taking over the Anastasia family, Gambino orchestrated Anastasia's assassination. In a scene well-reported at the time and later made famous in Mario Puzo's *The Godfather*, the ambitious underboss's henchmen riddled Anastasia's body with bullets as he sat in a barber's chair in New York's Park Sheraton Hotel. Following the murder Gambino disappointed his co-conspirator Genovese by keeping tight control of the Anastasia family himself while artfully remaining a staunch ally of Vito Genovese.

Their alliance continued through the Genoveses' fight with New York's Bonanno family in the '60s, during which Gambino earned the intense hatred of Lillo Galante, the infamous Bonanno underboss and Hoffa's jailhouse protector. When Lillo was paroled from Lewisburg in 1974, organized crime members thought him ready for war. "There was no doubt in my mind," said a fellow mafioso, that Galante, the volatile leader of cellblock G, "planned to take over the New York Mobs" when he left prison with Gambino as his chief target.[24] Galante's parting prison statements contributed to this widespread view of his intended conduct. "When I get out," he vowed, "I'll make Carlo Gambino shit in the middle of Times Square."[25]

Carlo Gambino knew of Galante's loathing for him, and of the latter's reputation for uncontrollable fierceness and cruelty. Well in advance of the Lillo's release Gambino learned the newly freed prisoner would be coming after him. To shore up his defenses he developed a plan to strengthen the power of his allies in the Genovese family, which was in decline. As the first of two suggestions he recommended that the Genoveses turn over some of their drug-trafficking operations to Meyer Lansky's people in New York City. This they did, thereby generating Lansky's goodwill while reinforcing Gambino's relationship with him. In this way the cagey Gambino also "developed stronger lines of communication to the Trafficante-Marcello-Bonanno criminal empire in the South" because they were Lansky's friends.[26] This tactic, in addition to widening Carlo's influence, was a signal to Galante that his enemy Gambino, along with the Genoveses, wanted cooperation not confrontation.

Gambino's second proposal to his allies in the Genovese family was that they offer some of their operations in Upstate New York to Russell Bufalino, who had recently replaced a Galante enemy as the head of the drug-trafficking business in the city of Buffalo. Because Bufalino himself had done nothing to alienate Galante, Gambino hoped that this favor from the Genovese family to the Pennsylvania don, in addition to strengthening their own power, would sit well with the mad-dog underboss of the Bonanno gang. His hope turned out to be well-founded.

Parlaying his new friendship with Bufalino, Gambino used it to further soften Galente's animosity toward him and his Genovese allies. Among the latter was Tony Provenzano, one of Galante's most outspoken enemies dating back to their time together as inmates at Lewisburg. Knowing of Tony Pro's various partnerships with Russell Bufalino, Gambino sought the latter's help. At Gambino's urging, Bufalino convinced Tony Pro, the part owner of a New Jersey bank, to authorize a $25,000 personal loan to Galante. This was a not-so-subtle signal that the Genoveses wanted to ease the tension between themselves and the Bonannos.

These Gambino-inspired chessboard moves of indirect support for Galante—through Lansky, Bufalino and Provenzano—had the desired effect. Containing his wrath, Lillo decided not to attack Gambino or Provenzano. He was on parole after serving only twelve years of his twenty-year sentence and did not want to risk a charge of instigating mob violence, a violation that would surely send him back to prison. In addition, now that the Trafficante-Marcello-Bonanno trio was more at ease with their New York City counterparts, Galante could concentrate on rebuilding his lucrative drug-trafficking business on the East Coast. In these circumstances the toughest mobster whose backing Hoffa most counted on gave up all thought, if ever he had been so inclined, of acting as the ex-Teamster boss's defender. This was a purely unintended result of Gambino's crafty moves but it left Hoffa with no serious Mob support.

****

His public campaign to regain the Teamster presidency continued unabated. In private, his promises to rid the union of Mob influence grew increasingly strident. Among the mafiosi feeling most threatened was Russell Bufalino. The Quiet Don was a prime benefactor of Teamster pension fund loans. He had multiple interests in legitimate businesses using Teamster labor, and in highly profitable, union-related scams. His principal partner in these latter enterprises, and in extortion and various other rackets in New York and New Jersey, was Tony Provenzano. In particular, their jointly owned "labor-leasing" companies put hundreds of union members out of work and tens of thousands of dollars in Bufalino's and Provenzano's pockets. There is no report of any conversation between the two mobsters about the Hoffa problem, but there can be little doubt they discussed it. They are "close … in everything," said one government lawyer. "Everywhere we find Bufalino we find Tony Pro."[27]

The Pennsylvania don took the lead in warning Hoffa directly that the Mob's opposition to his return to Teamster office was deadly serious. Bufalino saw the writing on the wall as early as mid-October, 1974. On October 18 more than a thousand people were expected at Philadelphia's Latin Quarter for dinner, entertainment and speeches at Frank Sheeran Appreciation Night. The keynote speaker was to be none other than Jimmy Hoffa. Bufalino sent his chief hitman to invite the former Teamster boss to dinner in Philly with the two of them and another "friend" on the night before the scheduled celebration. Hoffa accepted, and accompanied by Sheeran he joined Bufalino and Angelo Bruno, Philadelphia's crime boss, at a local bar and restaurant known as Broadway Eddie's.

As described by the Irishman, the four men sat side-by-side at a long table facing the bar, aligned in the order of Sheeran, Hoffa, Bufalino, Bruno. All four ate dinner, but for the short time they were together only the two principals spoke, turned toward each other and away from their companions. They quickly got down to business. "What are you running [now] for," asked Bufalino, "you don't need the money." "It's not about the money," Hoffa replied, "I'm not letting Fitz have the union. I'm going to take care of the people who have been fucking me." To make sure his guest understood the message the Quiet Don said, "There are people higher up than me that feel you are demonstrating a lack of appreciation. ..."[28] Hoffa heard him clearly but made no reply. Bufalino was not a man to repeat himself and the meeting soon ended. As they left, he took Sheeran aside. "Some people have a serious problem with your friend. Talk to your friend. Tell him what it is."[29] Both men knew what "it" meant.

The Irishman reported that he and Hoffa went back to the latter's room at the Warwick Hotel. "I didn't know what Russell was going to say to you tonight, Jimmy," he said, "but I know they mean it."[30] His bullheaded listener was unmoved. "If anything unnatural happens to Hoffa, I can tell you all hell will break loose. ... I've got records in the hands of the right people, and the motherfuckers know I've kept records on all of it. And I've got it all in safe places. ... Nobody scares Hoffa. I'm going after Fitz and I'm going to win this election." "You know what this means," the hit man insisted. Russell "himself told me to tell you what it is." "They wouldn't dare," was his friend's defiant retort.[31]

The clear-eyed judgment and perceptive instincts that had served Hoffa throughout his career now conflicted with his desperate need for recognition and revenge. Despite his changed circumstances he believed he could win his current battle with Fitzsimmons in the same way he had broken impasses in past labor contract negotiations: blast your opponent in public but cut a deal in private. A single thought, however, began to eat away at his confidence. Tony Provenzano, the former friend who had recently threatened to rip Hoffa's guts out, was the one mobster he knew would oppose him. Hostility from this high-ranking member of the powerful Genovese family would certainly complicate Hoffa's planned return. But if Tony Pro's anger could be assuaged and Galante's expected support retained, the less antagonistic gangster elements, he believed, would rally to his side.

The ex-Teamster boss was not alone in his thoughts about the crucial role Provenzano could play in Hoffa's effort to regain the IBT presidency. Beginning in the spring of 1975 Tony Giacalone, a friend to both men, encouraged Hoffa to agree to meet with Tony Pro in an effort to settle their differences. To convey that message Tony Jack used Louis Linteau, a mutual friend, as an intermediary. Linteau, the president of Teamster Local 614 in Pontiac, Michigan, also operated an airport limousine service. He faithfully relayed Giacolone's urgings but they fell on deaf ears. Hoffa did not trust Provenzano and knew the temperamental New Jersey capo's cooperation would bear a high price. Finally, however, in early June of 1975 he had a change of heart. Pressed by Linteau, and remembering Russell Bufalino's earlier warning of Mob retribution, the ex-Teamster boss told his friend to advise Giacalone that he was willing to try to work something out with Provenzano if the New Jersey mobster could be persuaded to approach Hoffa in the same spirit.

Giacalone took a few weeks to respond but his delayed reply through Linteau was positive: Tony Pro would be in town for the August 2 wedding of William Bufalino's daughter and would meet with Hoffa and Tony Jack on Wednesday, July 30. The plan, Giacalone said, was for the three men to rendezvous at 2:30 that afternoon in the parking lot of the Machus Red Fox, a restaurant on Telegraph Road in Bloomfield Township about twenty miles northwest of Detroit. The Red Fox was a popular suburban eatery but not a place where this trio would likely be recognized, particularly on a mid-week summer afternoon. Left unspecified was whether they would stay in the restaurant parking lot or proceed to another location for a private "sit-down."

Hoffa agreed, but his mind raced with thoughts of how to strengthen his hand and protect his flanks. His first step in that direction was to call Frank Sheeran to tell him of the proposed meeting, and to ask the

Irishman to join him at the Red Fox at 2:00 p.m., one-half hour before the scheduled meeting with the others. Sheeran would be an acceptable addition to their gathering, he reasoned, because the hit-man's boss, Russell Bufalino, would approve of Hoffa's attempt to negotiate a truce with the Quiet Don's business partner Provenzano. And it made sense for Hoffa to bring Sheeran along: what better ally to have with you at a Mob powwow than an experienced enforcer who had your absolute trust? Unknowingly, with this request Hoffa increased the apparent plausibility of his enemies' plan to entrap him.

About 1:00 p.m. on July 30th Hoffa left home alone in his 1974 dark green Grande Ville hardtop, telling his wife he was going to a meeting at the Red Fox restaurant. Josephine later disclosed that at the time he seemed unusually tense and jumpy. Instead of heading directly for the restaurant he stopped at the office of Linteau's limousine company, probably to get last-minute assurance that he was doing the right thing and possibly to ask his friend to come with him. Finding that Linteau had gone to lunch, Hoffa talked instead to the owner's assistant, Frank Reeves, who later told investigators that Hoffa had said he was on his way to a meeting with Giacalone and Provenzano. Further evidence of his intent to meet these two was a notation on his office calendar for July 30: "TG—2:00 p.m.—Red Fox."[32]

At two o'clock Hoffa stood outside his car at the Red Fox parking lot awaiting Sheeran's arrival. About a half-hour later, still alone and irked by the Irishman's failure to join him as promised, he grew impatient. Though Provenzano and Giacalone were not expected until 2:30, Hoffa called Josephine to complain. "Where the hell is Tony Giacalone?" he asked. "I'm being stood up!"[33] About twenty minutes later the labor boss, who normally would have been long gone from an unexplained no-show, was still there. Using the pay phone in the entranceway to the Red Fox he called Linteau, who had now returned to his office. Enraged, Hoffa griped bitterly to his friend that he was being stood up but did not say he was leaving. If the two mobsters ever showed up, his willingness to stay put for so long would work against him in their deliberations. In any case it revealed his belief that the outcome of their meeting would determine his future. His patience was rewarded minutes later, but not in the manner he had expected.

****

On the night of Tuesday, July 29, Russell Bufalino and Frank Sheeran dined early at Brutico's Restaurant in Old Forge, Pennsylvania, about ten miles southwest of Scranton. There the Irishman received his assignment for the following day: he was to whack Jimmy Hoffa. This would be his eighth hit in service to Bufalino, a task in which he had never failed. His mafioso boss then outlined the plan in full. The assassin and six others—only some of whom would know their objective—would carry out their mission via a tightly scheduled, intricately coordinated plan. This was serious business, but hardly an extraordinary matter for seasoned professionals. Understanding his instructions, Bufalino's husky gunman asked few if any questions and the two men parted company.

Leaving the restaurant that night in his car Sheeran headed west, alone with his thoughts. Known as "The Irishman," Frank Sheeran was perhaps the Quiet Don's most valuable asset. Born in Philadelphia in 1920 of a Swedish mother and Irish father, Sheeran was expelled from school while in the ninth grade. When his principal unwisely cuffed him for a minor offense the six-foot student retaliated by breaking the principal's jaw with one quick blow. At odds with an undemonstrative mother and a domineering father, the angry youngster decided to leave town accompanied by an older friend. Both got jobs at a traveling "honky-tonk carnival," Sheeran as a roustabout and part-time barker at the carnival's girlie show.[34] Three years later, taller and beefier, he signed on as a logger with a lumber company operating primarily in the Maine woods. For three more years he cut down trees by day and on many week nights fought in boxing matches with fellow workers for amusement, and for added income by betting on himself.

Days after Pearl Harbor, Sheeran enlisted in the army. Serving first as an MP and then as a dog-soldier infantryman, he endured fourteen continuous months of heavy fighting in Sicily, on Anzio's beaches and onward into Germany until the war's end. Back home as a civilian he took any job he could find: hauling ice, delivering coal, working as a construction laborer and keeping order as a nightclub bouncer. His intense combat experience had taken a toll; he began to drink heavily and to show a violent temper on slight provocation. He regularly sold his blood for ten dollars a pint and once fought, unsuccessfully, for the chance to win a hundred dollars by lasting three rounds with a carnival's kangaroo.

Finally settling down, Sheeran found employment as a truck-loader at the Swift Meat Company's dock in Philadelphia. This led to a better job as the driver of a meat truck for Food Fair, a Swift customer. In this occupation, naturally enough, he became a member of the city's local Teamsters union. Ruggedly good looking and now a strapping six foot four, he found a wife to whom he managed to stay permanently married, and with whom he had four daughters. But his problems and bad habits continued. For extra money he sold banned lottery tickets on commission and then moved into a larger game of illicitly selling partial truckloads of meat, hiding the diminished deliveries by secretly rearranging the hindquarters hanging at his employer's refrigerated receiving plant. He also began to keep company with some Italian friends among Food Fair's Teamster drivers, habituating their favorite bars, restaurants and social clubs. Coincidentally he met Russell Bufalino who immediately recognized the big man's potential and befriended him accordingly. In those days the Irishman also came into contact with Angelo Bruno, Philadelphia's Mafia boss.

Food Fair's detectives eventually figured out that Sheeran was stealing the company's product but were able to arrest only the Philadelphia Mob-connected thief who bought the truck driver's stolen meat. Company officials told the Irishman that they would have to subpoena him as a witness against his accomplice unless he silently resigned, in which case they would not press charges. Knowing he would regret the consequences of ratting on one of Bruno's men—even one this lowly—he walked off the job and kept his mouth shut. As he had hoped, this got him praise from his Mafia friends along with opportunities to earn bigger money. By accepting one such offering, however, he made a near-fatal mistake.

Sheeran had come to know a man named "Whispers" DiTulio, a small-time Philadelphia racketeer who made the Irishman an offer too tempting to ignore. DiTulio owned a small linen supply company facing stiff competition from a new competitor owned by Jews. If Sheeran would put these newcomers out of business by torching their plant he would receive $10,000, a huge sum compared to his ordinary earnings. Intrigued, the big man decided to case the new linen company's premises. On the night he chose to do so a watchman silently observed the Irishman's noticeable silhouette and reported it to his bosses. The next day Sheeran found himself before Bufalino and Bruno in an otherwise empty room, both in a decidedly hostile mood. From them he learned the owners of the new linen company were part of Philly's Jewish gang with Bufalino himself as one of their partners.

In a state of shock, and pleading ignorance and inexperience, Sheeran told his interrogators that Whispers had put him up to the job. This was the first and last mistake he could make without retribution, said the two mafiosi chiefs, who then gave him only one viable choice: "It's your responsibility," they told him, "to take care of this matter by tomorrow. That's the chance you get. Capish?" Nodding, Sheeran replied "Capish."[35] The next morning police found DiTulio's body on the sidewalk, dead from a .32-caliber bullet fired at close range. When the big Irishman met with Bruno a night or so later the Philadelphia boss·bought him dinner. Sheeran was now a made man.

****

On the night he received instructions from Bufalino, the gunman's destination was Port Clinton, Ohio, an out-of-the-way village on the southwestern shore of Lake Erie about twenty-five miles east of Toledo and forty miles due south, across the lake, from Detroit. He and Bufalino would meet there the next day in a designated restaurant to set the plan in motion. After a few hours behind the wheel he stopped at a Howard Johnson Inn in Western Pennsylvania. He tried to sleep but could not quiet his mind. He had no fear for his own life or the lives of his wife and daughters. His first loyalty was to Bufalino, for whom he must kill or be killed himself for disobedience. If he tried to run away someone else would do his assigned job and then come after him. If he performed now as in the past the Quiet Don would protect him in what was sure to be a tumultuous aftermath.

These rationalizations usually settled him down but this night was different. Unlike his usual target, Hoffa was Sheeran's business colleague, benefactor and personal friend. Shooting him at point-blank range would test the Irishman's nerves as never before. Lying awake, he could only tell himself that Bufalino's decision to "put [him] in the thing" was the best life insurance he could have asked for.[36] Rumors had previously surfaced that Hoffa might use his Irish friend to paint the houses of Provenzano and Fitzsimmons. If that speculation got stronger Sheeran's life would be in danger. Because the hit on the ex-Teamster boss had surely been cleared with Mob bosses in New York, Detroit and Chicago, whispers of the Irishman's role would spread among Hoffa's enemies, ending their fear of Sheeran coming after them. It might also lessen the chances that Bufalino would use him for future hits on the Quiet Don's gangland enemies. And most calming of all—though insufficient to induce immediate sleep—was the thought that Hoffa was already a dead man walking.

Early the next morning, ragged but adrenalin-energized, Sheeran settled into his black Lincoln and set out for Port Clinton. Bufalino, accompanied by his wife, her sister and the Irishman's wife, met him in the small restaurant there as planned. Around 12:30 p.m. the two men left in the gunman's car, ostensibly on business for two or three hours while the women talked and had lunch. A few minutes later the black Lincoln pulled up at an airport with one grass strip and a windsock where a two-seat propeller plane sat waiting. Sheeran got out, leaving his boss in the car's front passenger seat. As he took his place beside the pilot, whom he recognized, neither man looked directly at the other. As the plane began to roll, the gunman glanced through its right-side window at the parked car. "Russell," he noted, "had already started to nod off to sleep."[37]

About an hour later the plane landed at a small airport near Pontiac, Michigan. In its parking lot Sheeran found the aged Ford car which had been described to him, its keys under the driver's seat. It was a Mafia-acquired loaner, almost impossible to trace. Heading south he drove past the Red Fox restaurant on Telegraph Road and in a few more minutes, taking back roads as instructed, arrived at the house where the hit would take place. Located at 17841 Beaverland Street in greater Detroit's northwestern area, the home had been rented from an owner probably paid to be out of town that day and expecting no visitors. The Irishman turned into the driveway and parked behind a Buick, another nondescript loaner that had brought three Provenzano minions to the scene, all of whom were already inside the house. In the front hall to greet Sheeran was Salvatore "Sally Bugs" Briguglio, Tony Pro's chief enforcer who had once taken a rap for his boss and gone to prison for it. Briguglio's trim, five-foot-seven-inch frame belied his toughness. Nicknamed for his bug-eyed squint behind thick glasses he was also a business agent in New Jersey's Local 560, one of several Teamster unions controlled by his boss. Out of sight in the rear of the house was one of the Andretta brothers, either Thomas, an ex-con and labor racketeer, or Stephen, a business agent of Local 84, both of whom were Provenzano loyalists from New Jersey. With Andretta was another young man, also an "Italian guy."[38] They were the clean-up men who would wait in secret until needed.

Several minutes later a maroon Mercury drew up alongside the curb in front of the house. Its driver and sole occupant was Chuckie O'Brien, who had borrowed the car earlier that day from Joey Giacalone, Tony Jack's son. He would later tell the FBI he had borrowed the car in order to deliver to Robert Holmes Sr., who headed Teamster Joint Council 43, the gift of a twenty-pound Coho salmon packed in ice in a plastic bag inside a cardboard box.[39] That much was true, but O'Brien kept secret his directive to go from there to the house where Sheeran and Briguglio would be waiting. Nor did he ever say who told him to do so, though the likeliest source of that order was the elder Giacalone. Chuckie was probably told only that he was to pick up the Irishman and Sally Bugs and take them to the rendezvous with Hoffa at the Machus Red Fox. As always in such matters, the fewer who knew the truth the better.

Suspects in the Hoffa abduction arriving for lineup. Salvatore Briguglio, 45, of Paramus, New Jersey ,(R) and Thomas A. Andretta, 38, of Housbrouk Heights, New Jersey, arrive at the Oakland County jail to appear in a lineup for an eyewitness to the abduction of Jimmy Hoffa. December 6, 1975.

Sheeran squeezed his big frame into the Mercury's right front seat; Sally Bugs took a place in the back seat, behind the driver. "What the fuck is this?" Briguglio asked, wrinkling his nose and pointing to a wet spot at his feet. Chuckie explained that the package he had just delivered to Holmes had leaked onto the car's floor and he had not had a chance to wipe it up. Well, "The fuckin' seat is wet," too, said Provenzano's muscleman, wiping his hands with a handkerchief.[40] This prosaic detail was a happenstance, fortuitously helping to keep Hoffa calm when confronted a few minutes later by additional people bringing unexpected changes in the planned sit-down. The presence of Sheeran, his trusted friend, would also be comforting, particularly when he explained that his boss, Russell Bufalino, wanted to be part of the meeting. Briguglio's participation, though surprising to Hoffa, would seem to confirm Provenzano's attendance at the upcoming meeting. And despite their recent separation, O'Brien's role as their driver in a car owned by the son of Giacalone—whom Hoffa believed to be waiting for him—would look perfectly natural.

On their arrival at the Red Fox's parking lot, Sally Bugs spotted Hoffa's empty car and told Chuckie to park their vehicle between the green Pontiac and the restaurant. After all, the ex-Teamster boss might have a pistol under his front seat, so better to head him off in advance. The foursome waited, and moments later Hoffa appeared, walking towards his auto. O'Brien put his own car in gear and moved slowly toward their quarry. "I'm sorry I'm late," said the driver through his open window. Hoffa was furious. "What the fuck are you doing here? Who the fuck invited you?" he yelled, punching his finger into Chuckie's chest. And, "Who the hell is he?" Hoffa growled, pointing at Sally Bugs. "I'm with Tony Pro," said Briguglio.[41] Unintimidated by Hoffa's angry curses Provenzano's man asked him to lower his voice as it was drawing attention from a straggler or two in the lot at that hour. "Look who's here," he said, pointing at Sheeran. Bending down, Hoffa for the first time saw his Irish friend in the front seat, who waved at him familiarly. Briguglio continued, "His friend wanted to be at the thing. They're at the house waitin'."[42]

Sheeran could see the wheels turning in Hoffa's mind. Still frowning and tight-lipped, but a bit flustered by his own outbursts, the impatient labor leader walked around the car and got in the back seat next to Sally Bugs. As they drove off he said to the Irishman, "You were supposed to call me last night. I waited in front of the restaurant at two o'clock for you. You were going to be sitting in my car with me when they showed." "I just got in," the gunman replied. "There was a delay in plans. McGee (his code name for Russell Bufalino) had to rearrange things so ... we could do this meeting right, not sitting in a car." Glaring at Briguglio, Hoffa yelled, "Who the fuck is Pro, sending a fucking errand boy?"[43] Trying to calm the waters and noting the fish smell, O'Brien interjected, "We're almost there. I had to run an errand."[44] Hoffa's rhetorical question never got answered and they were at the house in a matter of minutes.

The two loaner autos—the New Jersey Buick and Sheeran's Ford— were still parked in the driveway. Sally Bugs, Hoffa and Sheeran got out of Chuckie's car. As the latter two walked toward the house Briguglio got back in O'Brien's Mercury, this time in the front seat beside the

Detroit house checked for clues in Hoffa's disappearance. Investigators look-ing into the disappearance of Teamster Union leader Jimmy Hoffa ripped up floor boards in this northwest Detroit home on May 28, 2004, looking for traces of blood. Photo dated June 1, 2004.

driver who immediately sped off. This appeared normal to Hoffa as neither was important enough to be included in the meeting. The real reason for their departure was so neither could later say what happened after they left.

With his Irish friend close behind, Hoffa entered the house through the front door expecting to be greeted by Bufalino, Provenzano and Giacalone. Shocked by the silent emptiness and instantly aware that something was seriously amiss, he wheeled and headed back towards the door, colliding with the burly Irishman but continuing his outward charge. With his adrenalin rushing and his mind in overdrive, he either failed to see the pistol in his trusted friend's hand or assumed it had been drawn for his protection, and did not look back. As he neared the front door two shots rang out, fired from what the assassin called a "decent range": close enough for accuracy but beyond the reach of spattering blood. Both bullets entered Hoffa's brain "behind his right ear," crumpling him to the floor, his life extinguished.[45]

Ever the professional, Sheeran looked back down the hall to make sure the clean-up team was not coming after him. Satisfied they were awaiting his exit he wiped his "piece" clean and placed it near Hoffa's fallen body. There was no rug or carpeting on the hallway's wooden floor, only a sheet of linoleum on the area near the doorway. Head down and breathing hard, the assassin walked hurriedly out the front door and back to his loaner car. Driving away he reflected on how well the day's planners had done their job. The neighboring houses were not particularly close, and no one from them seemed to be stirring. He learned later that Andretta and his helper, after a thorough house-cleaning, had put the victim in a body bag, taken their burden out the rear entrance and placed it in the trunk of the car that had brought them from New Jersey to Detroit. They drove with Hoffa's body to Central Sanitation Services, a Mob-controlled facility owned by Raffael Quasarano and Peter Vitale at 8215 Moran Street in Hamtramck, a northern suburb of Detroit. There Hoffa's body was cremated in the company's trash incinerator. The two men then picked up Sally Bugs, whom O'Brien had dropped off at some pre-arranged location. Their business done, the three mobsters drove back to New Jersey to report the day's events to their boss, Tony Provenzano.

Twenty minutes after leaving the death scene Sheeran arrived back at the Pontiac airport and his waiting plane. Again there was no communication between passenger and pilot. The Irishman consoled himself with the thought that "my friend didn't suffer."[46] They landed on Port Clinton's grass runway just over three hours after their first take-off. Neither airfield required the filing of a plan or kept a record of the two flights. The gunman's black roadster was where he had left it, with Bufalino dozing inside. They drove back to the small restaurant where the women patiently awaited their return, and the reunited party went into Detroit to spend the night. To that point, the two men had spoken of the hit-man's mission only once, back at the landing strip as the Irishman started up his car's engine. Russell "winked his good eye at me," noted the killer, "and said softly with his raspy voice, 'I hope you had a pleasant flight, my Irish friend.' " To which Sheeran replied, "I hope you had a good sleep."[47]

Epilogue

Hoffa's disappearance sparked the FBI's most intensive manhunt since the assassination of Martin Luther King Jr. Field agents spent thousands of hours pursuing leads and interviewing potential sources of information. Surveillance teams kept watches on everyone considered a suspect or material witness. Scores of staffers at the agency's regional offices and D.C. headquarters reviewed incoming reports, sending summaries to the agency's top brass. Six months later the Bureau reached a consensus: the missing labor leader—or "JRH," as FBI memos identified him—was the victim of a gangland slaying planned by the Mafia. The prime movers behind the assassination, said the FBI, were the two Anthonys: Provenzano and Giacalone. Tony Jack had lured Hoffa to the Red Fox restaurant on the false premise that Tony Pro would meet them there. Instead of showing up himself, Provenzano sent his underlings whose job was to convince their target they were taking him to the promised meeting. With Hoffa in the back seat of their car they probably drove to an isolated spot and beat or shot him to death. They then hid or destroyed his body in a manner calculated to mask their own identity and to deepen the mystery of his disappearance.

In short, the FBI essentially got it right. Details of the murder eluded them, however, as did hard evidence sufficient to support their theory. Two years later, in early 1978, an isolated incident brought into focus one of the FBI's "working theories" that Hoffa's body was

Rubble of sanitation company in Jimmy Hoffa case. LaRonda Friday and Royce Bramlet, who live next to the Central Sanitation Services Company which was destroyed by fire early in 1978, look through its remains after hearing the new theory of the disposal of Hoffa. September 10, 1978.

cremated at Central Sanitation Services in Hamtramck. Central's entire facility, buildings and equipment, was turned to rubble by a fire whose origin remains an ongoing mystery.

The Bureau set out its findings in an internal memorandum entitled "Hoffex Conference, FBI Headquarters, January 27 & 28, 1976." Six people claimed to have seen Hoffa in the parking lot of the Machus Red Fox restaurant on the afternoon of July 30.[1] One of these, a man, said the labor leader was sitting "in the right rear seat of a maroon Lincoln or Mercury" in the restaurant's parking lot, and that "three other individuals" were in the car with him.[2] From a group of photographs a woman identified Sally Bugs Briguglio as a passenger in the Mercury's other rear seat.[3] Another witness identified Chuckie O'Brien as the car's driver.[4] O'Brien told the FBI he had driven Joey Giacalone's maroon Mercury that afternoon but denied going to the Red Fox. Police dogs identified Hoffa's scent in the impounded Mercury's right rear passenger seat. Investigators found a "three-inch brown hair on the [car's] rear seat backrest with characteristics [of] known JRH hairs."[5] But not until twenty-six years later, using new techniques to analyze DNA material from Hoffa's hairbrush, was the FBI able to conclude that this single hair belonged, in fact, to the murder victim.

The Hoffex memo listed a dozen additional suspects thought to be connected with Hoffa's disappearance, including Provenzano and Giacalone. It also noted that Frank Sheeran, a "known associate of Russell Bufalino, La Cosa Nostra Chief," had been seen in Detroit in early August, but did not specifically put him in the car driven by O'Brien.[6] Persons reported by "sources" as "involved" or "likely to be involved" in the crime included two of Provenzano's "trusted associates," the brothers Thomas and Stephen Andretta. Also in this category were Rafael Quasarano and Paul Vitale, the owners of a sanitation company in the Detroit suburb of Hamtramck.[7]

In early December of 1975, ninety-five people obeyed subpoenas to appear before a Detroit grand jury investigating Hoffa's disappearance. Twenty-three of these prospective witnesses were known mobsters or Teamster officials, all but one of whom refused to answer questions, claiming a Fifth Amendment right against self-incrimination. The sole exception was Stephen Andretta, whose only apparent role in the suspected caper was to verify Tony Pro's presence in New Jersey on July 30. Andretta was granted immunity from prosecution in order to force him to answer prosecutors' questions. After first refusing to do so he was found in contempt of court and sent to prison for nine weeks. After serving his sentence he relented and agreed to take the stand. His testimony, if it could be called that, did nothing to break the log jam. During a mind-numbing six weeks he evaded direct answers by leaving the witness chair 1,157 times to consult with his lawyer, surely setting records in this category as well as in judicial and jurors' patience.[8] In the end, the grand jury's investigation failed to indict anyone as a participant or conspirator in Hoffa's disappearance.

The attorney representing Andretta in this farcical behavior was William Bufalino, who also served as counsel of record for Provenzano, both of the Andrettas, and the brothers Salvatore and Gabriel Briguglio. The FBI considered the Detroit lawyer's representation of Tony Pro and his four henchmen further evidence of the tie between the New Jersey gangster and Russell Bufalino. They likewise thought the appearance of a single lawyer for all of these men virtually confirmed the Provenzano gang's responsibility for Hoffa's murder. The Bureau's views were strengthened four months later when lawyer Bufalino added Frank Sheeran to his list of clients in the second round of the Detroit grand jury's ongoing inquiry.

Like the Provenzano claque, Chuckie O'Brien took the Fifth in appearances before grand juries but, unlike Tony Pro's men, he agreed to interviews with FBI agents. In unsworn statements O'Brien admitted using Joey Giacalone's car to deliver a fresh salmon to Robert Holmes Sr. in the early afternoon of July 30 but denied he had then gone to the Red Fox restaurant. The FBI could not move against or O'Brien or Sally Bugs, however, because accounts by persons claiming to have seen either or both men in the maroon Mercury at the Machus Red Fox parking lot were either inconclusive, inconsistent or arguably tainted by the witnesses having seen pictures of them in newspapers prior to being interviewed. And Hoffa's later disappearance was not sufficient, by itself, to prove that any of the Mercury's occupants were guilty of conspiracy to commit murder or of the act itself.

Also lacking was the identity of the maroon Mercury's fourth occupant. One witness said he had seen Hoffa in the car's back seat, a spot the hard-charging labor leader would never have accepted unless both front seats were taken. Perhaps someone should have suspected Sheeran as the man beside the driver. The FBI's mind-set, however, was that while others might have been peripherally involved, Provenzano had organized the hit and supplied the assassination team from his New Jersey gang. There was no apparent or necessary reason for the Irish mobster to have been in that group. Like O'Brien, he took the Fifth at grand jury appearances but talked informally to FBI agents. He had been in Motor City in early August, Sheeran plausibly explained, to attend the weekend wedding of William Bufalino's daughter.

Further weakening the government's case was the absence of a body. Rumors abounded on the whereabouts of Hoffa's remains. Some claimed it was in a barrel placed in a Japanese car that had been compacted and shipped overseas; others said his chain-weighted body lay at the bottom of Lake Michigan. One source reported him alive and well in Brazil, co-habiting with a black go-go dancer. As reflected in the Hoffex memo, the FBI saw no reason for the body to have been removed from the Motor City area. Why risk a long car or truck ride in the possession of a corpse "when Detroit organized crime people have proven in the past that they are capable of taking care of such things."[9] Rafael Quaransano and Paul Vitale, two Mob-associated businessmen, were among the FBI's suspects through their ownership of the Hamtramck sanitation company. A search of the company's premises by Bureau agents revealed no usable evidence but gave rise to credible speculation by author Steven Brill—in 1978, fifteen years before the publication of Sheeran's confession—that "the dead body was turned over to someone ..., maybe Sheeran, who took it ... to the Quasarano-Vitale incinerator."[10] But there was no evidence to support that assumption that would stand up in court.

Though the details of the Hoffa murder remained sketchy, a piece of information obtained during the first days of the FBI's investigation convinced J. Edgar Hoover and his subordinates that high-ranking Mafia bosses had authorized the hit. Strongly suspecting gangland participation in Hoffa's disappearance, FBI agents immediately put known Mafia bosses under heightened surveillance. On August 4, 1975, only five days after the labor icon's disappearance, Bureau agents observed the presence of five mafiosi in the Vesuvius Restaurant on West 45th Street, New York City. The assembled mobsters were Russell Bufalino, Tony Provenzano, Salvatore Briguglio, Frank Sheeran and Fat Tony Salerno, the head of New York's Genovese family and ranking member of this group. The conspirator's plan to eliminate Hoffa could not have gone forward without Salerno's prior approval. Though not overheard, the timing of their meeting was such that they could hardly have been discussing any other subject. As Sheeran described it many years later, "The purpose of this meeting was to report to ... Salerno ... how the thing was done, ... and he was very satisfied."[11] In hindsight the composition of the Mafia quintet points clearly to the roles each man played in bringing Hoffa down. At the time, however, it merely added to the law enforcers' frustration at the strength of *omerta*, the Mob's code of silence, and the government's inability to crack it.

As the FBI's investigation wore on and finally petered out, its picture of the crime remained fragmented like a digital video signal with half its pixels lost in transmission. DOJ lawyers were never able to make a case against any of the suspected participants free of reasonable doubt. Hoffa was officially declared dead in 1982 but until Sheeran's confession twenty-eight years after the fact, the disappearance of the Bureau's most famous missing man remained an unsolved mystery.

****

Frustrated at being unable to put the pieces together, the Department of Justice launched an all-out campaign against the mobsters identified as suspects in the Hoffa case. Begun in the Ford administration and continued under President Carter, an FBI-DOJ strikeforce went forward with a grim zeal that would have made Bob Kennedy proud. One by one their targeted culprits went down like tin ducks in a shooting gallery. Among those convicted and imprisoned were the six men thought to be most directly involved in Hoffa's disappearance.

Tony Provenzano headed the DOJ's most wanted list. The New Jersey capo had long been suspected of ordering the 1961 hit on Anthony Castellito, a dissident member of Teamster Local 560 who had challenged his boss for the office of secretary-treasurer in the New Jersey union. In 1976, fifteen years after the fact, an accomplice in Castellito's liquidation ratted on his boss. On this newly acquired evidence Provenzano was indicted in federal court for first-degree murder, and in a New York state court for conspiring to kill his foolhardy labor opponent. The murder case was eventually dismissed for delays in its prosecution, and a conviction in the conspiracy case was reversed on a legal error and not retried.

Undaunted by these setbacks, DOJ prosecutors convened another federal grand jury soon after Hoffa went missing. It indicted Provenzano, along with Stephen and Thomas Andretta, for violating a new federal law known as the Racketeer Influenced and Corrupt Organizations Act or "RICO" for short. The indictment charged the defendants with arranging a $300,000 kickback to a Teamster official in connection with $2.3 million loan from the union's New York State pension fund. The trial took place in New Jersey in 1978. Like the loan fraud charge against Hoffa in the Sun Valley case, the RICO charge grew out of transactions whose complexity made it difficult to connect the dots and prove criminal intent. As in Sun Valley, however, young but exceptionally talented DOJ lawyers—reminiscent of Kennedy's Get Hoffa

Squad—made the facts and the defendants' roles understandable to a jury, who found all three men guilty. Provenzano received a twenty-year prison sentence and his co-defendants ten years each. Tony Pro began serving his sentence in 1981 and died in prison of a heart attack seven years later at age seventy-one. The Andretta brothers served their sentences and were released. Stephen Andretta died of natural causes sometime thereafter. Thomas was last known to be alive and living in Florida.

Next in the prosecutors' sights was Tony Giacalone. The Detroit mobster, habitually at pains to operate in the shadows or behind closed doors, made almost comical efforts to highlight his presence at his hometown's Southfield Athletic Club on July 30. The Club's barber gave him a haircut; its masseur a long rubdown. A dozen others remembered Giacalone uncustomarily walking the Club's corridors between mid-morning and late afternoon of that day, glad-handing and talking with passersby. The circumstantial evidence of Tony Jack's involvement in Hoffa's disappearance thus suffered from weaknesses similar to those in the case against Provenzano, but the feds had other avenues of attack. As in the DOJ's earlier pursuit of Al Capone, Giacalone was charged with fraudulent tax evasion and like the iconic Chicago gangster was found guilty. He received a ten-year prison sentence in 1977 and went to jail in 1980 when his appeals ran out. In 1996, back in Detroit, the former "King of the Streets" was indicted on a RICO charge. In 1998, before going to trial, Tony Jack died of natural causes.

The DOJ prosecutors' third target was Provenzano's principal hit man Sally Bugs Briguglio, whom the FBI considered Hoffa's probable assassin. They sought and received from a New Jersey grand jury an indictment of Briguglio, alongside Tony Pro, for the 1961 murder of Tony Castellito. Those charges ultimately went for naught, but the feds stayed on Sally Bugs's trail. Aware of the Bureau's continuing interest, Provenzano and his mafiosi colleagues feared that Briguglio, in return for prosecutorial leniency, would implicate them in Hoffa's murder. Alert to his predicament, Sally Bugs had two choices, both unsatisfactory. By ratting on his cohorts he could gain a reduced sentence but every day in prison would bring fear of retribution in the form of a fellow inmate's shiv between his ribs. Alternatively he could keep quiet while free on bail and awaiting trial, but in doing so would risk a Mob hit to make sure he stayed silent.

Grasping the second horn of his dilemma, he kept quiet and thereby made himself a target. In the spring of 1978 Russell Bufalino and Tony Provenzano decided that Sally Bugs posed an intolerable risk. After clearing their plan with Salerno, they set about to implement it. On March 21 Briguglio was in the New York City neighborhood known as Little Italy. Around 10:30 that night he left the Andrea Doria Social Club, alone, and headed down Mulberry Street toward Umberto's Clam House, the scene of gangster Joey Gallo's murder six years earlier. Out of the shadows in front of him came two men, one of whom was a towering figure Sally Bugs recognized immediately. "Hi, Sal," said the big man. "Hi, Irish," came the reply. With these words barely out of his mouth, Briguglio took two bullets to the head from Sheeran's .38-caliber pistol and "went down dead."[12] The second man pumped three quick shots into the fallen body and the assailants disappeared into the night.

Two days later the *New York Times* described the assailants as "two men wearing jackets with pulled-up hoods … who ran a short distance [to their getaway car] and drove off in a blue Mercury with New Jersey license plates."[13] The second man was in fact John "the Redhead" Francis, a companion who usually took the role of Sheeran's driver. Neither of them, Sheeran wrote later, was wearing a hood, but otherwise the *Times* article was accurate. The Irishman further explained that the additional shots were fired into Briguglio's dead body to give "the impression of a shootout to scare away anybody who had an idea to look out his window after two shots."[14] Sheeran also confessed to having been the lone assassin of "Crazy Joey" Gallo at Umberto's Clam House in 1972, and to have "shot up the place … with two guns" to give the appearance of multiple assailants.[15]

Next on the prosecutors' list was Russell Bufalino. By 1976, the FBI had the goods on the Quiet Don for his participation in a protection racket based in New York. Jack Napoli, a petty thief charged with stealing jewelry from a Bufalino-affiliated seller, met with the Mafia boss wearing a wire supplied by the FBI. The hidden device recorded a conversation in which the crime chieftain "threatened to strangle Napoli with his bare hands" if he did not pay for the stolen goods.[16] Tried and convicted in 1977 on a charge of extortion, Bufalino received a sentence of four years in prison which he served in full. Upon his release at age seventy-six he vowed to kill Napoli for ratting on him. This plan was thwarted by another ill-chosen accomplice who agreed to testify against him as part of a plea-bargaining agreement with DOJ prosecutors. On this evidence the aging mafioso was found guilty of conspiring to commit murder and sentenced to fifteen years in jail. After serving part of his sentence, Bufalino's deteriorating health got him transferred to a nursing home where he died at age ninety.[17]

Though Frank Sheeran was not known to be Hoffa's assassin, government prosecutors pursued him as diligently as its other suspects. They first tried him on racketeering charges based on the testimony of Charlie Allen, a drinking buddy who had worn an FBI wire to get evidence against his fellow thug. Sheeran took the stand in his own defense and got a verdict of not guilty on the undisclosed but obvious ground of reasonable doubt. In the process of getting evidence from his criminal colleague, Allen had secretly tape-recorded Sheeran ordering him to rough-up an uncooperative manager of a company with whom the Irishman was having a labor dispute. "Break both of his legs. I want him to go to the hospital."[18] For these remarks Sheeran was tried in 1978 for conspiracy to commit assault and battery and sentenced to fourteen years in prison.

While that conviction was on appeal he was tried and convicted for accepting two Lincoln Town Cars "from a company that leased truck drivers to freight companies ... for substandard wages" in direct job competition with members of his own Teamsters union.[19] For that he got another eighteen years to be served on top of the fourteen already received. In 1991, after eleven years in prison, Sheeran was nearly paralyzed by severe arthritis. In that year he sought and was given parole on the ground of physical hardship. Three years later, he went back to prison for ten months for violating parole, gaining his final freedom in October, 1995. A crippled and broken man, Hoffa's assassin died in a nursing home in 2003 at age eighty-three.

The FBI felt that Chuckie O'Brien was probably an unknowing accomplice in his foster father's disappearance. They saw him, however, as a thoroughly unreliable witness, intentionally obstructing their efforts to solve the Hoffa mystery. Since his defection to the Fitzsimmons camp in 1974, O'Brien had gone steadily to seed. Relegated to a minor Teamster outpost in Florida, divorced and uncertain of his future, he nursed his anxieties with alcohol, food, expensive jewelry and tooled leather boots. His stocky five-foot-eight- inch frame and beer belly now required a size fifty jacket. Describing Chuckie's looks on the day of Hoffa's disappearance, Sheeran said that Hoffa's forty-two-year-old foster son sported "long sideburns, ... a paisley shirt with a wide collar, and lots of gold chains on his neck. He looked like he belonged in *Saturday Night Fever*."[20]

Hoffa's son Jim confronted Chuckie early in the family's frantic search for their missing relative. Nervous and obviously uncomfortable, O'Brien responded to his old friend's questions with contradictory accounts of his activities on July 30 and then promptly left town to avoid further interrogation. For the next several months he stayed basically on the run. During the IBT's international convention in Miami in 1976, hearing rumors that Tony Provenzano was looking for him, he took refuge in a friend's hotel room where he spent most of the next two days under the bed. This episode became an oft-repeated story, retold with scornful laughter at Teamster gatherings long after the event. Some months later the feds charged O'Brien with extortion of funds from a company resisting Teamster overtures, for which he was convicted and sentenced to a year in prison. Awaiting a decision on his appeal he was indicted and found guilty on a separate charge of making false statements in a bank loan application. In 1979, at age forty-five, he spent ten months in jail for the first conviction but was never imprisoned for the second.

Soon thereafter, "heavily in debt ... and [recently] married to [Brenda Berger], a go-go girl" about his age from West Memphis, Arkansas, Chuckie spent his next years alternating between Florida and Memphis, Tennessee, where his wife managed a family-owned Mexican restaurant.[21] O'Brien now lives in relative obscurity in the Miami, Florida, area and has never publicly admitted participation in his foster father's disappearance. When asked about it in recent years he said, "I loved this man more than anything ... and I agree with [young] Jimmy that [he and other family members] deserve closure ... I have my theories about what happened, but the FBI has always pooh-poohed them, and whenever I've tried to help, I get my brains bashed in."[22]

Perhaps, like Sheeran, the fickle O'Brien will one day confess, not that he knowingly aided his foster father's killers, but that he was only their innocent chauffeur. This would corroborate the Irishman's story, bring full closure to Hoffa's family and purge Chuckie's consciousness of its demon of guilt, if he has one. More likely, however, his secret will go with him to the grave.

Notes

Chapter 1: "The Sincerest Little Guy I've Ever Seen"

1. Oscar Fraley, *Hoffa: the Real Story* (New York: Stein and Day, 1975), pp. 34–35
2. Donald I. Rogers, *The Trials of Jimmy Hoffa* (Chicago: Henry Regnery Co., 1970), p. 23
3. Arthur A. Sloane, *Hoffa* (Cambridge, Massachusetts: MIT Press, 1991), p. 6
4. Jim Clay, *Hoffa! Ten Angels Swearing* (Beaverdam, Virginia: Beaverdam Books, 1965), p. 56
5. Ibid., p. 57
6. Ibid.
7. Op. cit., "Sloane," p. 8
8. Op. cit., "Clay," p. 59
9. Ibid.
10. John Barnard, *Walter Reuther and the Rise of the Auto Worker*, (Boston: Little Brown, 1983), p.29
11. Op. cit., "Rogers," p. 85
12. Op. cit., "Clay," p. 67
13. Ibid.
14. Op. cit., "Fraley," p. 42

15. Ibid., p. 43
16. Thaddeus Russell, *Out of the Jungle: Jimmy Hoffa and the Remaking of the Working Class* (New York: Knopf, 2001), p. 53
17. Op. cit., "Clay," pp. 64–65
18. Op. cit., "Sloane," p. 16
19. Ibid., p. 17
20. Ibid.
21. Op. cit., "Clay," p. 61
22. Op. cit., "Fraley," p. 49
23. Ibid., p. 53
24. Op. cit., "Sloane," p. 20
25. Op. cit., "Russell," p. 44
26. Op. cit., "Sloane," p. 22
27. Op. cit., "Russell," p. 79
28. Ibid.
29. Ibid., p. 27
30. Ibid., p. 91
31. Ibid., p. 135
32. Ibid., p. 89

Chapter 2: "If Hoffa's Acquitted I'll Jump Off the Capitol Dome"
1. Evan Thomas, *Robert Kennedy: His Life* (New York: Simon & Schuster, 2000), p. 35
2. Ibid., p. 51
3. Arthur M. Schlesinger Jr., *Robert Kennedy and His Times* (Boston: Houghton Mifflin, 1978), p. 67
4. Op. cit., "Thomas," p. 32
5. Ibid., p. 19
6. Robert F. Kennedy, *The Enemy Within* (New York: Popular Library, 1960), p. 285
7. Op. cit., *Enemy Within*, p. 18
8. Ibid., p. 19
9. Ibid., p. 20
10. Ibid.
11. Ibid., p. 19
12. Ibid., p. 20

13. Ibid., p. 46
14. Jim Clay, *Hoffa! Ten Angels Swearing* (Beaverdam,Virginia: Beaverdam Books, 1965), pp. 95–96
15. Ibid., p. 96
16. Lester & Irene David, *Bobby Kennedy: the Making of a Folk Hero* (UK: Sidgwick & Jackson, 1986), p. 98
17. Arthur A. Sloane, *Hoffa* (Cambridge, Massachusetts: MIT Press, 1991), p. 75
18. Ibid.
19. Ibid.
20. Op. cit., *Enemy Within*, p. 64
21. Op. cit., "Sloane," p. 76
22. Op. cit., "Thomas," p. 89. To Ethel, her husband was always "Bobby." "Carmine" Bellino was one of Kennedy's most trusted investigators.
23. Op. cit., "Sloane," p. 76
24. Ibid., p. 82
25. Op.cit., *Enemy Within*, pp. 80–81
26. Ibid., p. 81
27. Ibid., p. 83
28. Ibid.
29. Ibid., p. 76
30. Ibid., p. 77
31. Ibid.
32. Ibid., p. 83
33. Op.cit., "Sloane," p. 88
34. Ibid.
35. Ibid., p. 89
36. Op. cit., "Clay," p. 119
37. Ibid., p. 120
38. *Tennessean*, Nashville newspaper, April 13, 1958
39. *Tennessean*, December 27, 1957
40. John Seigenthaler, author's interview, April 18, 2005
41. Ibid.
42. Ibid.
43. Ibid.
44. Op. cit., *Tennessean*, March 28, 1958

45. Ibid.
46. *Tennessean*, December 18, 1957
47. Op. cit., *Enemy Within*, p. 303

Chapter 3: "Send a Reporter Down Here If You Want a Story"
1. The *Tennessean*, Nashville newspaper, October 5, 1954
2. James S. Neal, author's interview, April 20, 2005
3. Ibid.

Chapter 4: "Will Someone Please Wipe Up All That Blood"
1. John B. Martin, *Jimmy Hoffa's Hot* (Greenwich, CT: Fawcett Publications, 1959), p. 104
2. Op. cit., *Enemy Within*, p. 303
3. *New York Times*, March 5, 1964
4. Op. cit., *Enemy Within*, p. 168
5. Ibid., p. 96
6. This group included, among others, Secretary of Defense Robert McNamara, Treasury Secretary Douglas Dillon, National Security Advisor McGeorge Bundy, Washington Post Editor Ben Bradlee, Syndicated News Columnists Roland Evans and Charles Bartlett, and uber-lawyer Clark Clifford
7. Walter Sheridan, *The Fall and Rise of Jimmy Hoffa* (New York: Saturday Review Press, 1972), p. 105
8. Thaddeus Russell, *Out of the Jungle* (New York: Knopf, 2001), p. 88
9. James D. Squires, *The Secrets of the Hopewell Box* (New York: Times Books, 1996), p. 185
10. Op. cit., *Fall and Rise*, p. 204
11. Ibid., p. 205
12. Ibid.
13. Ibid., p. 224
14. Ibid., p. 227
15. Ibid., p. 215
16. Ibid., p. 226
17. James F. Neal, author's interview, April 20, 2005
18. Op. cit., "Sloane," p. 264

19. Op. cit., James F. Neal
20. Ibid.
21. Op. cit., "Sloane," p. 264
22. Op. cit., *Fall and Rise*, p. 249
23. Ibid., pp. 253–54
24. Op. cit., "Sloane," p. 267
25. p. cit., *Fall and Rise*, p. 255

Chapter 5: "They're Fixin' to Get at the Jury"

1. Op. cit., "Sloane," p. 266
2. Op. cit., *Fall and Rise*, p. 216
3. Ibid., p. 217
4. Ibid.
5. Ibid., p. 219
6. Ibid., p. 220
7. Ibid., p. 224
8. Ibid.
9. Ibid., p. 225
10. Ibid., p. 227
11. Ibid., p. 229
12. Ibid., p. 230
13. Ibid., p. 234
14. Ibid., p. 235
15. Ibid., p. 251

Chapter 6: "Bobby Kennedy's Just Another Lawyer Now

1. Op. cit, "Sloane," p. 268
2. Op. cit., *Fall and Rise*, pp. 258, 262
3. *The Banner*, Nashville newspaper, January 18, 1969
4. Op. cit., *Fall and Rise*, 276
5. Ibid., p. 278
6. Ibid., pp. 279–80
7. Ibid., p. 280
8. Op. cit., "Sloane," p. 277
9. Op. cit., *Fall and Rise*, p. 287
10. Ibid., p. 288

11. Op. cit., "Sloane," p. 280
12. Ibid.
13. Evan Thomas, *Robert Kennedy: His Life* (New York: Simon & Schuster, 2000), p. 21
14. Ibid.
15. Op. Cit., "Sloane," p. 280
16. Ibid.
17. Op. cit., *Fall and Rise*, p. 304

Chapter 7: "My God, It's Partin"

1. Op. cit., *Fall and Rise*, p. 306
2. The *Commercial Appeal*, Memphis newspaper, May 11, 2008
3. Op. cit., *Fall and Rise*, p. 201
4. Frank Ragano and Selwyn Raab, Mob Lawyer ((New York: Charles Scribner's & Sons, 1994), front-cover flap
5. Op. cit., *Fall and Rise*, p. 311
6. Op. cit., "Sloane," p. 294
7. Op. cit., "*Enemy Within*, p. 78
8. *US v. Hoffa*, US District Court, Eastern District of Tennessee, Southern Division, No. 11,989, trial transcript, p. 2964
9. Ibid.
10. Ibid., p. 2965
11. Ibid., p. 3212
12. Op. cit., *Fall and Rise*, p. cit., pp. 328–29
13. Ibid., p. 195
14. Ibid., p. 330
15. Op. cit., "Sloane," p. 297
16. Op. cit., *Fall and Rise*, p. 334
17. Ibid.
18. Ibid., p. 334
19. Ibid., p. 347
20. Op. cit., "Hoffa trial transcript," p. 7345
21. Ibid.
22. Ibid., p. 7348
23. Ibid., p. 7332
24. Ibid., pp. 7352–53

25. Op. cit., *Fall and Rise*, p. 350
26. Ibid., p. 352
27. Ibid., p. 351
28. Op. cit., "Sloane," p. 299
29. Op. cit., *Fall and Rise*, p. 351
30. Ibid.
31. Ibid., p. 352
32. Ibid.
33. Op. cit., "Sloane," p. 301
34. Juror Patrick J. Haverty, author's interview, February 6, 2007
35. Ibid.
36. Ibid.
37. Ibid.
38. Op. cit., "Sloane," p. 301
39. Op. cit., *Fall and Rise*, p. 354
40. Op. cit., "Hoffa trial transcript," p. 9289
41. Ibid., p. 9290
42. Ibid., pp. 9290–91
43. Ibid., p. 9293
44. Op. cit., *Commercial Appeal*, May 11, 2008

Chapter 8: "The Most Contemptible Piece of Trickery and Fraud"

1. Op. cit., *Fall and Rise*, p. 293
2. *The Tennessean*, Nashville newspaper, May 27, 1964
3. Op. cit., *Fall and Rise*, p. 297
4. Ibid., p. 299
5. Ibid.
6. John Seigenthaler, author's interview, April 18, 2005
7. James D. Squires, *Secrets of the Hopewell Box*, (New York: The Times Books, 1996), p. 214
8. Ibid., pp. 216–17
9. Op. cit., *Fall and Rise*, p. 300
10. *US v. Z. Thomas Osborn*, US District Court, Middle District of Tennessee, No. 13,484, trial transcript, p. 430
11. Ibid., p. 303
12. Ibid., p, 377

13. Ibid., pp. 399–400
14. Op. cit., "Squires," p. 205
15. Op. cit., Osborn trial transcript, p. 698
16. Ibid., p. 1097
17. Ibid., p. 1098
18. Ibid., p. 1105
19. Ibid., pp. 1172–73
20. Ibid., pp. 1197, 1176–77
21. Ibid., p. 1190
22. Ibid., p. 1196
23. Ibid., p. 1201
24. Op. cit., "Squires," p. 235
25. John Seigenthaler, author's interview, June, 2009
26. Op. cit., "Squires," p. 279
27. Ibid., p. 280

Chapter 9: "Like Jesus Christ on the Cross"

1. Steven Brill, *The Teamsters* (New York: Pocket Books, 1978), p. 368
2. Ibid., pp. 378–79
3. Op. cit., "Sloane," p. 140
4. Ibid., p. 141
5. *Time Magazine*, July 7, 1959
6. Ibid.
7. Ibid, August 31, 1959
8. Op. cit., *Enemy Within*, pp. 302–03
9. Op. cit., *Fall and Rise*, p. 218
10. *The Independent*, London newspaper, May 9, 2003
11. www.thenation.com/section/fred-j.-cook
12. *The Nation*, weekly journal, archives, New York, p. 417
13. Ibid.
14. Ibid.
15. Ibid., p. 438
16. Ibid.
17. Op. cit., *Fall and Rise*, p. 363
18. Ibid., p. 377
19. Ibid., p. 378

20. Ibid.
21. Op. cit., "Sloane," p.
22. Op. cit., *Fall and Rise*, p. 382
23. Op. cit., "Sloane," p. 313
24. Ibid., p. 314
25. Op. cit., *Fall and Rise*, p. 387
26. Ibid.
27. Ibid., p. 392
28. Op. cit., "Sloane," p. 316
29. Ibid., p. 319
30. Op. cit., *Fall and Rise*, pp. 396–97
31. *ACLU Brief*, September 2, 1966, p. 8, filed in *Hoffa v. US*, 385 US 293 (1966)
32. *Atlantic Monthly*, November 1966, pp. 118, 122
33. *Hoffa v. US*, US Supreme Court, 385 US 293, December 12, 1966, p. 302
34. Ibid., p.
35. Ibid., p. 304
36. Ibid., pp. 308
37. Ibid., pp. 311–12
38. Ibid., pp. 317
39. Ibid., p. 319
40. Ibid., p. 320
41. Ibid., p. 321
42. Fred J. Cook, *The Nation*, February 20, 1967, p. 231
43. Ibid., p. 230
44. Ibid., p. 236
45. Op. cit., *Fall and Rise*, p. 406
46. Ibid., p. 356
47. Ibid., p. 389
48. Op. cit., "Sloane," p. 328
49. Ibid.

Chapter 10: "Booked, Fingerprinted, Showered and Deloused"

1. Lester Velie, *Desperate Bargain: Why Jimmy Hoffa had to Die* (New York: Thomas Y. Crowell, 1977), p. 109
2. Ibid., p. 110

3. Op. cit., "Sloane," p. 330
4. Ibid.
5. Oscar Fraley, *Hoffa: the Real Story*, (New York: Stein and Day, 1975), p. 182
6. Ibid.
7. *Tribune*, Fort Scott, Kansas newspaper, June 21, 1973, pp. 1, 8
8. Op. cit., "Fraley," p. 187
9. Ibid., pp. 207, 189
10. Op. cit., "Sloane," pp. 332–33
12. Op. cit., "Fraley," p. 208
13. Ibid., p. 209
14. Op. cit., "Sloane," p. 340
15. Op. cit., "Velie," p. 120
16. Op. cit., "Sloane," p. 342
17. Ibid., p. 343
18. Dan. E. Moldea, *The Hoffa Wars*, (New York: S.P.I. Books, 1978), p. 257
19. Op. cit., "Sloane," p. 343
20. Ibid., p. 346
21. Ibid., p. 347
22. Op. cit., *Fall and Rise*, p. 518
23. Ibid., p. 519
24. Op. cit., "Moldea," p. 313
25. Steven Brill, *The Teamsters* (New York: Pocket Books, 1978), p. 101
26. Clark R. Mollenhoff, *Game Plan For Disaster* (New York: W.W. Horton, 1976), p. 175
27. Ibid., p. 177
28. Op. cit., "Fraley," p. 17
29. Op. cit., "Brill," p. 102

Chapter 11: "Some Day, Somehow, I Will Return

1. Op. cit., "Fraley," p. 187
2. Op.cit., *Fall and Rise*, p. 430
3. Ibid., p. 500
4. Op. cit., "Velie," p. 135

5. Ibid.
6. Charles Brandt, *I Heard You Paint Houses* (Hanover, N.H.: Steerforth Press, 2004) p. 197
7. Op. cit., "Brill," p. 181
8. Ibid., p. 216
9. John Seigenthaler, author's interview, June, 2009
10. Op. cit., "Brill," p. 215
11. Op. cit., "Moldea," p. 263
12. Op. cit., "Brandt," p. 163
13. Op. cit., "Moldea," p. 367
14. Op. cit., "Brandt," p. 214
15. Op. cit., "Velie," p. 167
16. Ibid., p. 26
17. Op. cit., "Moldea," p. 177
18. Ibid., p. 347
19. Christopher Davis, *Esquire Magazine*, March 1975, pp. 145–46
20. Ibid., p. 146
21. James R. Hoffa v. William B. Saxbe, US District Court for the District of Columbia, 378 F. Supp. 1221, 1974, p. 1224
22. Oval Office Conversations 16–60, December 8, 1971, 5:08–5:14 p.m., US National Archives, College Park, Maryland
23. Op. cit., "Oval office Conversations," 640–11, December 22, 1971, 1:16–1:50 p.m.
24. Op. cit., "Moldea," p. 361
25. Ibid., p. 362

Chapter 12: "My Friend Didn't Suffer"
1. Christopher Davis, *Esquire Magazine*, March 1975, p. 95
2. Ibid.
3. Jerry Stanecki, *Playboy Magazine*, December 1975, p. 75
4. Op. cit., *Esquire*, p. 145
5. Ibid., p, 146
6. Op. cit., *Playboy*, p. 74
7. Ibid.
8. Ibid.
9. Ibid., p. 83

10. Ibid., p. 82
11. Ibid.
12. Ibid.
13. Ibid., pp. 86–87
14. Ibid., p. 83
15. Op, cit., "Fraley," p. 13
16. Ibid., p. 15
17. Ibid., p. 17
18. Ibid., p. 237
19. Ibid., p. 16
20. Vincent Teresa with Thos. C. Renner, *My Life in the Mafia* (New York: Doubleday & Co., 1973), pp. 4–5
21. Ibid.
22. www.gangstersinc.tripod.com
23. Charles Brandt, *I Heard You Paint Houses* (Hanover, N.H.: Steerforth Press, 2004), p. 11
24. Op. cit., "Teresa," p. 4
25. Ibid.
26. Op. cit., "Moldea," p. 365
27. Op. cit., "Brill," p. 55
28. Op. cit., "Brandt," p. 240
29. Ibid.
30. Ibid., p. 241
31. Ibid., pp. 242–43
32. Op. cit., "Sloane," p. 378
33. Ibid., p. 375
34. Op. cit., "Brandt," p. 32
35. Ibid., p. 84
36. Ibid., p. 249
37. Ibid., p. 248
38. Ibid., p. 251
39. Op. cit., "Sloane," p. 382
40. Op. cit., "Brandt," p. 253
41. Ibid., p. 254
42. Ibid.
43. Ibid., p. 255
44. Ibid., p. 256

45. Ibid., p. 257
46. Ibid.
47. Ibid., p. 258

Epilogue
1. F.B.I. Headquarters, *Report of Hoffex Conference*, January 26–28, 1976, p. 19
2. Ibid., p. 43
3. Ibid., p. 45
4. Ibid., p. 31
5. Ibid., p. 45
6. Ibid., p. 3
7. Ibid., pp. 2–3
8. Op. cit., "Brill," p. 34
9. Op. cit., *Hoffex Report*, p. 38
10. Op. cit., "Brill," p. 64
11. Op. cit., "Brandt," p. 259
12. Ibid. p. 268
13. *New York Times*, March 23, 1978
14. Op. cit., "Brandt," p. 260
15. Ibid., p. 300
16. Ibid., p. 265
17. Ibid., p. 266
18. Ibid., p. 274
19. Ibid., p. 275
20. Ibid., p. 252
21. www.time.com/magazine
22. *The Commercial Appeal*, Memphis newspaper, September 21, 2010

Index

Organized Crime, Individuals: (*Cont.*)

Salvatore ("Sally Bugs") 252–54, 266, 256, 260 262, 263, 265–66; Bruno, Angelo 246, 250–51; Bufalino, Russell ("the Quiet Don") 24, 220, 240–42, 245–47, 248–49, 252, 254–55, 256–57, 261, 263, 266–69; Capone, Al ("Scarface") 216, 239; Corallo, Anthony ("Tony Ducks") 29; Castello, Frank 237; Coppola, Frank 239; Dalitz, Moe 237; Dioguardi, Giovanni ("Johnny Dio") 24, 29, 41–42, 68, 77, 237, 239; Dorfman, Paul ("Red") 24, 16, 217, 239; Galente, Carmine ("Lillo") 240, 241, 243–45, 247; Gallo, Joey, 266; Gambino, Carlo 243–45; Genovese, Vito 240, 243; Anthony Giacalone ("Tony Jack") 222, 223–35, 239, 242, 246, 247–48, 254, 256, 259, 265; Giancana, Momo Salvatore ("Sam") 174, 239; Glimco, Joey 239; Lansky, Meyer 237; Marcello, Carlos 24, 127 215, 240; Meli, Angelo 239; Perrone, Santo 73, 239; Provenzano, Anthony ("Tony Pro") 24, 117, 199, 200–01, 204, 207 219–20, 225, 240–41,

244–48, 254, 256, 259, 262–65, 268; Salerno, Anthony ("Fat Tony") 240, 263; Sheeran, Frank ("the Irishman") 220, 240, 242, 245, 246–48, 249–51, 252, 255–57, 261, 263, 266–69; Trafficante, Santos 24, 127, 240; Other Detroit Gangsters and Families: Harry Ames, Tom Burke, James Cassidy, 23; East Side Sicilians, 14; Jewish Purple Gang, 14; Zerilli Family, 223–24

O'Rourke, John J. 177

Osborn Jr., Z. Thomas 79–81, 85, 96, 101–02, 109, 146, 147–161, 185

Parks, Thomas Ewing 93, 109, 126, 141–43, 145

Partin, Edward Grady 91, 92–105, 129, 172, 173, 178–79, 182–184, 214, 215; courageous decision to incriminate Hoffa 124

Paschal, James M. 97, 98, 100, 135

Paschal, Mrs. James 99, 100, 136–37, 142

Pearson, Drew 207

Pepper, Rep. Claude 171

Piersante, Vincent 217

Pitcher, Sargent 91

Pitts, Oscar "Mutt" 99, 100, 101, 135